SEARCH FOR THE FOUNTAIN

SEARCH FOR THE FOUNTAIN

The Secret to Youthful Aging

Linda J. Falkner

iUniverse, Inc.

New York Lincoln Shanghai

Search For The Fountain
The Secret to Youthful Aging

iUniverse, Inc.

For information address:
iUniverse, Inc.
2021 Pine Lake Road, Suite 100
Lincoln, NE 68512
www.iuniverse.com

ISBN: 0-595-27079-4

Printed in the United States of America

You Are Old Father William

by Lewis Carroll

"You are old, Father William," the young man said,
    "And your hair has become very white;
And yet you incessantly stand on your head—
    Do you think, at your age, it is right?"

"In my youth," Father William replied to his son,
    "I feared it might injure the brain;
But, now that I'm perfectly sure I have none,
    Why, I do it again and again."

"You are old," said the youth, "as I mentioned before,
    And have grown most uncommonly fat;
Yet you turned a back-somersault in at the door—
    Pray, what is the reason of that?"

"In my youth," said the sage, as he shook his gray locks,
    "I kept all my limbs very supple
By the use of this ointment—one shilling the box—
    Allow me to sell you a couple?"

"You are old," said the youth, "and your jaws are too weak
    For anything tougher than suet;
Yet you finished the goose, with the bones and the beak—
    Pray how did you manage to do it?"

"In my youth," said his father, "I took to the law,
    And argued each case with my wife;
And the muscular strength, which it gave to my jaw,
    Has lasted the rest of my life."

"You are old," said the youth, "one would hardly suppose
    That your eye was as steady as ever;
Yet you balanced an eel on the end of your nose—
    What made you so awfully clever?"

"I have answered three questions, and that is enough,"
    Said his father; "don't give yourself airs!
Do you think I can listen all day to such stuff?
    Be off, or I'll kick you down stairs!"

C ONTENTS

▼

Introduction

▼

G rowing up, I saw my grandparents enter nursing homes and came to believe that getting old means becoming feeble and needing care. Yet, I heard many stories about somebody's mother, uncle, or cousin who was still active and healthy in their late eighties or nineties. Over time, I began to suspect that active, healthy, self-sufficient seniors are far more common than I had previously believed. But until I began writing this book, I had no idea how active and healthy they actually are. Retired, and free from the day-to-day job of earning a living, these seniors fly. They love what they're doing, and many are more active than they were in their younger years.

I wrote this book, hoping I can change a stereotype of what people think seniors are like as they age. I interviewed the experts on healthy aging, people who were eighty years and older. The people I spoke with were not exceptional people. None were famous or well known, expect possibly within their own community. My goal was to find "ordinary" people. However, I believe I failed, as each person I spoke with had an "extraordinary" story to tell.

Florida includes a huge population of retired people. Finding active seniors turned out to be much easier than I had thought it would be, and it wasn't long until they were finding me. I spoke to over fifty people born between 1898 and 1921, with the youngest being eighty and the oldest a hundred and three. I chose thirty-four individuals from varied socio-economic incomes to include in this book. Most people I interviewed live at least half a year in the Tampa Bay area of Florida. This includes St. Petersburg, Tampa, Brandon, and Sun City Center. One woman lives in Haynes City on the East Coast and one man in Miami, which was a five-hour drive for me, each way. The place where they were born and/or raised is at the beginning of each chapter along with a few details on how I found them, or they found me.

The people I spoke with had certain characteristics in common. Many, such as long-lived parents and a healthy life-style, I had anticipated. The two surprising factors I hadn't expected were a predominance of first born or only children, and traveling.

I found that religion was not a factor for long life and health. I spoke to some deeply religious individuals, but also a surprising number of people who felt no need for religion in their lives. Considering that my interviews took place in a strongly religious part of the country referred to as the Bible belt, the number of people who were not religious was higher than I had anticipated.

Diet was one feature I asked about. Their eating habits differed, but the one thing they had in common was a widely varied diet. I didn't meet one person who claimed to be a picky eater, and not one vegetarian, although most mentioned that vegetables are an important part of their diet and most ate meat sparingly. The majority of the seniors were at an ideal weight, or slightly overweight. Very few were underweight, and if so, by just a few pounds. I've read research theorizing that people will live longer if they limit their food and keep themselves underweight. However, I did not find any seniors who followed a strict diet regime to keep themselves underweight. Enjoyable meals and eating out were an important part of their lives.

Although several had smoked when they were younger, no one whom I spoke to smoked presently and the few who drank alcohol were light drinkers.

Exercise seemed to be another important factor, and everyone had a regular exercise or activity routine. They were involved with activities that they loved, and kept busy throughout the day, often with projects that helped others.

By looking for active people, I had expected to find healthy people. However, many people had overcome serious diseases including heart attacks, diabetes, osteoporosis, and resulting broken hips. The majority had their share of aches and pains, with arthritis and cataract surgery being almost universal among this population.

Extensive travel was a theme that came up with nearly every person I spoke to. At first I thought it was a coincidence that each person told me travel stories, but soon it became apparent that this was a pattern, and an important aspect of their lives. This population put a great importance on reading and continued learning. Everyone had at least a few books and many had large collections. Many, but not all, had also entered the computer world.

Lastly, every person I spoke with had a genuine outgoing, happy personality. I heard very little about their illnesses, and they spoke at length about their good friends and loving family. Each one took an interest in me, wanting to know as much about me as they told me about themselves. Although I did tell them about myself, I didn't include my answers in each chapter. I regret that I had to leave out most of the stories about friends and families, as that would have more than doubled the length of this book. Many people showed me full activity calendars with my name penciled in between a morning activity and an evening of dancing.

I couldn't write about everyone, but deciding whom to leave out was difficult, as every person I spoke to had a story worth telling. Had I left in every fascinating person I met, I would have had to write a second book. The people I chose to write about were those I remembered most clearly months later after interviewing and transcribing the tapes. These were people who stuck in my mind and my dreams. I want to thank everyone who welcomed me in their homes and shared their stories with me. I also want to thank Ann Cook for her hard work proofreading this book and Diane Brazas for her illustrations.

DOROTHY APGAR, AGE 83

The Nearly New Shop
West Bend, Wisconsin

I read an article in the paper about a thrift shop called the Nearly New Shop and about Dorothy who manages it. I called her and we set up an appointment to meet at the store in Sun City Center. Dorothy was difficult to interview. She wanted to know everything about me, and she wanted to tell me the best things about her friends and co-workers. She didn't want to talk about herself much, and I had to ask many questions to bring her back to her own life.

The day we met was Dorothy's day off. I arrived at the Nearly New Shop about ten minutes before she did so I had time to look around the cluttered, two-room store. The shop looked like a typical thrift store with a variety of adult clothes, hats, and sweaters in one room. The second room was filled with knick-knacks, linen, books, tapes, glassware, and plates. The prices were low, with a coffee pot going for three dollars, and a set of three Pyrex bowls for ten dollars.

Dorothy entered the store, but since I was looking for someone over eighty, I failed to recognize her. She appears much younger. She was wearing a sports suit with tennis shoes and a sweater. Her hair is white, and she wore light pink lipstick. The smile lines surrounding her eyes appeared more a reflection of her happy mood than age.

"Life has been very good to me," Dorothy began. "If you think young, you will stay healthy. People come down here and they sit and don't keep busy. They have someone do their housework, their yard work, and they just sit. They go out to breakfast and lunch, but they don't do much. People can become negative as they get older. You can talk yourself into being sick. You won't get old if you don't think that way.

I keep active and I don't let things bother me. If I can change something or help somebody, I will. Another thing, older folks need to learn to help one another. Just like the farmer, you can't keep planting corn in the same field. You have to give back to the soil or pretty soon you don't get any corn. Life is the same thing. You have to keep acting healthy to stay healthy. Get your rest and don't let things bother you.

Jealousy, hate, and prejudice are cancers that nobody needs. People are people. You have to give them a chance because you never know. Just one thing might help them. When someone believes in you, you can do anything.

I found that out when I was seventeen. I used to stutter very badly, but I overcame it.

Life is what you make it. If you're going to be old and crotchy, then be old and crotchy, but you won't have a life. Everyone will stay away from you. It's important to have friends.

The Nearly New shop started in '71 in Wimauma. We started it with the Community Church to help the migrant workers. We're part of the Interfaith Counsel of Churches, although our Temple helps too. The Council is in charge of the store. I can't join because you have to belong to a church and I don't profess to be anything. That's all right. It's a fun place to be.

Nobody owns the store. We're all volunteers. Most are retired and many are over eighty. These people are great. All of our people are volunteers, and they're all wonderful. There isn't one bad apple in this whole group. They're happy, and they enjoy what they're doing. They're super! They do a good job and they're special—they're givers and not takers. It isn't what you want life to give to you, but it's what you make it, and you've got to do right by other people.

We stayed in Wimauma until the first of November. The rent was much less out there, but it's okay. It's easy coming here because I'm only two blocks away. I'm glad I don't have to run out to Wimauma anymore. We moved because we were broken into four times and were tired of it. They didn't have to break in and steal things from us, if they needed something, we would have given it to them.

There was a man who got out of jail and we outfitted him twice. I didn't ask him what he was in jail for, but each time I said, "Please Mike, take care of yourself." I think he can do it. Sometimes it only takes someone believing in you.

I'm just managing the store until they find someone else to take it over. I work over forty hours and rarely take a day off. I wish a man and woman would volunteer because there's a lot of lifting. It would be easier if a couple would come along and take this over. They put it in the Church bulletin, but so far nobody's come forward. When they find someone else to take over, I'll still help them. Last year I only missed working on Christmas and Thanksgiving.

I enjoy it. I think everybody here enjoys it, and they all do their own thing. I just can't tell you how good they are. We don't have one bad apple in the whole bushel. I like working, and there are such wonderful people here.

Everything in the Nearly New Shop is donated. We sell it, and we use the money for charity. We gave twenty-five scholarships last year. We gave a thousand dollars to East Bay High School. Our prices are much lower than all the other thrift shops, and we have very nice things. We're crowded so we have specials. We sell three pairs of shorts, slacks, or blouses for five dollars. Our shoes are one or two dollars.

We put an ad in once in a while, but mostly our business comes from word of mouth. All of our volunteers and many Sun City Center people buy their things here. In fact, a year ago a semi ran into me at a light. A man ran up to me and said, "I saw it all. I'm your witness. It sure wasn't your fault." Then he pulled over in the courtyard and said, "My mother-in-law is dying and I'm looking for a new shop and a Dorothy." I said it must be the Nearly New, and I'm Dorothy. He gave us all her clothes and furniture. He left an electric cart that I put in my house and sold for him. He sent me one hundred dollars for the shop then, and this Christmas he sent me a Christmas present, another hundred dollars for the shop.

People know we do a lot of good here. A lot of people buy winter things for their children and send them up north. People from Wimauma find their way in here, too.

People donate everything we have. If they can't get down to the donation box they call us and a volunteer picks it up. We are packed on Saturdays so we started opening Friday and Wednesday mornings."

$$*\qquad*\qquad*\qquad*$$

"I'm by myself. I don't have family because I was orphaned at four."

"Did you live in an orphanage?" I asked.

"No, I wasn't that lucky. I lived with relatives in West Bend, Wisconsin, until I was thirteen.

I went to a country school. Back then we had a cook stove and we boiled water for hot water. We washed clothes with a washtub and a board. They was no linoleum, just plain wood floors. If they got wet they'd leave a ring. I had to scrub it, and if I didn't scrub it and rinse it right, it showed a ring. Our light came from kerosene lamps. We had to trim the wick and wash the globes. We had outside toilets and maybe one winter coat. I had one or two dresses and one pair of shoes.

They keep a child in a foster home a couple of years, and then they transfer to another place. I feel we should have homes where brothers and sisters are together. Siblings shouldn't go separate ways and not know each other. You go to bed at night, and you don't know if you're going to be there the next day. When holidays came, no matter how excited, I knew I was just staying with this family. Foster homes didn't send you on to high school and college either.

When I was thirteen, I got a job on a turkey farm for fifty cents a week and my room and board. I dropped out of school, did house-work, washed clothes and ironed. I worked so hard at the turkey farm that I damaged my tubes and never could have children. I wanted children, but it's worked out all right.

I went up to Wisconsin and worked in a dime store. I got paid five one-dollar bills a week, which was quite a raise up from fifty cents. A man came in my first day and wanted a jockey strap.

I said, "I don't know if we have a horse department or not," so I called the manager and asked, "Do we have a horse department?"

"What do you want?"

"This man wants a jockey strap."

"Oh, I'll take care of that. Before you go home tonight, go see Miss Williams in the office."

She said, "You did the right thing. Don't ever let anybody walk away. That doesn't belong in the horse department—a man wears it like a brassier." I still didn't know what it was, but that's a bit of how I learned.

I finished the first year in high school. I quit because my appendix ruptured. Nobody would sign for me, so the juvenile judge said to go ahead and operate. I was hospitalized for eleven days if I remember right. In those days they kept you longer. It cost ninety-nine dollars and my father's sister gave me the money. Her husband was in the banking business. I left school and it took me three years to pay off my debt. My boss said, "Here's a dollar, I want you to see a play."

I said, "No." I worked and I never took charity. He said, "I'll lend it to you."

I needed glasses, so I added that onto the fourteen dollars he had loaned me. When I went to Wisconsin, I sent him fifteen dollars. He wrote thanking me and saying it wasn't necessary. I still have the letter.

When I was seventeen, I lived with a family who had three children aged four, two, and one month. They became my god family. One boy went to college and finished at MIT. He is out in California and has done very well. Another went to college for a couple of months but then went into the service for two years. He was nineteen when he went to Korea..." Dorothy tried holding back tears, but they flowed down her cheeks, "...and didn't come back. It's one of those things. The girl has five children. Of course both parents are gone now. We just lost the father a few years ago at ninety-seven. They were wonderful people."

"It sounds like you were real close to them. They were your family."

"Oh, yes. They hired me for two months, then it got to be three months. I went to the poor house and got a job for thirty-eight dollars a month. When I told Mother on Saturday that I was leaving Sunday, she started crying. She called Father and he said, "Young lady, I want to talk to you. Understand that this is your home and you never leave home. If you want to do housework you can get another job, but when I come through that door, you will be here."

I did housework there until I got the job at Penny's. I started working at Penny's the week before I was nineteen. We bought strips of paper and put the little swatches of paper with the dresses, in the back and front, and I checked the stock. I earned one hundred and thirty dollars a month. I eventually became a buyer for JC Penny's in Wisconsin. I lived with a nice family, which saved me three dollars a week. That's what they charged for a boarding home in those days.

"Could you live comfortably on that?"

"Yes, I didn't spend money at home for my room and board and I worked six days a week, so I didn't have time to run around. It's what you make it.

I played the stock market. I bought my first shares when I was seventeen, in 1935 and 1936. The depression was just getting over. I don't know what the young people would do today if there were a depression. They don't know how to make stew, or vegetable soup. They don't know how to manage. It's always, give-me, give-me, give-me. My generation wasn't like that. They didn't want everything. They were happy with what they had.

I ran a roadside stand in Minnesota. I had baskets of tomatoes and stuff on a table. I modeled a couple of years for Dolphin, sold furniture, and decorated for ten years. I worked in an office for four years where I learned computers and the payroll machine. I didn't like it. I prefer helping people.

I came down here in '68 because my husband and I had never been to Tampa. I wouldn't want to go back up north to freeze. I moved to Naples, but it was such a dead place, so I came to Tampa and opened the First Oriental Rug shop.

I think about the wonderful things I've been able to do. I've met wonderful people. I've had wonderful friends. I'm there for them, but I don't belong to one person. I belong to many people. If they need me, I'll be there. I'm the American mother to a foreign girl since 1963. She has two sons, one is a doctor and the other will be an architect.

Life has been good to me. I had a wonderful husband for four and a half years before he died. I didn't ask for it, but you have to move on. I cried…" Dorothy didn't finish her sentence as her voice choked and she wiped tears from her eyes. "I have to put his death behind me. I was married three times.

My second husband, Willie, was fourteen years older than me. We had a lovely home, six and a half acres. I was forty and wanted to adopt, but he was never around children and wouldn't have been the father type.

A man who volunteers in the Nearly New Shop adopted children. Those people are special to me, especially the men. Women are born to be nurturers, but when a man takes in a child as his own, loves and supports it, he's pretty special.

Anyway, I was too late to adopt. In those days they wouldn't give you children at my age. There were a lot of black babies, but protestant, uh-uh. There just weren't any available. It was very difficult to adopt children, and it took a long time.

My present husband is eighty-five. I don't think he'll be here too long. He gets nothing out of life. He complains. I shouldn't have been so foolish as to marry him.

I'm an usher at the performing arts center on Wednesday nights, and sometimes Friday nights. Since I volunteer there, I get to see all the shows. I've also joined hospice. There's a patient I visit. I do my housework. That's about it. I keep busy and the store takes a lot of my time. I moved the first of November and I still don't have the house ready to have people in. I haven't had time. That's how life is.

I hope I can stay healthy and continue helping people. I'll stay with the store as long as I'm able to do my share.

I was on the volunteer emergency squad five years. We need people in the emergency squad. We have two units of three. Two of my volunteers are there on twenty-four hour duty. They have the ambulance, which is free to the people in Sun City Center, and they also have two vans to take people to dental appointments. There's a driver, an EMT, and a First Aider on the emergency squad. It's a wonderful service. I just can't say enough good things about the emergency squad. I had to quit because I have arthritis in my hands. I can't lift the gurney any more. We have mostly old people because the young people who are coming down here aren't volunteering.

I think one of the biggest changes I've seen is that people have more than they need. They don't know the value of the dollar like we do. Also, people aren't as giving as they used to be. A handshake doesn't mean what it used to mean. Today you have to put it in writing and put some money down. Years ago you shook hands and made a bargain. Years ago, if someone needed help we would stop and help. The young people can't be bothered and drive on by. You have to remember that every human being needs to be needed, and if someone needs help, that's our duty.

People say, "You're a good Christian." I don't like that label. You're a good *person*.

There are a lot of good Moslems, a lot of good Jewish people. It doesn't cover all people.

I'm a little prejudiced because my last husband was Jewish. He was wonderful. He was super, superman! I was born Presbyterian and was baptized, but I like the Jewish faith. I like how they believe. I get perturbed when I hear people say someone Jewed them."

"I don't hear that expression that much any more," I said.

"You hear it more among the older crowd. That was their expression and they meant nothing by it.

Coming from small towns, people weren't associated with other nationalities. I don't think there were any Jewish people in my little town, so I wasn't exposed to other cultures, which was sad. When I was a child I knew one Jewish art dealer, so I thought all Jewish people were art dealers. I thought all Chinese people were bootleggers because that was in the paper and I heard people say that. Because I never knew any, I thought all Chinese had a long braid down the back of their necks.

Back when I lived in Wisconsin, I took my first husband to the Mayo clinic. I was going to stay there some time, so I asked someone if they knew where there was a restaurant and a hotel. They said, "Yes, but I don't think you want to stay here." It was a kosher place. I couldn't understand what that meant.

If people don't tell you, how do you learn? Dr. Glicksman at Mayo clinic explained it to me. I was ignorant because I hadn't had any exposure. I was around twenty-five years old.

Since then I've traveled all over Europe. There's no favorite country. When I saw Switzerland, I thought it was the most beautiful country but my husband said, "Wait till you see Norway."

Wherever you go, it's the people who make it. The people are all special in their own way. You could go to the most beautiful place in the world, but if the people aren't nice, you won't like it. I've never been to New Zealand or Australia. When I retire I'd like to go to New Zealand. They say it's a lovely place, and the people are so nice. I don't care if I take a tour or not. I hope to travel more, but the store is growing and there's work to do.

Life has been good to me. I'm going on eighty-four in a few months. I won't push it, but when it comes, it comes. I'm happy for every year I have. I'm happy I can reach that. My mother and father weren't so lucky.

If I'd had children, I wouldn't worry about my daughter. I would have impressed on her over the years that she would use good judgment. I'd explain that whom you marry is who your children will become. If you marry a ditch digger, your children will be with ditch diggers and won't have a push for education. If I had children I would say, "This is what you will be when you go to college." I wasn't that lucky, but my life is better than I ever thought it would be.

I wear glasses to read now, but my vision and hearing are very good."

"What is your secret for keeping you complexion so smooth?" I asked.

"I don't use any cream, just soap and water, and a little lipstick. My health is good." Dorothy knocked on the wooden table. "You never know what's around the corner. If it's something bad, I'll handle it. I am writing notes of my life, and when I get it all put together I want to make it into a book. I've had a very different life. I've learned a lot of different things about life."

Map—India

Leon Boucher, age 81

Agricultural Specialist
Green Springs, Ohio

Leon is a volunteer at the Newly Near Shop in Sun City Center, Florida. Dorothy gave me his phone number and recommended I call him.

Leon and his wife Ginger live in Sun City Center. Their white house with gray brick trim is neatly landscaped with grass, flowers, and bushes. There is a large recreational vehicle in the open carport.

Leon greeted me at the door. He has an average build and the black hair trimming the back of his head is beginning to show a hint of gray. He was dressed casually in a striped cotton shirt, wore wire-rim glasses, and two hearing aids. His smooth, wrinkle-free face had a smile during most of our interview.

Ginger had recently broken her hip and was using a walker to get around the house. She was busy getting dressed as she was expecting a friend to visit and said that she didn't have time to talk to me right now. Consequently, this interview is only with Leon, who began by telling me about his travel experiences.

"We lived in India two years and worked there. Girls didn't count and they didn't even send them to school. The boys went because they are considered part of a joint family. Anything the son earned went into the dad's pocket. They had arranged marriages. When the next son got married, you'd just build another three walls onto the house. The new bride got all the dirty detail and she moved up, or down, the hierarchy. There wasn't much for her to look forward to.

I wanted to hire a secretary and I advertised in the paper. I went down to the college Monday morning and saw all these men out in the hall.

I asked the head of the college, "What's going on?"

He said, "You've got interviews. They're your secretaries."

Not a lady in the bunch. Some of them weren't qualified and they'd cry. "You've got to help me, my family is depending on you to hire me."

India is making progress. Girls now are going to school. I'm on the doctoral committee at the University of Bhubaneswar in India. That means, City of Temples. It's about three-hundred miles south of Calcutta. In fact, I'm the advisor for a girl who is getting her doctorate.

I am on a dissertation committee at Ohio State. One girl was here two years and had to write her dissertation. She is trying to help homemakers in her country, and I am advising her in agriculture. She set up her program. I look at it, make any comments, and send it back. It's taken quite a while, but within the next six months she'll get her doctorate. I'm just helping this one woman now but in Kabala, Africa, I handled the Masters students.

We agreed to help India build four teacher-training colleges. We helped train the people and get started. We were hands-on in home economics, agriculture, industrial arts, and business and office. We followed the Gandhi approach, where he said that if people travel around the country they'd become smarter. Gandhi set up four holy cities, one up at Kashmir in the North, one at Bangalore in the South, and at Bhubaneswar in the South and Bhopal, which is Central. Gandhi thought if you get to these four places, you have a better chance of getting to Heaven. His theory was that by traveling they would learn and pick up ideas. It's a sound approach. We put the colleges in those same cities. Each college takes up four states. India is made up of sixteen states. I had charge of agriculture at the college in Bangalore. College graduates from India came to Ohio State, where I trained them for a year.

I have a doctorate in agricultural education. We train agricultural agents, extension agents, agriculture teachers, and foreign agricultural workers from Africa. My co-workers said, "You ought to go back with us." My wife and I had a ten-year-old boy, and an eight-year-old girl. Of course, we took them with us.

My association in Africa was short time stuff. Kabala in Sierra Leon had the old British system. They wanted to avoid nepotism and favors so they wouldn't let the professor examine his own students. You needed to have outside examinations. They recommended me to be on the doctoral committee and sent me the syllabus. The professor would write an examination that he thought was fair, I'd make suggestions for minor changes to add or delete material and send it back until finally we agreed on the exam. The professor didn't get to grade the papers. They administered the three-day written exam and sent them to me. After I read them, I packed my suitcase and headed for Sierra Leon. I would be over there about a month giving oral exams. I'd have their exam paper, we'd get acquainted, talk about their ambitions, and so forth. Then we'd go over the test.

This was in English, although they had their own dialect. In India they learn three languages, Hindi, English, and their state language. One is not more than the other. I learned enough Hindi to get along, but I'm not proficient. They grew up with English, so there was no problem. My kids enrolled in school and had to take English, Hindi and the state language. We were in the State of Orissa, and the kids had to learn that language. Most states spoke English more than anything else.

Another pleasant experience was in South Africa, Swaziland. Look on the map, clear down on the bottom of Africa, on the right hand side of the country there are two little dots—one is Swaziland and the other is Lesotho. They're land-locked kingdoms within South Africa. Although they have a king, they are pretty well controlled by South Africa. When you think of Africa, you think of wild animals. Swaziland is about five-thousand feet high, like Denver, Colorado. Five thousand foot ridges run down the country, forming a big valley. They have corn, cotton, pineapple, and dairy farms. People were poor, but they were happy.

The University of Swaziland in Africa was trying to teach agricultural agents and teachers by lecturing. There was no hands-on experience. Ohio State thought that we could help them build a better program, so I was selected to do that. I set up the farm and we changed the whole way we went about teaching those people.

They had plenty of land, so we took six-hundred and seventy acres, divided it into cropland and animal pastures. We bought livestock and poultry, swine, dairy and beef cattle, electric milkers and coolers for the milk. It took mechanics and a lot of machinery. We trained those young people how to run and care for the equipment. We taught them artificial insemination so they could inseminate their own cattle, and we didn't have to ship semen from the United States to Africa. Their farms have prospered. That was a fine experience and I enjoyed it.

Although I'm retired, I still serve on some committees at the University, and I still work with farm organizations, farm bureau, and the scholarship aspect. We give scholarships, and we have alumni meetings.

I've always volunteered. Ginger and I are quite active in the church. We help out with little league, and the ballgames. We feel good about it because we're helping somebody have a better quality life and they appreciate it.

I volunteer in the men's shop at the Nearly New Shop. Monday, Wednesday, and Saturday. Yesterday they got in quite a bit of stuff.

The tables were piled high with men's clothing so I helped with that. I've worked there for about ten or eleven years now. Seven churches and a Jewish synagogue make up the Interfaith Counsel. Last winter there were people living in a trailer without heat. I gathered up blankets and corduroy pants, heavy wool stuff that we couldn't sell, and I took them out to Beth El, which is part of our counsel. I just took out two bags yesterday again, and I'm continuing to try to meet the men's needs. Last week Dorothy and another lady sorted out a big bag of heavy sweaters. I took those out for the ladies. They emptied the bags out, and began looking and measuring. We used to just be open on Saturdays. We'd size and separate and so forth on Wednesday. Now she has it open on Wednesday and Saturday—I've got my schedule built around that.

I serve on the scholarship committee here, selecting kids for scholarships. Last year the shop gave twenty-three scholarships. We interview at East Bay, and also at the Baptist school in Ruskin. We give five kids one-thousand dollar college scholarships. If we can get them started, there's enough money to get them through. There are grants, loans, and internships. They need somebody to clean up the laboratory, and kids can almost pay their way through school if they get one of those jobs.

Ginger and I are both eighty-one. We're active in a lot of things. We belong to Kiwanis club—that's a service organization. We're up there six months and down here six months. We started coming down here because Ginger had three sisters here.

I help with the Historical Society back home in Hilliard, Ohio. I'm a director with the society and take care of the buildings. There's always work out there to do. We moved a church that's over a hundred years old and built a historical village, including a schoolhouse, in our hometown. Painting and repairing the schoolhouse is almost a full time job. We have a log cabin. We couldn't find one good log cabin, but three people donated log cabins. We tore them down, took the timbers, and built one in the village with an inside staircase and an upstairs bedroom. None of them had that. They'd sleep upstairs but they had a window up there, and a ladder. Back there in those early times, you'd crawl up the ladder, go in, and then pull the ladder in so the Indians couldn't get in. Besides the staircase, we have a fireplace in there now. It's very cozy. The Hilliard City Museum helped us build a church. They gave us fifty-thousand dollars. We earned the other monies. We have a barn with all kinds of hand tools and farm machinery from the 1800 vintage. We have a railroad depot with flashing red lights and everything. The latest thing was voting booths. Florida was having so much trouble voting, so we wanted to save one for prosperity.

I have a computer, mailing lists, and e-mail. I head up a thing called the Hilliard Reunion. I just got the invitations out last week. You'd be surprised how many people from that little town come to Florida. We'll meet down at Buddy Freddie's. This is the fifth year, and we'll have seventy-five people there just from that little town.

We're sports fans, and I am in the alumni group. We've traveled around the Southwest, Midwest, Wisconsin, and Minnesota to all the Big Ten university football games. We've been to all the universities at least once, some many times during football season."

Ginger walked into the room using her walker. "Ginger fell and broke her hip. That takes some time because now I need to do all the cleaning, washing, cooking. Ginger has had one knee replacement, a hip replacement, and broke the other hip. That's what's healing now. They put in a stem and socket. We have a home care lady who comes three times a week to bathe her and teach her how to handle that broken hip. Another lady comes and helps her with exercises, and there's a home nurse who comes to draw blood, and so forth. She checks that the Coumadin blood level is right. Ginger had a couple blood clots. They gave her too much Coumadin in the hospital, and we almost lost her. Cumin is rat poison, a blood thinner. They got it right now, but it needs to be checked. An overdose of that is bad news.

"Ginger, turn your walker around here so I can show my stones." Ginger had a cloth pocket decorated with polished stones hanging from the front of her walker. She got them out of the jewelry box and said, "I'm going to fancy this up a little bit".

Silver smithing is one of my hobbies," Leon continued. "When I first retired from the University in '84, we thought we'd move to Arizona. It's a great place to be. They have the international gem show in February every year. They come from all over the world. I thought I'd learn silver smithing from the Indians. I sat with old Tom down there is Tuscan, Arizona, and he taught me.

I do a little photography, too. I judged photography at the Ohio State Fair for twenty-two years. Here's a picture of my little granddaughter," Leon brought out a photo album to show me his family photos.

"I have a big flower garden back home in Ohio. This was a jungle out here in the back before I pulled out two truckloads of snake plant. I planted flowers and bougainvillea and will put my Christmas flowers out there. I just put seeds out here yesterday.

I have many things, but not enough time to do it all. I like lawn bowling; it's an English game. You can't roll the balls straight because they're weighted. It's a great time.

Life has been good to us. We had the kids with us, lived around the world, including India and the United States. Probably the prettiest tour we've ever been on was not the Taj Mahal, which is one of the Seven Wonders of the World, but the trip to Boston the first week in October, route 3 between Vermont and Mount Washington and then Bangor, Maine. There isn't any artist that paints the colors we saw. We've always made a fishing trip up into Canada in the summer time. Now it's mainly between Ohio and here. We do some side trips, saw New Brunswick, Prince Edward Island, or Nova Scotia.

We'll travel this summer if we're both hail and hearty. I've had two open-heart operations, so I can't do some of the things I used to do, or go as hard and fast as I used to go. We still would like to go to Nashville or Brandon, Missouri."

*   *   *   *

"My hometown was in Green Springs, near Columbus. I served in the Navy in World War two, in the terror task force in the South Pacific. I got an award and some battle scars. I wouldn't take a nickel to go back and do it again, but I wouldn't take anything for the experience.

I had two brothers and three sisters and I was number one. We were just coming out of the depression, and we were scratching...doing everything we could do to make a living on the farm. Instead of hauling hogs to the packing plant, we butchered them and sold meat. We cut them up, smoked it, and made hams. We raised melons, and pickles, and cabbage. That's all stoop labor. You have to bend over. With three boys, Dad thought we should make our contribution.

I worked with horses during the depression time. We bred and raised our own colts. We broke them and trained them for teams. In 1936, when I was sixteen years old, I drove them in a pulling contest and I broke a world record—the heavy weight team in Mariana, Ohio, 4th of July. It didn't last long. Only three weeks later a team out of Indiana broke my record.

My dad was working at the local elevator, where they grind feed, sell fertilizer, and so forth. Rural elevator, they call them, for a dollar and a half a day during the depression. I'm about twelve years old, and I was picking strawberries at two cents a quart. I could pick two hundred quarts a day, earning four dollars a day, and he was working for one dollar and fifty cents a day. I thought I was really big stuff. Of course, to survive, all the boys gave to the family. I can still remember that. I was making more than Dad did, but strawberries are a short season crop. It didn't last too long. We worked hard. I graduated in '38. We were poor and it was the depression time so there was no chance of going to college.

I had an agricultural teacher who, unbeknown to me, filled out a scholarship application. I was out in the field working when he came to the house and said, "I want to talk to you and your parents."

We went back to the house, and he said "I have a scholarship for Leon." First thing Dad thought was he was losing a hired hand. Teacher said, "I think he's college material and he ought to go. This will pay his tuition at Ohio State."

Without him I'd be on that farm picking pickles yet. The guy gave me a chance.

It was a Sears and Roebuck scholarship. It paid three hundred dollars. Back then in 1938, the tuition at Ohio State University was a hundred dollars a quarter. It paid for three quarters, and the fourth quarter was summer vacation.

My parents finally said, "Yah, we think he should go, but we can't afford to pay his room and board."

The next week my teacher took me to Columbus, and I got a job washing dishes. It was a white tablecloth restaurant, good eats. I washed dishes three hours every evening, and that gave me three meals and twenty-five cents an hour, which paid my room rent. Sears and Roebuck scholarship paid my tuition

I worked summers. I got a job with a contractor working in concrete and block laying, carrying mud and mixing mud (mortar). That paid 80 cents an hour. So, I got through school, taught two years, and then went into the Navy.

A boy named Carmen, which sounds like a girl's name, was absent. I hadn't seen him in about a week.

I said, "Where's Carmen, is he sick?"

Someone said, "No, he joined the army."

This was in 1942. About a week or two later, I asked about Val C. He had joined the aircorp.

I thought, "here's high school kids going into the service. What am I doing here?" I was teaching and these were my students signing up. So that weekend I went to Detroit and asked if I could get into the navy. That was my motivation to volunteer and join the service.

I'm a long timer in a lot of things. I've been with the American Legion fifty-six years continued membership. Masonic Lodge, fifty-two years. Helping with college, fifty-one years. I've been on committees and so forth at Ohio State.

Ginger and I went to school together. We grew up together as kids. Her family moved near me when she was in eighth grade. We were high school sweethearts and graduated from the same class in '38. We got married in '45 after our graduation from college and I got out of the Navy. We've been married one hundred and twelve years, fifty-six for her, and fifty-six for me. We get along great on that. We argue, we question, and don't accept anything.

We were arguing some point and had a grandson in the rear seat of the car. He leaned forward and said "Grandpa, Grandma, I don't know how this marriage ever lasted." He thought we were fighting. She votes one side, I vote the other. We cancel each other's votes. She's the Democrat, I'm the Republican.

I inherited that from my Grandpa. He was politically active and Republican. Back in those early days you had a straight ticket. You only voted one way and didn't even look at the other side. I'm not that way, I read up on them, go meetings and learn, then pick the best one. So when I say we cancel each other's vote, that's not quite true. We discuss who we think the best people are.

I taught for forty-five years. I got the student advisor award at the college at agriculture, and also the one for outstanding teaching. I tried to help my students just like my teacher helped me. It's worked out pretty well.

I got an e-mail come in from St. Louis from a previous student. He's the president of grain marketing and big grain exporting all over the world. He sent a note saying, "I had an agricultural teacher once who helped me get where I am now."

Another student had a lot of spunk to him, a feisty little guy. He'd try hard. He had never milked a cow in his life, but I taught him how to judge milk, to taste it and smell it. They had dairy products judging for butter and milk. I trained him, and he's a state champion. I encouraged him and got a loan for him to start school. He just retired as Corporate Vice President, Buick Motor Division, USA.

Two years ago this fellow came up to see me and introduced himself. I recognized the name. I had him in high school. He said, "I came up to tell me you were the best teacher I ever had."

When I taught, I visited every family. I sat in the kitchen with Mom and Dad, and talked about where the child was going to go, on the farm, or off the farm, and opportunities. I never had to worry about discipline. If anything happened, I just called Dad and he would take care of it. Parents were involved. When I came home from school, I had chores to do and responsibilities. Today when kids come home from school nobody's there. Both mom and dad are working. That's too bad.

I'm disappointed in our education system. The kids who come from Asia whip our kids in mathematics. There's something we're not doing as good as we should. I wish there was some way to solve it, but it just isn't spending more money. We have to get the parents involved in the process, with parents and teachers. Yep. I used to have groups of students from the college come out to the house.

You don't teach class like you feed a pen of steers, take it out and throw it in. Each one of those kids is an individual, and they have goals, and aims, and experiences they can build upon. You treat them as worthwhile individuals. You don't just throw it out and let them come and eat.

I'm living off the successes of everybody I touched, people I worked with, people I taught. To see them grow and bloom, that's great, makes you think you did something right. That's one thing that keeps me young.

I have some grand kids that I want to help get into college. One boy was in the Navy. He's married now and has a child. I have a granddaughter eleven, another six, and a great grandchild who's one. They are great—yah.

My grandson asked me "Grandpa, why do you work all day at the Historical Village? You don't get paid for it."

Young people today don't seem to want to volunteer to pick up paper or anything to make the community look better. I even sense this here in Sun City Center. I don't think the younger people here are volunteering as much for emergency squad, or volunteering for service clubs. That's not a hundred percent true as there are schools that adopt a highway or a mile.

I don't sit down, I keep moving. I eat anything that I want. Ginger does a good job preparing meals, and I like to cook also. We stay away from the fats because of building up plaque, and the two open hearts I had. They won't operate anymore. Now if I have a block they go up there and put a stent in. I have five stents in me. We enjoy people, we like bridge, people came in and play cards. One lady brings us oranges. Come strawberry season, I'll pick her some strawberries. When I go to the berry patch, I pick about twenty quarts of berries and bring them for people.

There's so much to do here in Sun City Center that you can't do it all. I can't imagine anybody could live in Sun City Center and be bored. I'm in lapidary (jewelry making, grinding and polishing stones) over here. I'm on a committee with the church. I golf, lawn bowl, work out on the fitness machines, sort clothes, pick tomatoes and strawberries. Now I've got to do the washing, and housecleaning, and meals. I need more hours.

The key to a healthy retirement is *don't sit down*. In the summer time I taught at Cornel, Michigan State, and so forth. I was on a train coming back from Colorado. There was a man with a notebook on the plane, and I asked him what kind of work he was in. He was an actuary. The fellow took care of death payments for the railroaders.

I asked, "What kind of program do you have?"

He told me about the policies. He said, "Let me show you something."

He showed me pages with two year's results. The people who work railroads only average nineteen checks from the time they retired until they die a year and a half later.

He said, "They did in retirement the same thing they did when they worked—they sat."

They were engineers or conductors on the train—they sat. They just sat. That will shake you up.

Maybe I'm too much the other way. I can't sit down. I don't need exercise because I have enough work to do.

There probably isn't anything I'm going to upset the world with from now on. I'll just stay healthy and active and contribute where I can. Ginger and I have a good life. Getting a broken hip slows her down a little, but we will continue doing the things we enjoy doing. I'm a people person. I enjoy being with groups, church groups, this mission work that we're doing, the university, and committees. My most productive days are probably gone, but as long as they want me to serve, and I can function, I'll keep going."

Aurora, age 80

Demo Sales
West Virginia

I met Aurora at the Sunbird Extravaganza, a yearly activity where companies display services geared towards seniors. She was managing an information booth about a liquid product for heartburn and passing out samples. I wanted to set up an appointment at her home, but she said she was too busy, so we talked in the rear of her display booth as best we could over the background noise and interruptions from people looking at the booth and asking questions.

"They say that Capricorns are hard workers but they bitch about it, and I'm a Capricorn," Aurora laughed.

Aurora has pure white hair, was dressed in a white shirt and blue pants, and wore a volunteer ribbon which somebody had given her, even though she told me she was being paid for managing the booth. Although she is short, she stands straight with perfect posture.

"I'm five feet, and have always been five feet," she explained. "I don't have osteoporosis. When I was younger, I enjoyed getting tan, but now I'm too busy working outside to worry about it. The sun gave me wrinkles." She smiled pleasantly, showing her own perfect teeth.

"I worked here last year and am working here this weekend. The rest of the year I do demos in the stores on Saturdays, and sometimes Fridays. I love doing this kind of work—I get to travel and meet people.

I own six apartments and do all the yard work outside, cut the grass, weeding, planting, and making sure that everybody's yard looks okay. I have to keep them nice because they're in a nice section of Haynes City. The apartments are always rented, and I could rent more if I had them. They're nice apartments.

On weekdays, I care for five ladies in an elderly home. I do cooking and sometimes spend five to ten hours a day cooking and putting stuff in the freezer. If the woman who owns the home is gone, I take care of the ladies, take them to the bathroom, and make sure they're okay. I live one block away and walk there. I'm up by six-thirty and go all day long until six at night. After six o'clock, don't bother me—it's time for me to rest. I work now more than I ever did in my life. As long as I can have my health, I'll keep working. I went to church one Sunday and the minister pointed to me because I do so much."

*   *   *   *

"I'm Italian. There were ten of us kids when I was growing up, five boys and five girls. I was in the middle. My mother was married twice, to two brothers. She lived to be ninety-six, but was in a nursing home for seven and a half years. My father lived to be ninety-four and was in a nursing home for only one month. My sister had him for four or five years before that.

Life was rough growing up during the depression. We were lucky we had a farm. We got everything out of the garden, and had a cow, pigs, chicken, and rabbits. We didn't want for anything.

I went through high school and was married when we were both nineteen. We had a little house and a car. I stayed home with my kid, although I went to work in the steel mill when we went to war. I was about twenty then. My first husband burned to death. We were married ten years and had one seven-year-old son. We were both thirty years old. When my son was thirteen I got a job working in a store where they sold dryers and refrigerators.

I had no children from my second marriage. We were married thirty-seven years. He was a construction worker and his work took him from coast to coast, including Hawaii and Alaska. I went with him of, course. We came down here to retire, but we were here only one year when he went back up north to work in the summer. He'd come home every winter. One day, six years ago, I went to Wal-Mart, and when I came back my husband was dead.

My husband always wanted to buy property down here. When I said that I was going to buy the three duplexes, he was so happy, but he only lived one year. The rent helps pay for them, but they have a first and a second mortgage, so I've got to work. When I get my apartments paid off, I will give them to my son.

Thursday is my day to get my hair done. I do that much for myself. I'm a beauty operator too. I went to beauty school. I cut my son's and his wife's brother's hair. I've got too much work to do anybody else.

My son is fifty-seven now, and he's very good to me. This is his third wife. She is very good to him—and to me too, so we get along real well. They gave me a surprise birthday party, and I really was surprised.

I help my daughter-in-law. She sells costume jewelry, and I go with her to the home parties. I do the packing and unpacking, and she does the talking.

My daughter-in-law is a very big girl and weighs over three hundred pounds. If I go into her house and there's a pile of clothes, I wash them and hang them on the line. I make her bed, clean her house, and cook for her. When I see her struggling to do something, I get up and do it myself. I know that's not right, she should be doing it, she needs the exercise, but I get impatient. I wash floors on my hands and knees. My daughter-in-law has three or four new mops and they're all in the corner while I'm on my hands and knees scrubbing her kitchen floor. She says, "Mom, you don't have to get down." I don't like it dirty—I have to get in the corners. I don't believe in mops. My mother never believed in mops. I do things the way my mother did.

When my son first moved into the apartment, there were two fellows helping him. They asked who did the upkeep and my son said, "My mother does."

About that time, I came down the driveway carrying a sheet of plywood, and they asked, "Who's that?"

He said, "That's my mother."

When it comes to working, I'll attempt anything—I'll take the wheelbarrow and go. If I can do something myself, I'll do it. I get on the stepladder, change the light bulb, change the filter in the air conditioner, take down my Christmas decorations, and take down his, too. My son gets mad and says, "Why don't you ask me to help you?"

I think my secret for staying healthy is to stay busy. I get up at six-thirty and go to work. If you're busy you don't have time to think, this is hurting me and that is hurting me. I'm not on any medication, except for a little Aleve for arthritis. I had my blood pressure taken today and it's pretty good. I used to walk a mile a day, but I don't have time for it now. I don't travel much, although I go up to West Virginia to see my sisters.

As for my future, there's not going to be another man—that's for sure. Two were enough.

I have a little Pekingese dog, and he's the love of my life. I have a lot of friends but I don't really have time to go out. I go to church and I visit my sisters once in a while. I have two sisters and one brother left. We're a close-knit family. My sister was very surprised that I have so many friends down here because I'm from West Virginia. I'm not a snowbird, as I've been down here twenty years. I came down here and stayed. At eighty I'm starting to slow down but I don't feel old. I feel well enough to attempt anything."

Wertha Smith, age 80

University Student
Corning, Ohio

Wertha had picked up a flyer that I left with the University of South Florida gerontology department. "I saw your advertisement in one of the rooms where I took a class, and noticed a copy on the table, so I decided to call you," she said. Having just turned eighty, she was the youngest person I interviewed.

Wertha has a soft, husky, carefully modulated voice, light brown skin, and high cheekbones. She is thin and her face smooth, giving her the appearance of a much younger person. Her dark gray hair is short and tightly curled, but not nappy. She wore a professional matching outfit consisting of black slacks, a white sweater, and a vest with real gold thread weaved into the cloth to form designs. Around her neck was a large necklace with an oddly crooked, alien face. The words that came to my mind describing her were sophisticated, proper, and regal.

Her immaculate apartment in an upper-middle-class neighborhood was decorated with African designs, artificial plants, wooden statues, a variety of both wooden and stuffed animals, and a life-sized stuffed tiger. I had the feeling I had walked into an African museum display.

"I enjoy collecting," said Wertha, "and have had the pleasure of visiting Africa three times. I have more statues back home but not as many animals there. This collection here isn't as big as the one in my home in Dayton. I enjoy things other people do in art and music.

I spend three or four months here in the wintertime, but I keep in touch with people at home. I often make phone calls to keep up with what's going on. One of my friends told my daughter, "You know, you mother's missing all the funerals." Unfortunately, there have been four since I've been here, in less than four weeks. That's not something I look forward to.

When I came to Tampa I left twenty-degree weather, and it was eighty some degrees this week. I had to make a mental adjustment to the change. I brought some clothing but I didn't bring the right things, Nevertheless, I'll make it through because I anticipated that it would be cool in February.

I've been taking classes at the university. The instructors are volunteers. I took a course last year where the instructor was a retired surgeon who had an amputation due to diabetes. Another fellow had worked for the government in the justice system. I had one course in African-American art, taught by an African professor. Right now I'm taking one on the wonders of ancient Egypt, which interests me because I've never been to Egypt, and another in cultural diversity. I go to a Bible study group on Monday morning and another group on Wednesday evening. I was in a bookstore today, and the owner of the store said, "Why don't you come to yoga—we have a class on Tuesday."

Wertha showed me the necklace with the odd figure that reminded me of a space alien and explained, "This grotesque figure is a Maori symbol of an ancestor and is made of whalebone. The Maori are the indigenous people of New Zealand. This is a female figure with green eyes made of jade. Many times this kind of ancestor symbol is shown with the tongue sticking out and the head twisted to the side. Ancestors are important. Without them, we wouldn't be here. Ancestors are prevalent in the Indian and African cultures, and I'm sure other cultures as well.

I try to maintain a fair degree of exercise. Walking is one of my favorite exercises along with aerobics and yoga. I also read a lot. When I go to the library I usually come back with a bag of books. Right now I'm reading about women in the Bible, and the Nile. I do things with a friend who's interested in art, drama, and theatre. My friend prepared Jamaican food and invited me to dinner.

I find ethnic cooking interesting, not just my culture, but other cultures as well. I like many things—I'm not a picky eater. I enjoy making preparations, and sharing. Cooking for myself isn't as much fun as cooking for others. I have many choices of food that I enjoy. Today I wanted a certain seasoning and went to a store that sells Caribbean food to get it there, and some goat, as a matter of fact. Last time I was there I talked to someone who told me about cooking goat. It's crazy things like that." She laughed, "So those are some of the things I do."

*   *   *   *

"There have been some mixes in my background. My French ancestor was an indentured servant who came to this country. When he had worked out his services, and the person responsible for him said that he could leave, he went to southern Ohio. My mixture is American Indian and African, and most likely there is Caucasian, too, and who knows what that might be. My first name, Wertha, is of German derivation. I come by it because my mother had a friend by that name.

I took a course in jewelry making and the teacher said to me one day, "How do you come by your name?" The next week she came to class and had done research on my name. Wertha was the goddess of small plants and animals and the sister of the goddess of nature. I thought that was interesting information that I would not have gotten otherwise.

I have two children that had unusual names. My older daughter is Kountez, which means, "to give comfort", and my younger daughter has the name Wrise. I made it up. I enjoyed an opera singer named Rise Stevens but I wanted my daughter to have my initials. It's a mother's privilege to make up names. I also have a son, Edward III.

There are many different considerations for what people include in children's names. There is a new trend to choose African names. In later years I did some volunteer work at a school, and the teacher wanted me to take the child outside the classroom door. I began working with the child outside the door, but I hesitated to pronounce his unusual name.

The first time I went to Europe, the tour guide met us in England. We were all black, educated people. The tour guide seemed unsure and asked the group what we were interested in seeing. I told him, "I'm interested in everything that you have to show anybody. Even though I'm whatever term you want to use, African American, or black, I'm an American. I have mixed heritage, so I'm interested in everything."

I was born and grew up in Corning, a small country town in southern Ohio. I had a brother five years older than I. He was in an age group with older children and I was like an only child. I lived on a hill where I spent long lonely evenings, so having nothing else to do, I learned how to find constellations. As a matter of fact, I think some of my traveling came from my lonely evenings at home. I remember the rhyme, "Star light, star bright, first star that I see tonight, I wish I may, I wish I might, have the wish I wish tonight." I looked at the stars and wished to travel to far away places. Fortunately, my wishes came true. I still remember the constellations.

As a child, I loved traveling to family reunions and church conventions. My parents were actively involved in church, and I grew up in that environment. My father said to me one time "your middle name should have been GO." I have always enjoyed going.

My mother tutored me so I skipped a grade and finished high school at fifteen. While growing up, my thought was to be a teacher. I started college at sixteen, graduated with a bachelor's degree at nineteen, and started teaching at twenty. I taught first and second grades. I got administrative experience, first with the primary grades—kindergarten, one, two, and three, and then in elementary school.

My parents both died at eighty-four. My father died of a heart attack and my mother had cancer and an amputation. She had complications later in life. I have both those things that I need to be aware of. That's part of my heritage, too.

I thought it was important to have my advanced degree, so when my oldest daughter was about ready to enter college, I returned to school and got my Masters degree. Learning never ceases. I've maintained an interest in always doing something, trying to find out more about the world we live in, and what it's all about. There's a lot to learn.

My first husband was an athlete and an engineer. He was the first engineer to go to Lake Patterson Air Force Base. He competed to go to the Olympics in '48 and came in fourth place but they were only taking the first three. Then he developed kidney failure and was a dialysis patient for five years. He was fortunate to have a transplant but there were complications and he passed at age fifty-four. It was hard losing him.

People have different motives for looking for a mate. People need to have a companion to talk to and do things with. When I met my second husband, I wasn't looking for someone to keep, or to keep me. It would just be nice to have someone to talk with.

My second husband was born and raised in Toledo, Ohio, which is north of Dayton. We met through mutual friends in a religious organization. My husband was a Shriner and at one time he was the international head of his Shrine. He traveled a good bit both by car and by air.

In my early years I was a social smoker—I'd buy a pack of cigarettes, have a couple and throw the pack away. Although I have smoked, I don't consider myself to have been a smoker. I don't think I am plagued by the results of smoking. However, my husband was a heavy smoker and developed emphysema. Even though he used oxygen, he maintained a positive attitude about it, and we maintained a good relationship. He was sixty-eight when he passed. He hadn't smoked for many years, but the damage was done.

My daughter in California has her own business, a consulting firm, and my son owns a company that gives aid to minority businesses. My older daughter works in accounting with General Motors. She will be retiring in the next month. I have a grandchild graduating from college in San Juan Academy, so I'll be going to Boston where they live. I have two grandchildren, and their husbands suggested that we travel together.

I have been to many states in the United States and have gone to Europe about four times and to Central America. I've gone to countries on the East Coast of South America, the Soviet Union, Africa three times, the Orient two or three times, the Caribbean, San Juan, Mexico, and my most recent experience has been in New Zealand.

Having lost two husbands, I thought that was the end of traveling but I was active in church activities and the Bishop asked me if I wanted to go to Africa. Two weeks after he spoke to me we were enroute. That was a joyous occasion, and totally unexpected.

Although I attend church here, and they always welcome me with open arms, I'm affiliated with an Episcopal church in Ohio. My home church has a vision and we are planning a home for independent living, assisted living, and a clinic on the church site. So with that dream, there's lots to be done. I'm on the banquet committee, and I'm serving now on the school committee. This is a long-term plan, maybe twelve to fifteen years. Recently I helped publish a newspaper about many interesting things, including columbaria. This is a burial place for remains, which are put into receptacles, and sometimes put in gardens or in the walls.

I'm also interested in stained glass windows. I'm look forward to presenting my contribution, which will be the stained glass windows. I've called companies that do this kind of work, and as of today, I have received responses from two companies. To learn what others are doing, I have made phone calls to some Episcopal schools and have made appointments to visit them.

I don't find the time to do it all, but I share in whatever way I can. I participate in the advanced gift committee for soliciting funds. Even though I'm here rather than in Ohio, I have been trying to make contacts and suggest activities. I meet with other committees because this is one way that I can learn what his happening, how it's happening, and what support I can give.

The world has changed a lot in my lifetime. Children are off and running. Even babies know how to use the computer, but many of my friends don't use computers and e-mails. I got a little e-mail only computer, but it didn't work and I ended up bringing it back. I have a fax machine, but not a computer. I end up making a lot of phone calls. My phone bill—I don't want to see it.

I think people are becoming more tolerant in relationships and are working towards being less judgmental of many cultures, although there are still cultures where women are held back. Young people are more open than people my age. They have more acceptance of this American dream of people being equal.

Travel experiences in this country were not always positive in earlier years because of discrimination. You went to the back of the bus, you didn't drink at the white fountain, and you didn't try on a hat. I had these experiences traveling in Florida. My own children have more opportunities and better economics for making their own living.

When I was growing up, the history books did not present various cultures in a positive manner. The African back and Pigmies were shown with unusual things like rings in their lips and markings. That is what you saw—I wasn't championing black history at that time because it wasn't taught. Yes, there were some people who were mentioned and brought out, but there certainly wasn't the proliferation of materials that there is now, that makes us very aware.

That takes me back to something my father said to me in reference to color. He said, "You're not colored—nobody colors you." That's something I remember. I listened to what my father had to say, and I thought, "I'm really not colored, like crayons or ink. I'm a person." I emphasize the fact that you are who you are, you're a person, and you don't have to have that for identification. Black or African American, or what have you. There are continuing to be more opportunities for people to get and use an education. That has been a good change.

I enjoyed my travel and haven't had many negative experiences. Even in South Africa, during apartheid, my experiences were positive.

Some of my opportunities to travel were arranged by friends who had leadership in the AME (African Methodist Episcopal) Church. A lot of my travels have been church related.

You've probably heard that the most segregated place in this country is the church. Growing up, we were not welcome in my small home-town Catholic church. That is changing for the better. To my amazement, there are now opportunities for church visitation. I would like to visit a Catholic church and a Greek Orthodox church. When I traveled in the Soviet Union and through the US, I visited many churches and other denominations including the Russian Orthodox church. A woman who I sit on a committee with interviewed me about my experiences. She did research in theological theory. I'm grateful to have had the opportunity to travel.

I have so many reasons to be positive. I have a strong faith, and a belief that I cannot change what is, and I can always expect some change. I don't take the time to get unhappy with people. I try to find the positive and don't waste my time complaining. People talk about their frustrations in occupations and relationships, but you try to work through for the best and it makes for happier living.

Sometimes I wonder how much longer I will be coming to Tampa. I realize there will come a time when I will not be able to drive south, so I enjoy each day and look forward to seeing the people I've met. Life changes and I hope that I'll be able to keep my faculties, because I have plans. There but for the grace of God go I.

My health is good. I take some medication for blood pressure and cholesterol and a heart related pill. About four years ago, I was working with children in a summer program and had an uncomfortable feeling. I checked with the hospital but didn't have a heart attack. They gave me some medication to correct the pain, and so far so good. My philosophy is to check it out and find out. I think that has proven to be my advantage. I had chemo for cancer and recently the doctor said, "Your five years are up. You're doing well, no traces." Staying healthy certainly has to do with what you take into your body, what you do, and your genes. I'm certainly thankful for my health, and hope that I will grow old gracefully. I enjoy being active, and being involved, and I try to help other people. I've been very fortunate. I've made no specific plans for traveling, and heaven knows what is in my future."

Map of Papua, New Guinea

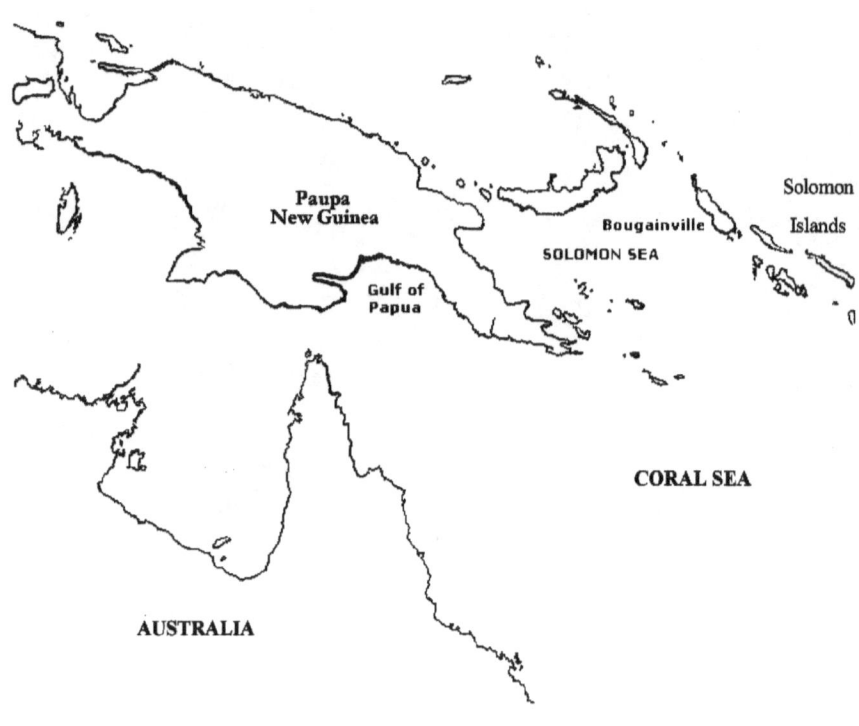

Sister Michaeline, age 80

Marist Sisters—Society of Mary
Cleveland, Ohio

I met Sister Michaeline at the Senior Companion program where I was invited to speak. Senior Companions is a program that allows low-income seniors to volunteer in various positions. They work twenty hours a week and earn a stipend of $2.50 an hour. Senior Companions generally care for sick or disabled seniors. Sister Michaeline works at the veteran's hospital.

Sister Michaeline, or Mike for short, is small, frail, and aged looking. Her face is a mass of fine, deep wrinkles, making her look much older than her eighty years. The wrinkled, but smiling face, and white veil covering her salt and pepper hair, remind me of Mother Theresa. Although sister Mike appears thin and fragile, with a pronounced kyphosis, or humped back, she is remarkably strong, agile, and quick. Along with the white, scarf-like veil covering her head, she wore a white blouse, dark blue skirt, and an orange volunteer jacket from the Veterans Administration (VA) hospital. She bent down easily, and demonstrated how she touches her toes as part of her daily exercises.

When I arrived at her doublewide mobile home, subdivided into three, one bedroom efficiency apartments, Sister Michaeline was standing outside waiting for me. She spoke at a rapid pace, barely taking a breath, chatting even before we entered her apartment.

The apartment was small and sparsely furnished with a dining table for two and a rocking chair. Although it was already March, Sister Mike's Christmas decorations, plastic holly, pinecones, and angels, were still up. A small American flag was taped to the wall. Hand crocheted magnets of flags and religious symbols stuck on her refrigerator, and several pictures and figures of Jesus and the Virgin Mary hung on the walls. She had numerous books and magazines, both religious and secular in nature, scattered about a small coffee table.

"All these things are coming down. They are Christmas decorations," Sister Mike explained. "I put up all the decorations for myself and another Sister. I had to go up and down the ladder and take everything off the walls. I did hers first but never got around to mine. I don't have time to sit down.

At Christmas my house was full because people brought me things. Christmas Day there was so much stuff—it didn't look like this. I covered it up, and I had to finish decorating when I came back from brunch. The only other thing I had to do was meet with my sisters for open house in the afternoon. I got feeling so down, so I said, "I'm going to see if there is anybody who doesn't have anything." The man next door didn't have a thing, and he was so pleased. He thought that I'd be visiting him regularly, but I told him "I can't take any more people, I just don't have the time." I'm not taking care of him, but I give him cake or gifts sometimes.

I learned to drive in Australia where they didn't have expressways. When I came here at seventy, I was afraid of the traffic. I was forty-seven years old when I began to drive, so I didn't have the confidence a young person would have. We have a couple cars for emergencies, and we have other Sisters who drive.

I walk to the bus stop. My program is on Monday and I leave here at six-ten in the morning to start work about seven-thirty or a quarter to eight. I don't get back here until five o'clock. I do chaplain work at the VA hospital. I don't have to go to the VA that early every morning, just two mornings a week.

I am Catholic and take communion. I have prayer requests come down from other denominations because I pray really from the heart. I don't use a book or anything. Some people like that—they say it's so nice to hear somebody praying. I gather them together in a room and we all pray together. Sometimes I listen to what they have to say. If they have a diagnosis, such as cancer, they may need someone to talk to.

My chief work on Monday is giving communion. I'm a volunteer, not a staff member, so I don't get involved in medical things. They tell me their problems and I have to be compassionate with them.

I take the elevator up but I walk through seven floors to give communion. If I don't see someone, they have therapy or another commitment, then I keep walking back until I finish everybody on my list. I have anything from twenty to twenty-five, maybe thirty people to see on Monday. Then I make a report and give it to Father. I tell him if they want to see the priest.

Tuesday is a freer day. I have a couple living here whom I help. He's a veteran of the war, and she's schizophrenic. She just sits there, very depressed. She's doing better now because I encouraged her to see a doctor and she's on medication. She asked me to pray for her and I brought her a Bible. Her husband is very, very good to her. He does as much as he can, because she can't do anything. I wash their clothes, fold clothes, and bring it to them. We have a laundry room. I carried their clothes, and my own, until last week when somebody gave me a cart.

On Wednesday I clean for them. They cannot stoop down. They think it's just marvelous that I can get on my hands and knees to scrub floors, stoop under the sink, and wash the dishes.

I put in three hours of prayer everyday. I have meditation to make and mass for half an hour each. That's a required thing. Usually I try to get my rosary in the morning before I go. I can get some done on the bus if I can't do it here. Later, we have a longer time for prayer. I have to do my Divine Office, and there are different kinds of prayers in the Bible. In the morning is Matins, and Lauds. We don't have to say this one because it's every ten minutes until noontime. Most of us can't do that because we're working. Then there are prayers at noon. At four o'clock, we stop and say Vespers, which is about a fifteen-minute prayer, and then at night we say Compline. We have adoration, quiet time with God every night for at least a half hour, but I try to put in an hour. I find my strength in the Lord. Without prayer, I couldn't do what I do. I get really down when it's just too much. Then I say "Lord, if you want me to continue doing this work, give me the strength to do it."

I give things to people who need it, but that takes time. I want to stay more with spiritual things, but if material needs happen I can't say, "I'm so sorry you're hungry. I'll pray for you," and not give anything to eat. That's not doing what God wants you to do. I need to see if I can get that man something to eat, or someplace to sleep, medicine. Whatever it is. You know what I mean? One day I saw a lady on the ground. I couldn't really bypass her, so even though I was going somewhere else, I stayed with her until I found someone to get her up.

I work with the AIDS people. That's really where I do most of my work I help people spiritually, do dishes, and play cards. I've had some very, very good experiences. I've stayed with people who are dying. My goal is to bring them comfort. AIDS is very confidential work. I have pictures of AIDS people, but newspapers can't publish the pictures, or come to the hospital.

One man was a drinking man. He asked me "Did you come here to preach the word of God?" I said, "No, I came here to see you," because I knew him, and I said, "you're drinking."

He said, "Sure, I'm drinking. You can stay if you want, but don't preach the word of God to me."

I said, "I'm not preaching the word of God to you." Finally I asked, "Do you have a Bible?"

"No I don't want a Bible."

"Oh, it's very interesting reading,"

Finally at the end he said, "Why don't you bring that Bible next time you come, and I'll consider it as a history book."

I really don't go in to preach, that's not what we have to do. We bring goodness and kindness. He said, "I'm not worth anything,"

"Yes you are,"

"Do you like me?"

"Yes I do. I love you as a Christian."

I can get words in like that. He felt very down on himself. He was gay and worried about not having a lover. I said, "It's not wrong, any friendship is okay. But if you go against the law of God it's wrong."

"How do you feel about gay people?" I asked.

"They're people of God. They were created by God, like I was. So therefore, when I went there to work with the AIDS, it must have been for some reason. Eight years ago, AIDS people were very much rejected. Now there's medication and different ways of looking at things. Some people still reject them, but if they take care of themselves they have a long life span. They can look quite good, better than some other people look.

I became so tired this past year that I decided I would give up the AIDS work at Tampa AIDS Network, but they called me and asked me to come back. I work mostly with men, but there are children and women who have AIDS.

I never worked much with children. When I was younger I didn't mind them making noises, but now that I'm older, I'm less tolerant with little children. Most of my people come in from the prison, or drug rehab. They don't have bedding or sheeting, so I buy it. I buy clothes when I see people who don't have clothes.

I have a man who has been helping me financially the past four years, although I didn't meet him until two years ago. He comes whenever I need him for something special. Now he's involved with homeless people. He's very generous, but the demands on him are too great.

There are so many people with problems. Sometimes I get home and I'm so drained. Then someone calls me over the phone and I say, "I don't know what to do. Lets pray."

"What do you do for yourself to get your energy back up?" I asked.

"We have to have three hours of prayer every day. That includes our Mass. We have Mass every morning, then we have meditation, then the rosary. Sometimes I put that on a tape and I listen to the adoration. Sometimes I pray at ten at night. When I'm really stressed and don't know what to do, I go before the Lord and say, "I'm so tired." or "I don't know what to do with this situation." God gives me patience and a different insight into things.

Every year we are required to make a retreat. I usually go to Clearwater and take ten days, all quiet, nothing, just to be with the Lord. I find my treasure in the silence.

We need to have a break in order to function better. Sometimes somebody gives us money to go out to lunch. Sometimes when my AIDS people are really down and out, I say, "Lets go out for a lunch," and we go to a cafeteria. I do different things to uplift them. Sometimes I get pictures or Bibles. They see my cross and ask if I can give them one. I always give them crosses. Then if I find something spiritual, I talk to them about it. I ask, "Do you read your Bible?"

If I offer to give them a cross and a chain, then it's very precious for them. I remember one man had a statue of a naked man. I gave him a chain and a rosary, and when I visited I saw that he had it draped over that naked statue. I felt really hot and bothered by that. If they take anything spiritual, they have to give respect to it. If they don't want to do that, they should return it to me. They want to have Jesus on the wall, but on another wall they may have nothing but naked women. You know what I mean?"

"What do you do if you need money?" I asked.

"Do you mean for the clients?"

"No for yourself?"

"The government subsidizes me at this mobile home park for seniors. We get our meals here. If I have to get to the doctor, they have transportation."

"If I open your refrigerator, would it be empty?"

"No, because I people give me things. I helped someone and he brought me a cake."

Sister Mike opened the refrigerator to show me.

"I don't really have a lot here. I don't have any meat, just a few vegetables because I get my meals. I'm not a big eater and only take one meal down there. I have eggs and some things that people give me. We get a hundred dollars a month allowance to buy what we need."

"You get fifty dollars a week from the Senior Companion program (the VA visitations) don't you?" I asked.

"Yes, but I have to turn that in to the Mother House. I can't spend any money from what I earn. We just get enough to keep us going. They give us a subsidy, but I don't get to keep any money. If you gave me ten dollars now, I'd have to put it in a savings account, and then if I need to take it out, ask somebody for it—or myself. I happen to be the bookkeeper. All our money…we take the vow of poverty, chastity, and obedience. No matter what we earn, it's not ours, but we're not wanting. If we need money for our teeth, our society will give us money to have our teeth cared for."

Sister Mike smiled to show me that she has her own teeth, laughed, and then bent under her coffee table to retrieve a folder filled with newspaper clippings.

"Do you read much?" I asked, noticing numerous magazines scattered around and a small overfilled bookshelf.

"I have spiritual things I have to read. I don't get the paper because I don't have time to read it. I get the news from TV, but I never just sit here and look at the TV. I always have to be eating, or doing something while I'm watching TV. I go to bed between twelve and one in the morning, and I'm up between five and six at the latest. Unless if I'm really tired, I don't need more than four hours sleep. If I get four to five hours of sleep I'm very good. I get up and do my desk work over there."

*   *   *   *

"My mother and father came from Czechoslovakia and migrated to Cleveland, Ohio to their own ghetto on the west side of town. My mother was fourteen and my father seventeen when they came to this country. They met in the ghetto. My mother went through sixth grade and my father finished eighth grade.

Mom and Dad were both Catholic. We had a very strict Catholic upbringing. My family went to church, and we prayed at the meals. We had a wonderful family life because my father was most devoted to my mother. They had the idea that if their children could go to Catholic school, it would be like getting a college education. We did everything that Catholic people would do, and my mother was very strict on that. If we didn't go to church…we just never thought of not going because my mother and father always went to church. My family was very devoted, and I learned a lot from them. My father was born a very angry man and we obeyed him.

They had six children, each a year and a half apart. The first-born, named after my father, died at two years old. She took him to the doctor, who gave him some medicine, and it turned black. She didn't understand the language and thought the doctor gave her poison. She was very, very upset. She was grieving. I remember the picture my mother had, and I remember my brother in the coffin. That picture hung on the wall. I don't remember what year someone finally took it down, but anyway, I knew Louie in the coffin. My sister was next in rank. I came next, and my name was Irene, then my brother Joe. I cared for him until I was eighteen.

My mother cleaned buildings at night for…I don't know how many years. She came home in the morning and slept until ten, and then did things with her children. I had to work and I helped my parents.

My parents both worked, so we were never destitute. My father had a Ford in the early days of Ford. I remember we had nice kitchen, nice furniture in the living room, and we had nice clothes. We had one of the first radios.

During the depression my father lost his job, but my mother kept hers. My father was a very proud man, and when he lost his job he wouldn't stand in line, so my mother stood in line for flour and sugar. To this day I remember my mother giving us sandwiches that had green pepper on it. We didn't have any meat.

My mother had a terrible experience when she almost drowned. She related a horror story how the water came in on her, and she never went into the water—so we were afraid of the water. None of us ever learned how to swim, although my father took me to the beach one day.

We had a big hose in the backyard, and if we wanted to get cooled off in the summer time, we ran under the hose. The other thing we used to do is dance the polka. Every Sunday we went on picnics or we had people over, because polka was part of our nationality. People came over and we were happy. My parents were always helping people.

My sister was a year and a half older and went out a lot—she smoked and drank. Not to excess, but she did the ordinary things that young girls did, and I was always the "good one." I didn't do any of that stuff. I'd get very angry with her because I kept my clothes in much better order, and she would borrow my clothes.

My mother depended on me. In later years I found out my sister was very hurt and said, "They always depended on you." I was the responsible one. I never missed a day in school, and I never missed a day at work. I went to high school for four years. I was seventeen when I finished school, and then I worked for six years.

My father worked in a bank building as a maintenance supervisor and there was one lawyer there who was willing to give me work experience. I worked for the lawyer for nine months. It meant a lot to me to have a job. No matter how good my grades were, nobody would take me because I had to be eighteen to work. So I worked for nothing, and that was okay. At night I worked for a plumber. I took a course at night in advanced commercial training. I did some night credits after high school in advanced bookkeeping, but didn't go to college.

My mother lived until she was fifty-eight. She was diabetic. After my mother died, my father lost ground. He had never been sick before, as far as I knew. Five years later my father had a stroke and died of loneliness at age sixty-one. That's one of the things I like to remember about my family. I was home at that time because I had returned from Jamaica.

When my mother died, I wasn't allowed to come home. I didn't resent that because I knew those rules when I entered the convent. The rule was changed later on to say that we could go home if it wasn't too far, and I would have been able to come home. Whenever I came home I would pray.

It wasn't part of our culture to kiss. We were not a demonstrative family, but there was devotedness. They were always concerned if somebody was sick, or if they didn't have something. My mother was a very loving person, but when we went to school in the morning we didn't kiss. I think it's a nice thing for children to be hugged and kissed, so they don't feel rejected."

*   *   *   *

"My first assignment was with the leprosarium in Jamaica. I was there ten years. We had to learn to be domestic. I learned to cook for the people in the convent. At home, my mother always made the meals. Although I didn't like sewing, I had to learn how to make my dress. I used to paint. I painted a whole house. I painted and varnished the floors by kerosene lamp. I can repair a typewriter."

Sister Mike brought out several photo albums.

"What made you decide to become a nun?" I asked.

"I had always wanted to help people," she replied. "I was attracted to the order because I wanted to help people who were rejected, and I still do. In my day, the thinking was that when you enter a religious society you become another person. Your life becomes dedicated to God and you leave the world behind, so you take on another name. You can choose the name as long as no one else has it in the society. About 1975 that rule changed. The thinking now is that you were created by God as Irene, (that's my name), and you're still Irene. I'm still Irene. My characteristics and things that I was born with are still there. The things that are not so good, I try to work on and overcome. I have my father's temper. We all have our vices, and we have to discipline ourselves.

I finished high school, and then took some postgraduate work in the convent. After I finished my studies, I was trained for financial administration and stayed in that work until I was fifty years old. Then I did two and a half years of study and pastoral work at the East Asian Pastoral institute in Manila, in the Philippines.

I got many, many credits when I went over to Manila to study. If I had applied that to my education, I could have had my college degree. I took a lot of courses through my society. I did a six-week course in cannon law. We never bothered with credits until later on, when our society decided we needed educated women to send to the missions. Our Sisters went to the mission and although they were nurses, they did doctors work like suturing, and they delivered babies all the time.

Later on in the sixties and seventies, we called the Sisters back and gave them education. I taught school when I went over there because I had business abilities, and I knew how to organize. I just taught school without any degree.

In the missions you have to be very, very adaptable. You have to do without and you have to walk. They wanted to give me bush training. Although I can't swim, I remember crossing the rivers. A native man helped me. I was petrified. He said, "This *latorn* Sister, what for she come along this place?" *Latorn* means you're old. Most of the Sisters were there in their late twenties or early thirties, and I was forty-seven. I had already done ten years of work in Jamaica, and ten years in America. I really wasn't old, but I was to them because the native person's lifespan was between forty-six and fifty.

I've visited all the little islands, but I did not work there. I was in Fiji, Tonga, and Samoa. I've also been in Australia, and New Zealand, where I did my renewal for six months. I've been to San Francisco, Hawaii, and Washington DC. I visited Rome for my fiftieth anniversary as a sister. I went to France where we were founded. That's our heritage. Then I came back here for a while and started a prayer group in the church for women and children.

"That's what we used to wear," she said, showing me a picture of herself wearing a habit with elaborate lace surrounding her face. "It was changed to a veil so we could see when we were driving. We had a very simplified habit here. This is one of the native Sisters on the island wearing the whole dress."

"Now all you wear is the veil," I stated.

"Oh, no. I wear a skirt and blouse."

"I know. You're not naked." We both laughed.

"We changed in 1963 because it was too cumbersome for the people to work on the islands. When we crossed the river, our dresses got wet. I still like the habit though. I think it's better to be the same in your order, but most people don't like it.

These are different places that I've worked." She continued showing me pictures. "My first mission, with leprosy, was in Jamaica. Hospital people have always attracted me because of the various diseases that they have. You see everything there. People with their noses off, or maybe their leg was cut off, or they burned their body. It brings out all the compassion I have in my heart. Then of course, all the sad stories that go along with that.

I was a missionary in Papua, New Guinea, a little island called Bougainville that the Japanese invaded in the Second World War. The British government ran it. I didn't get there until 1967, and I stayed there until 1990, when we were evacuated.

I did the administration there because everything had to be in order. I had to do a lot of paperwork. I used to get a lot of things free. I would spend my time trying to find people who would help us, give us charity. Americans are very generous and gave many, many things. I would crate them myself, and mark the crates. When the missionaries returned, they took the cargo back.

One or two evenings during the week, and on Sunday, I went over to be with the leprous people, show movies, and do different things to be a part of their life. I wanted to be a nurse, but my order kept me in administration. As time went on and there were fewer Sisters, we became more people oriented, rather than administration oriented. You can hire people to help. Right now we are short of Priests. The Priest that spends all his time in administration doesn't have time to care for people who need him to be with them. Just a kind word.

I was then sent to the mission in Papua New Guinea, where I worked with the Bishop in administration. It was much needed. A lot of people would send us things. We had to get papers through the customs, and then we had to do shipping, and get rice and carrots, medicines. A lot of local people ran the office.

It took from 1957–1970 to build the mine in Bougainville. I was assigned to the mining area to the town, way up in the mountains. They had to put a powerhouse there.

We had to wash by hand because we didn't have any washing machines. Washing clothes by hand is hard physical work, but we had girls who helped us. We had kerosene refrigerators. Our lights went off at nine. I usually worked until about midnight to prepare classes and whatever. I had to work by kerosene light until generators came, and then we had neon lights in our rooms. This priest generated power for three hours, so we could use the washing machine at night and we didn't have to wash by hand anymore.

I walked a lot in Papua, New Guinea even though I had a chauffeur. I learned to drive on the mountains when I was forty-seven, and was very cautious. The parish bought me a car because I had to travel distances, but I still walked a lot. We were in the sun all the time and I never put on lotion or anything. Then when I came home I said, "Oh, my gosh, I've got all these wrinkles." They never worried me. This is the last picture taken by a photographer—the wrinkles are there, and everything. They were much deeper when I first came home twelve years ago. Without having that much sun here, I'm not as wrinkled as I was.

I needed a car there because I did a lot of counseling work. People had so many problems that I often came home late at night. The Mission station was right outside the mining town. It changed the whole picture of the island when the minors came in. We had food come in, so they wanted the best of food. Once they became independent in 1976, Papua, New Guinea had its own currency, kina and toea. The supermarket food was terribly expensive. I remember Christmas time we liked to make stuffing. We wanted to have celery, but it cost six kina. We bought one quarter of the celery. The whole thing would have cost something like seven dollars. Cherries were four or five dollars a pound. We could never buy that.

There were some people who worked in the mine and were well to do. They found this mineral called copper ore. It was a cheap mineral there, and it yielded millions of dollars from the mine. They were mining this until about 1982, and as they got deeper into the mine they found gold and silver. Then someone instigated the tribal people, who owned and rented the land, to demand twenty billion dollars more from the mining authorities. The mining company said no, but little by little they returned to negotiating. By 1990, they brought two thousand men into the militia to protect us, but they went to the villages and they raped the women and devastated everything over there.

We didn't come there to run the country for them. We gave them education and taught hygiene. We didn't go there first to evangelize—we went there first to help them to be able to eat better, to help them with their sores and their sick bodies, and to give them education. Then gradually we began taking second place. Instead of a Sister being the school principal, the locals started training teachers and running the school. We also formed a nurse's training school. Other people with different religions came to help, and the place grew.

We were so proud of three men who studied at the Oxford University. One became a doctor. It just shows that these people are not stupid people. They have a great intellect and can do great things if they have the education. Their farming became better. At first, they were doing everything by hand. They even built a golf course because the white man wanted to have one, of course. Some local people learned to play golf too. They became educated, sophisticated, people. They dressed up their little children in western clothes—we started that.

Things became desperate because the white man brought in the drink. When drinking became a problem during the mining time, I did triple purpose prayer instructions with all the different denominations. It was a big climb up the mountain so I used to drive there. We asked God to take pity on them because the white man did this. Then they started with the baby garden. There was lots of devastation. After awhile, they formed a rebel Army who shot people going to the mine. The mine was destroyed.

The mine is closed to this day. Because they didn't want anybody to run the mine, the rebel army started killing people. They wanted more people, so they went into homes and ordered people to join the army, or they would kill them. There was a lot of bitterness. They burnt the hospital, burnt the school, the airport closed, the big supermarket closed, everything was devastated. A bishop, and missionaries come to help the people learn to run their own country. Finally, in 1990, the bishop said it wasn't safe for us to stay and brought us out.

I find my work here fulfilling, but I am disappointed that I can't return to the islands—there's so much devastation, and so much work to do. Circumstances won't allow me to go back there. I didn't want to just sit so I found prayer work here. I'm resigned to do whatever God wants me to do. If I had a dream come true, I'd like to go back to the islands."

"What do you attribute your good health to?" I asked.

"I don't know. I never drank, even when I was young and could drink. I used to enjoy dancing and horseback riding very much. I went out with boys, but I was never interested in anybody particularly. We had four friends and we always went together. We had different boy-friends and went out to parties, but I didn't focus on that. I already knew I was going to enter the convent. I didn't know where. Then I read about the lepers, and there was a Sister Michael who was six years older than me. I know her because she was my classmate's sister. When Michael came back from the mission, I heard all these stories about what they were doing with the leprosy patients and knew that's where I wanted to go. I made a pact with myself that I would help my mother financially, so I didn't go to the training house in Massachusetts until the following year. I was twenty-four when I entered the convent.

Poverty and chastity isn't hard for me. Obedience isn't hard for me, but not being independent is very hard for me. I'm a very independent person. I always had to make things do. In the mission it's the same way. If I don't have eggs, I'm not going to try to make a cake. If I don't have carrots, we pick the greens and make *pumu* with coconut milk instead.

We had girls to help us in the house. You never want to be so tired that we wouldn't be…when I get tired like that I get grumpy, and then I'm not understanding to other people. I try to watch that. Just recently I was grumpy. I had a cold and don't know how many people

I talked to that day. Then someone called at ten at night, and I said, "I really can't talk anymore."

This man said, "What do you think I should do when I go to the University, tell me what you think I'm good for?"

I said, "You've got to make that decision." That upset me. I did try to give him guide points. I said, "You know what you've suited for. Don't put that burden on me to say you should be doing this. I think you have talents, but in your heart, you know what you should do." I told him there are counselors. In my day they didn't have that.

Being independent, I don't ask for help because I can do it myself. Sometimes the Sister asks me, "Can we take you somewhere in the car?" But I can't wait. I find that hard to do. When I decide to go, I have to go right now.

If you're really trying to serve the Lord, you want to give to people all the time, but sometimes it's very good to allow people to give to you, because they feel good about doing something. Last Sunday I had to prepare for the twelve Sisters to come to this house for prayer. I didn't want to ask the Sisters to bring chairs, so I borrowed from this lady next door.

She said, "You don't know how happy it made me to contribute to your meeting."

Some people think I'm too busy to help them, so they don't ask me. The saying is true, "A busy man always finds time to do one more thing."

How do I find time to do it all? I never say no. That's one of my…it could be a fault as I'm getting older. Sometimes I really do have to ask for help. Sometimes I ask a male friend to bring me. I don't want to ask the Sisters—they're all old. They're not as old as I am though.

As for now, walking is important in what I do. If I'm not able to do that in the future, I could do telephone work with people. I'm not really an artist, but I can get things together. If your mind is creative, you can think of lots to do. I have a lot of things to do for my congregation. If I didn't have anything to do, I'd find a lot to do. I really have a creative mind, although I'm not a brilliant person.

I like vegetables, soup, and fruit. I'm not really a dessert person, although I eat it on occasion for energy. I really like fried food, but I don't eat it too often. I take vitamins, Centrum A to Z, but I recently started taking Ginkgo Biloba for memory.

I never smoked, and because of that my lungs and heart are good. I wear reading glasses when I work, but I can see well, and my hearing is fine. When I find that I can't do something, I try to exercise. When I'm droopy, I go against this wall, and straighten up and exercise, [demonstrates standing straight against the wall]. This is the other one I have to do." Sister Mike held her arms out sideways to demonstrate.

"Generally, I'm in very good health. I don't have any problems now. In the past I was anemic from overwork. My blood count was four, but I had some blood transfusions. I had low fever malaria, and inflammation in my legs, but I never had too much trouble. I have a bit of trouble with my neck. I have this curvature. I was always 5'6, but I've shrunk in my old age. Now I'm 5'3 ½. I go to a chiropractor, which helps me be the best that I can. I have osteoporosis but no pain. I'm lucky. If I have arthritis, I don't have pain with it. I went to the doctor for pain last month and he said its arthritis, but I'm okay now. I have very strong hands—I can get down on my hands and knees and wash the floor. I don't use a mop. I think it's important to be able to get up and down. I've done that all my life. If I don't get enough sleep, and I work hard, then my energy gets low. I hardly ever have a headache, but I have a low pain tolerance. I pray to the Lord that I don't have pain before I die. People don't know that I think about that, but I do.

I try to keep my mind sharp. Sometimes there's a lecture going on, sometimes we have a meeting, or sometimes we go out for a good time. It's very stimulating for me to meet younger people. I'm not always in the same group. I've learned a little bit about the computer and moving the mouse around. There is a class I can take. I think I'll do that. You cannot be ignorant about something that is going to be part of your life. I'm concerned about spending too much time with a machine, when I should be spending time with people.

I like living with other people, but having my own place works out well for me because I work at night and need the quiet time. I have my father's anger, but I have learned to control that. Sometimes in the house, I'm just so upset, or go to a quiet place like the chapel and pray. They say sometimes just screaming in the shower will relieve the tension. I do it where I can't hurt anybody. I feel my inadequacy.

In the future as I get older, and less able to do…maybe I'll spend more time in prayer and in being quiet. I may have the option to return to the Mother House and finish up my days there. I have the option of going to a nursing home to be cared for. Most of us need to be cared for as we get older—you have to have that foresight. Our bodies will be shipped back to Boston. We will be buried with all the Sisters in our plot. We don't live in isolation—there are twelve Sisters here in my order. We have meetings and form a community."

OLGA, AGE 81

(With a little help from her husband,
Dick, age 81)
Painter
Guatemala, Central America

*Olga, who lives in Sun City Center with her husband Dick,
found my flyer at the neighborhood recreation center. She called
me and invited me to her home.*

Olga and Dick are both eighty-one but they could pass for sixty. Olga's dark brown hair with only a few stray gray hairs in the front, smooth complexion, and svelte figure does nothing to give away her age. She dressed in a green and white shirt and pants. She told me she had been born in France, so her Spanish accent puzzled me until she said she'd been raised in Guatemala. Dick was casually dressed in a sweater and pants. Although his hair is pure white, there is no sign of balding

Their spacious home is surrounded by flower gardens outside. The first thing Olga did was to give me a tour of her house. The décor was casual and comfortable. There was a basket of shells and numerous elephant statues. The walls were covered pictures of her family, children, and grandchildren as well as numerous oil and watercolor paintings. Some appeared professional, but most looked as though a talented amateur had done them.

"They are gorgeous," I commented, noting one especially well done oil painting of a bird.

"My daughter did that. She's a professional painter. Here we are in Switzerland." Olga pointed to a photograph. "I'm going to have to stop painting because I don't have any more room on the walls." She laughed.

"You painted all these?" I asked.

Olga nodded yes. "I always painted by myself, but now I go to class. I can see from the pictures that I've improved. I learned by copying the masters. I like to paint Monet.

"This is beautiful," I exclaimed.

"This picture of the Tetons is done with the yolk of an egg in the paint. My neighbor took a photo and put it in the computer. I painted it. I also drew this family tree. This is a collage of my family, my husband, and our children.

"Do you know what this is?" She pointed to a detailed watercolor of a large cottage home with a huge stairway. "Before the revolution, Marie Antoinette was a doctor in Formosa. She was doctor to Katherine the Great. She loved the countryside and left Paris for a little cottage. This picture shows the stairway that was large enough for the carriage with six horses to pass through it.

Painting satisfies me, and so does gardening. I love gardening.

"Who likes elephants?" I asked.

"One of my boys went to India and brought the table, glass, and ivory elephants. This table had inlaid elephants carried from India. These elephants are holding up the world." She pointed to a statue of six elephants supporting a bowling ball sized Earth. "This is a dragon from China. This boat is Hindu. It shows six wise men, woman, and a child. These are just little things but they mean something to me.

Dick and I are newly weds. We have a wonderful time." Olga changed the topic.

"We'd known each other for a few years," Dick began. "We met up here at the community center. There was a crowd. We knew each other only enough to say, 'Hi, how are you doing?' Her husband had died earlier, and then my wife died. When I met Olga, she said, 'Why don't you come up to the golf and racket club and meet some people up there?' I said, 'No, I'm not going to a singles club.' Then I started thinking that I needed to get out of my house, so I said, 'If you still want me I'll go'. We went up to dance. Coming back from the dance floor, we were holding hands, and we've been holding hands ever since. We will be married four years."

"Five years," Olga said.

After a few minutes of light-hearted discussion, they still couldn't agree on the year they were married.

"How is romance in your older years?" I queried.

"Terrible," Dick laughed. "I go to sleep and she goes to sleep. No, I'm only kidding, it's been wonderful."

"So you're not over the hill?"

"Oh, no."

"We will never be. We will die before getting over the hill," Olga added. "It shows when you live life rather than just existing. We have good basic moral religious principles, but we don't go to church. Religion isn't going to church. What keeps you young is your faith in life."

"It's nice that we met at an older age and that we're both the same age," said Dick. "Let me show you a calendar. Thursday she has her hair done," he read from the calendar, "We play bridge and pinochle. I play golf three times a week, and we go out to dinner three or four times a week. I also belong to a golf club and have a lot of friends and social engagements with them. There are over forty people in my golfing club."

"Every Saturday we go to the Alpha house in Apollo Beach," Olga added. 'It's a Greek dinner and a dance place which looks like a little dump, but it's filled with the most wonderful people you can imagine. We get together with a big group there.

Sometimes Dick goes around in the evening, in his golf cart, to look at alligators. I do Ti Chi three times a week. I do tap dancing twice a week, and paint two days a week for two or three hours. I used to do line-dance, but I don't anymore because my other half complains that I do too much."

"Every solitary night we play pinochle," Dick stated. "We don't go to bed until one or two in the morning. I usually get up by seven, but she may sleep till ten."

"Sometimes it's two or three in the morning before we get to sleep," Olga said. "On the days I have to go to class, I get up early, eight or nine.

Every two years we have a family reunion. I had seven children but only five are still alive. They come with their husbands and children. We had the last family reunion in Vegas."

"We go to the casino three or four times a year," Dick said. "We go to Mississippi now because it's so much closer. My daughters meet us there."

"Dick and I love dancing. I go to the pool and go swimming, aqua-size in the water. It's fun." Olga began laughing. "We have boxing gloves and we fight. We are lively and express our likings."

"What do you fight about?" I asked.

"Who won playing cards."

"Sometimes you don't obey me." Dick laughed.

"My mother and father are the only ones I ever obeyed in my life." Olga returned his laugh.

"Are you sure of that?"

"I spoil you. I do your footsies, pedicure. I spank you when you do something wrong."

"This was my house," said Dick. "This being the better house…"

"…No, my house was better, but I still had a mortgage, and his house was free. This is the largest house that you could buy in 1983, but now they have larger.

I love to cook special dishes. He loves crab casserole and stuffed salmon with crab. We go together once a month to buy meats, and a whole fillet of fish. We love raw oysters. I went to Japan and learned to love sushi. I've been to Singapore, Malaysia, and Oceania."

"Sushi is the only thing we don't agree on," Dick said. "I traveled overseas during the war. I've been to Canada and Mexico. I was in Japan during the war. When I sold my business, I went on a six-month trip. That's enough travel for me."

*   *   *   *

"I was born in France, and was the fourth child of ten," said Olga. "My father was a doctor and we traveled to many places. He came to America to treat Yellow Fever. He didn't stay in the United States but went to Guatemala. He liked it there. My mother wasn't sure about the education, so we studied with her and didn't go to school until later. My mother spoke Spanish and French to me. Spanish in Guatemala is a little difference from the Spanish here. I learned English in secondary school. After her children were grown, my mother formed a school which now has twenty-six thousand girls. There are many schools for the very rich, but she helped poor people. She went to the orphanages and got five children every year. The school gave room and board to the children until they graduated, and supported them until they found a job or got married. She kept this a secret and even my father didn't know about it. We found out when they nominated her "Woman of the Year."

My first husband's parents knew each other in Paris but their families fled Paris during the revolution. They were close to the fighting. His father's family, the Arce, went to Mauritius Island, which is between Africa and Madagascar. They eventually came to America.

It's a funny idea that you belong to the country where you were born. My parents were not French. My father was from Spain, but as a doctor he studied in France, and he took two or three weeks every year to visit poor people in the little villages. I went with him all the time. That fascinated me and I decided I wanted to work in that field. That's how I became a nurse.

I came to this country in 1950 and attended the university from 1951–1953. I earned two college degrees, a Masters in education and in nursing. Nursing was different then—there was no rehabilitation.

My husband graduated from the NYU in engineering before we got married in Connecticut. We lived in New Jersey and New York.

We moved to Arizona, but I didn't like it. I don't like crawling creatures. There were scorpions in the living room, and snakes all over. Once I was moving a sprinkler and a tarantula went onto my hands. I hated that place. It was terrible. I was glad when we moved from there.

We took the kids to Yellowstone when they were young. We drove to Yellowstone and camped out. I hated every single night because of the crawling things, but I couldn't say anything because I didn't want to make the kids afraid too. I would never sleep on the ground so we made up a story that my back was bothering me, and I got a cot with a mattress. They climbed mountains with their father, not with me.

I wanted to study medicine but my children attracted me to settle down. I have seven children and twenty-five grandchildren. I belonged to things that had to do with children, like the Children's Theatre Guild and clubs for children.

Later on when my children were older, I started a private school of my own in New Port Beach, California. I was the owner and principal. Only my youngest boy attended the school. The older ones were already in high school. The school was trilingual. We spoke French one day and Spanish one day every week. We had shows and plays in all three languages. We did the same play in each language so people could follow it. It was fun. When the people I was renting the building from decided to sell it, I couldn't afford to buy. Instead, I taught secondary school in a convent in California.

A friend of mine established summer studies in Europe. We started in England, Spain, France, Italy, and Switzerland. We have three professors come from each University, and the children earn eighteen units. The last time, the students compared the difference between communist countries. We went to five countries: Yugoslavia, Hungary, Czechoslovakia, Bulgaria, and Germany. The kids learned the culture of each country.

Later, I ran a pediatric clinic in Texas. It was wonderful. I worked in occupational therapy teaching people to do things that help psychologically with disability. I need to take care of people and I need to be giving. I was the head nurse and handled everything."

"She's good at everything but hanging pictures," stated Dick who was nailing a picture hanger into the wall for Olga's most recent painting.

"That's what she's got you for." I laughed.

"There were four boys and two girls in my family," Dick said. "My father was a printer. I was the second child. There really isn't anything novel about my life. I went to school and then I went into the war. After the war I started my own printing business. I was in there for forty years. I got married and we had two children. After I reached retirement age, I sold my house and my business up north. My wife and I came down here to Florida. She passed away five years ago."

"My husband was looking for a warm place because he wasn't feeling good," Olga said. "We came down to Florida but I don't like the heat. Six months after we moved here he passed away. I was getting ready to move back up north when I met Dick. He saved me from lonely days and nights. I met his wife and she was wonderful. He never met my husband."

"I think the secret to living a long, healthy life is good genes," Dick said. "My mother missed being one hundred by two months, and my father was ninety-six when he passed away. My aunt lived to a hundred-and-two."

"My father was eighty-nine and my mother was sixty-nine," Olga added. "She never had a wrinkle in her face. That isn't a sign of age. My health is excellent. I believe in vitamins and in maintaining your health. We have a highball every night and if the evening is long, we might have two. We don't smoke.

You know, I wrote my memoirs and printed it. I didn't have a computer, but I had an electric typewriter with memory. But when I started reading it and relived my life, it made me cry, so I threw it away. I'm sorry now. My son came last year with a video camera. He talked to me about my life and made a videocassette.

I love to read. I read scientific things, and recently I read a book about a doctor at the Mayo clinic. I also like to read historical novels like Ruska and Rutherford. Now I'm reading *The Writing On The Wall*. It's about the wall in Germany. They take a family and develop the whole story of this family that gets separated, and it's wonderful."

"I read, but not as much as she does. Most of my reading is about the stock market. I study the stock market at least half-an-hour a day. But she's into many, many different types of reading."

"As to my future," Olga concluded. "I'm going to Guatemala next month. One of my boys lived in Germany. My granddaughter who lives there is getting married, but Germany would be too far for everybody to go, so we're having a reunion in Guatemala."

Dick had been pacing the floor for the past few minutes and looking at his watch. "Don't forget, we're going to the wooden nickel tonight. If we are going to go dancing, we have to leave pretty soon," he reminded Olga.

Ken Delaney, age 81

Retired FBI agent
Buffalo, New York

The Kids and Kubs is a softball team that meets three times a week in St. Petersburg Florida. The players have to be at least seventy-four to try out. There is no maximum age.

K en, like all the players in the Kids and Kubs, wore a white uniform and cap. He is a tall, thin man with smile lines around his eyes, who gestures as he talks.

After ending a game, Ken joined me at a picnic table with Australian green parrots and native Floridian birds flying past. We talked, interrupted only by an occasional squirrel checking to see if we had peanuts to share.

"I'm retired," he began. "I play here three days a week on Tuesdays, Thursdays, and Saturdays. I also go to tournaments.

After I retired from the FBI in 1977, I came down here and have been playing ball ever since. At first I played in the half-century club, which is fifty and older. I won the batting title and about four world championships with them. Then when I turned seventy-four, I had the option to stay with them or move onto the Kids and Kubs. I've been playing with the Kids since '94. We went to Pennsylvania on a tour where we played in several cities with the local teams. We don't get any pay and go at our own expense.

I'm the luckiest guy I know. I played semi-pro ball starting at the age of sixteen. I got out of high school at seventeen and played semi-pro ball in New York. We got paid three dollars a game. I wanted to make the majors but they didn't have it organized like they do today. Each team put up a hundred dollars a game and the winning team got the money. We either got six dollars or nothing. In order to make some money, I played on three different teams with three different names."

✳   ✳   ✳   ✳

"My parents were two great people. My mother lived to ninety-seven and my father was ninety-one. Today he probably would have lived longer but he smoked. In those days smoking was nothing. I had a younger brother and sister. We were brought up during the depression and I was lucky that my father was with the post office, so he wasn't out of work. He was getting twenty dollars a week in the thirties. When I look back at it that must have been tough, but we didn't know we were giving anything up. We didn't have a telephone, but we had a radio, and we'd listen to the old programs.

I've always read a lot. I'm inundated with baseball books every Christmas and Father's Day. I think I've got every baseball book ever written. I've got books on Hall of Fame stars and every baseball player who ever wrote a book about himself. I don't get time to read them all.

In college you have to read. I majored in literature. I read all the Greek plays and American literature. I always tried to get my kids and grandkids to read because reading really helps. You learn geography, history, and a lot of things. I used to do talks in high schools.

In high school I wanted to get a letter in every sport. I've always been playing ball. I don't know what I would do if I couldn't play ball. I played football in high school and they broke my leg. I used to say "I" broke my leg, but now I say "they" broke my leg because somebody tripped me. I couldn't play either football or baseball that year. The following season I joined the swimming team and got my letter in swimming and a scholarship, but unfortunately, the war broke out and I didn't get a chance to use it.

I made an application to the FBI and joined when I was only twenty years old. I decided to be an agent, but I needed to get a college degree. I had only gone for one summer in Washington when I started as a photographer in Washington, DC. When Pearl Harbor was attacked, I was transferred from Washington to New York because we needed photographers and that was the biggest office. I went back to college at night in New York, and then into the Third Naval District Team.

I was taken into the Navy Intelligence Office because I was a photographer and worked for the FBI. I was stationed at Floyd Bennett Field and never got out of New York. I photographed the ships coming in and out, plane crashes in the area, airways contests, things like that. We found out in September that they were going to use the Army Signal Corps instead of the Navy to photograph the atomic bomb dropping. We were assigned a special assignment just to do that, and thus we were all discharged from the Navy.

I went back into the FBI and into college and then went from photographer to special employee photographer. I was assigned to be a special agent in 1951, the day after graduating from New York Emigrations with a B.S. degree. Now I had a college degree and all those years in the FBI, so I became an agent. They sent me down to Quantico, near Washington DC, for training. Since I was older than most of the class, who were in their twenties, I became an instructor.

I was on the Skippy Peanut Butter program "You Asked for it." People used to write in and ask questions like, "What do FBI agents do if someone attacks them?" There were four of us taking turns showing defense tactics (they call it karate now) taking the guns and knives away, and flipping people over.

Then from Quantico, I was transferred to Buffalo, New York. I spent two years there freezing my head off and worked a few cases. You worked whatever assignment you were given. Then I got transferred to Pittsburgh.

I was married in 1941 and had six daughters and three sons. My oldest son lives in Costa Rica, my next oldest son is vice president of a corporation in California, and my next son works in construction. My oldest daughter will be sixty years old next February. I can't lie about my age anymore. I used to tell people I was sixty-nine, and she was born when I was nine years old. Anyway, the reason I mention this is because two of my daughters married people from the Pittsburgh area.

I went to Pittsburgh, got transferred to Newark, then Camden, New Jersey and then St. Louis, Missouri. From St. Louis, Missouri, I worked the Hoffa case in Chattanooga, Tennessee.

Hoffa was in jail and he made an application for parole. He had depositions from many different people. We had to check all the depositions to find out if he was worthwhile. Well unfortunately, there were a lot of gangsters involved and they intimidated people, made false statements, and gave prostitutes a thousand dollars each to make depositions against the juries, marshals, judges, and everyone else. We proved that these were all false, so he went back to jail.

Myself and fifty-four others were transferred to Birmingham when the Baptist Church was bombed, because we were all mature, experienced agents. I'll never forget that. That gave me a wonderful perspective on the civil rights movement. For example, Collie Leroy Wilkins, along with three others, was acquitted of killing a Mrs. Viola Liuzzo.

She came down from Detroit with two kids and her husband. She joined the civil rights marching, and one day she decided to drive this black boy home. Three Klan members want to kill the black boy—they fire a shotgun, he ducks, and she gets killed.

I don't know if you know about this, but they have what you call Southern Justice. You can have all the evidence in the world against these people and the jury won't convict them. They all went to trial on the charge of murder. Now, murder is a state, not a federal crime. They were brought into court and all acquitted. At that point, the United States government said, "This is atrocious," so we got a warrant out for violating civil rights. That's the only thing we could get them on. I arrested Collie Leroy Wilkins. When I arrested him, I interviewed him of course.

I said, "I'm trying to understand you Klansman. I can understand how you get angry about these people coming down here, considering that your life-style is to hate blacks, hate Jews, hate everybody. I can understand that. I'm from New York where we're all pretty liberal. But how can you possibly condone throwing a bomb in a church with these young black girls?"

There were four, six and seven years olds killed. He looked at me with a straight face and went, "They were niggers."

I said, "Okay, now I know the way you think."

I was never so happy as to grab this guy and put handcuffs on him. You know, they all got convicted and sentenced to six years. That's it, because the civil rights act didn't include murder. Later, one guy got convicted again.

After that case, Mr. Hoover died, and they transferred me back to Philadelphia. I spent my last seven years with the FBI in Philadelphia.

I used to recruit FBI agents, and I'd talk to colleges. I'd tell them that the one important thing about my job as an FBI agent is that I never had a boring day, or a day that when I went to work knowing what would happen. I never knew if I was going to be working a bank robbery or picking up a fugitive. We had one hundred and sixty-four violations, and as an FBI agent, I might be investigating any one of those on any given day. It could be car thefts, interstate transportation, stolen property, white slavery, obscenities, even the migratory bird act, for Gods sake.

Most people don't even know that the FBI has the migratory bird act. It was made an act by a member of the Audubon society who became a senator. He said, "I want killing or holding up a migratory birds to be a federal violation." So they said, "Okay what agency do you want to give it to?" He said, "Give it to the best agency available." So we got the migratory bird act. I only had one of those cases in my entire career.

We have the Red Cross Act. Anybody falsely representing themselves as a member of the Red Cross would be in violation. Of course, you have impersonation. Every one of these cases was so interesting.

I've had bank robberies that turned out to be sad. I had a bank robbery that was faked by a young fellow, an eighteen-year-old teller. We get a call that the bank had been robbed. So we all go running up there. We interviewed the kid. We asked him questions such as, "What kind of weapons, describe exactly what this guy looked like, how did he get the money?"

This kid was so nervous and scared that he hesitated on almost everything. Finally, I said, "I'm going to have to present this to the attorney to see if we are even going to work on it. Do you want me to do this?"

He broke down and said, "No, I'll tell you the truth. My girlfriend told me the other day she's pregnant, and I had to get money for an abortion. I took the money out of the till, put it in a brown paper bag in the trunk of my car, came back inside and said I'd been robbed."

I said, "Okay, lets talk"

I talked to the kid and his father. The attorney said, "I want to see him." He gave the money back, of course. They never prosecuted. I felt good about that.

Another case backfired on me. I told the attorney, "He seems like a good kid, and he's going to get a job. It was impulse that made him do that." The attorney declined prosecution.

I left this kid my card and I said, "Now look, if you get an urge to do a stupid thing, call me and I'll talk to you." I was out in my car and the office calls me on the radio and tells me to contact Captain so and so at the Washington State police, so I call him up.

"Hey Kenny what the heck are you giving burglars your card and your telephone number?"

"You don't mean Richey A?"

"Oh, yah, we have him in jail right now for burglarizing eight houses."

"I tried to give the guy a break. You people do your job."

I did everything I could. Sometimes it works, sometimes it doesn't. Sometimes you hear a story about something minor like writing bad checks, which is interstate forgery. You can get five years for every count.

There was a young girl I arrested one time. Her husband was in prison for murder. When he went to prison, he turned her over to his buddies who talked her into a free trip with stolen money orders. She had to go into a motel, pay with a fifty-dollar money order and give the change back to the guys. She had to go into the stores with a twenty-dollar money order and buy something for a dollar. All the money went back to them. Cashing these things made her guilty of interstate forgery, although she was a victim.

I have a fellow still in prison who killed eight kids. Everytime I read in the newspaper that some little boy is missing, I check with friends that he is still in. The only thing he said to me, and this almost made me hit him, was, "Well, I beat the gas chamber didn't I?"

He escaped and disappeared. When we finally caught him, they had done away with the death penalty in Missouri, so he got life in prison. Life in prison sometimes doesn't mean life in prison."

"Are you ever fearful that somebody is going to come after you?" I asked.

"No. The Kids and Kubs asked me that before putting me in their brochure. I've been in these brochures since 1977. I've never heard any repercussions from anybody. When I was a kid I saw a policeman go up to a young fellow, grab him, and smack him in the face. "You'd better tell me now who did that." Well I put myself in…if he hit me I wasn't going to tell him anything. That made an impression on me.

When I was in the FBI, I had a policy to talk to people by using common sense and telling them what their alternatives were. I've met people who did three, maybe five years, and they always said the same thing. "I was wrong, but I remember you treated me fairly. You presented the thing right to me."

The guys would tell me their story and I'd say, "Look, your fingerprints were found. You go to the attorney and you'll get the minimum."

The media makes bank robbery into a glamorous thing. They glamorize John Dillinger and all these people. In fact, my own kids said to me, "Boy, we saw Bonnie and Clyde. How can you guys shoot these young people?"

When you actually knew these people, you knew Clyde was the lowest form of life on earth. In the movie, he was dressed up and his wife and children were crying. You forget they were not the nice loving couple shown in the movie. They killed policemen and bank employees. But the movie they made them out to be such a nice couple. That used to drive me crazy when I'd see it on TV.

A movie was made from a case I handled. Jack Lord from Hawaii 5-0 played one of my subjects and they romanticized this guy. He was the biggest piece of trash. He beat up his wife, killed people, then in order to get a car, stopped a salesman on the highway, killed him, kept on traveling and traveling, and we were after him all the time.

We had a warrant against him in New York, but he fled the state. We finally caught up to him, and agents killed him. I was glad that this guy had been killed. They would have put him in prison for life. He was like Manson. You can't have any love for a man like that. He was a really terrible murderer.

Here's what they did in this show. They had his wife cheating on him. He captures her with another man and that's why he killed her. That's not true at all. Now, they do have him taking this car away from the salesman, but they don't show him killing him. Then he's traveling and stops in a diner. In order to put a little romance in this program, he starts talking to the waitress. She's Mexican and she falls in love with him. He talks her into going with him so now they're traveling together, they have romance, and he buys her things.

She says, "Oh, you're so nice to me. I came from Mexico and my people didn't treat me good."

Now they end up in Utah and the FBI guys discover them and they kill him. In the last scene, which made me sick, she came over to hold him up, and turns to Efram Zimbalist, Jr., who played the inspector, and says to him "You killed the only man I could ever love."

I was in court with another agent's subject, and I wrote a note and said, "You've got the wrong man." Ken laughed. "They convicted him, but put him on probation. He must have been the wrong man because the priest said he was a wonderful man. This is real life and it's unbelievable.

Remember the Bundy case, where he'd killed all these college girls? They had people marching and saying they were treating him inhumanly. The women were out there saying, "He's such a nice looking guy."

The world is changing. It's getting to the point if you're going to arrest a guy and he has a gun, you have to go up to him and say, "Excuse me." You can't approach him the way we used to do. We'd out gun him, out man him, we would dominate him. We'd have four men with shotguns and we'd say, "Joe Blow, you're under arrest, put your hands up. If you make a move we'll blow you to pieces." Can't do that anymore. Now you have to say, "Excuse me, you're under arrest."

*   *   *   *

Both my parents lived here in St. Pete, and when I visited them, I came down to the ballpark and watched these people play softball. I swore that I was not going to spend another winter up in New Jersey where I froze to death. The month after I retired, I came down here, and I've been here ever since.

I was married to my first wife for fifty-one years. My wife died in 1991 and I never dated anybody. I wasn't interested in getting married again. From '91 to '96 I was single and living with my sister.

I was playing down here four years ago when I met my current wife. She came down to see us play. I came off the field and met her through another player, Nick. His wife, Maria, a feisty Italian, said, "Kenny, you had a great game today, give me a hug."

I said "No, Nicky's going to punch me in the nose if you keep hugging me like that."

So Maria turns to this woman, Fran, who I didn't know and says, "Okay you give him a hug."

She did, and I felt so weird. Do you believe in love at first sight? I now believe in angels. I was hugging her in the parking lot, and one of the ball players comes by and yells, "Cut that out, you're going to get arrested," because I wouldn't let her go.

When I finally let go, I apologized to her. She later said, "I didn't know who you were, but I talked to Maria and she said you weren't a bad guy."

So now, she takes off and I figure I'll never see her again. I could have been an ax murderer, and she could have had a husband, or boyfriend. But the next game she shows up with them again. I found out that she was a widow. Her husband died the same year that my wife died, and her maiden name, Anderson, is the same name as my wife's maiden name. We both had grown children, she had five sons, and I had three sons and six daughters. We both came down here in 1977 from New Jersey where we had lived only a mile apart. I must have gone by her house a thousand times on my way to the FBI office. It was like…it was bound to happen.

Our romance life is beautiful. I like to tell people I met Fran because she asked Nicky, "Who's that cute looking third baseman and is he single?" She gets mad when I say that.

It didn't take long, we got married and here I am. I've been married three years to Fran. Everybody in this club is crazy about her. She brings down cookies for the fellows and makes lemon cakes. She loves to cook. The guys say to me, "We don't care if you show up, but we hope Fran comes down with her cookies."

The secret for staying healthy? Diet and exercise is ninety percent of it. I weigh now what I weighed when I was eighteen years old. I'm five foot eleven and I weigh one-seventy. I used to be half an inch taller. In the FBI, we took a physical every single year, and agents were weighed every single month because we had to keep in shape. We had a lot of former athletes.

I've never been in the hospital in my life. I don't go to doctors. I don't take pills. My wife was kidding me and said, "You know, the hospitalization plan that you have with the FBI ought to give you all the money back that you paid in." I've never used it. I take a vitamin in the morning but I don't go to a doctor. I gave up smoking cigarettes in 1950. Staying healthy isn't just genes—my brother is three years younger than me and is in terrible shape.

Here's another story. I retired with fourteen other men, all at the same time and all from the FBI. Five years later when I went up to New Jersey for a meeting of former special agents, only two were still alive. They retired and didn't do anything. They stopped living and rocked.

We get retirement. I get eighty-six percent of my highest pay for the rest of my life. I'm comfortable, almost uncomfortable. One fellow got another job with the county, and when I first saw him a year later I ask him, "How are you doing?"

He said, "I hate it. The politics is driving me crazy."

I asked, "Why are you doing it?"

"Do you realize I get this money added to my retirement pay? If I spend five years with them, I'll get their retirement too, and I'll have it made."

"Marty, what good is all this money if you're so miserable?" I asked.

The following year I went up there, and he had died of a heart attack.

I have a big house, swimming pool, and a wonderful patio. I do the gardening, and put in all the stones and a birdbath area. I don't have enough time to myself to do everything I want.

I have breakfast and dinner and I'm very careful about what I eat. I don't drink and I don't eat lunch. We eat out a lot. I told people not to send me any more books, so we received four hundred dollars or more in gift certificates for restaurants. Last night we went to the Cracker Barrel, and three nights ago we went to the Olive Gardens, and the Outback. We went to Biloxi twice, and we go on boat rides. Whatever she wants to do.

On my off days, either we have a meeting, or I do my shopping. I take my wife or sister or their friends to their doctors appointments. The women have to arrange their lives around my games. Their appointments have to be on Monday, Wednesday, or Friday. My wife drives, but there are times when she needs somebody to drive her home. She has to go for annual scopes. She had a colonostomy before I met her, and now she goes back for check-ups.

During baseball season I watch baseball and football, but otherwise I don't watch much television.

We go to banquets and picnics. We have a lot of friends—we visit them, they visit us. Fran has five sons, and three of them live here with their wives. They're always coming over. She loves to cook big dinners. We go up to visit one of her sons in New Jersey.

One time my grandson asked me, "Grandpa, how old are you?"

"I'm seventy-five."

"Oh, that means you're going to die soon."

He thought anybody over thirty is an old person and you're not supposed to be alive at seventy-five.

Then he said, "Grandpa, my Mommy says when I get older I'm going to look like you."

"That's possible."

"I'm doomed."

I had to laugh at that. I still have my hair, and all my teeth, which makes some people mad. They seem surprised that I'm eighty-one years old and still playing ball.

During the summer we travel all around Pennsylvania, and I've been invited to play on different teams as exhibitions for charity. I can't even remember how many charity games I've played—over a hundred. I plan to keep playing ball and grow old gracefully."

George Humiston,
age 83

Caned Chair Repair
Tampa, Florida

I discovered George when he was featured in a newspaper article about caned chairs. When I called him, he invited me to come over anytime.

At age 83, George Humiston has a smooth face, marred only with age spots and deep wrinkles in his chin. The day I visited, he was wearing a brown, long-sleeved Scottish checkered shirt and matching pants with a tan apron. He had wire-rimed glasses, a full head of silky white hair, and a ready smile.

When I arrived at his red brick home with white trim, a life-sized plywood cowboy greeted me in the driveway. Nearby, a plywood dog was chasing a cat up the fence. George Humiston had cut and painted these figures. He had also had planted flowers around the house and built birdfeeders, which hung from a tree in the front yard.

"There aren't any birds out now," he explained. "The cardinals have left for the winter."

I entered his small but neatly kept cottage-like house through the kitchen where he was repairing a caned rocking chair. The chair was turned upside down on a stool.

A small red and brown daschund, Max, greeted me with jumps and then ran to get his bone for me to throw.

"Max, come here," George called. "He wants attention. He's six years old, but still acts like a puppy."

George took me into his living room. When we sat down, Max jumped into George's lap and sat quietly looking at me.

A cat meowed, and I looked around, but all I saw was a stuffed cat on the piano. There were several old-fashioned china dolls and a large stuffed tiger on the floor next to the piano. The cat meowed again, but I still couldn't find it.

"Do you have a cat?"

"No. That's a stuffed cat. When there's a certain noise it meows, and when you pet it, it purrs."

"Does your wife collect dolls?" I asked. The newspaper article where I got George's name had mentioned him and his wife doing caning.

"No, my daughter and I live here—I have two daughters. One has always lived with me and she collects these dolls. The other one is married. I have two granddaughters. One of my granddaughters lives in Ft. Myers. She's married and a lawyer. The other is in Orlando.

My wife died a couple of years ago. She had Alzheimer's and was in a nursing home for two and a half years. My daughter and I went to visit her at least twice a week. I think it was worse putting her in a nursing home than it was having her die. She didn't know who I was. I was her father, or her brother, or someone. When she died, my daughter and I both agreed it was a relief. I told somebody "I'm not mourning— I'm just happy it's over with." She just kept getting worse. I hated to see her suffering.

My wife grew up with caning in her family. When her father died, we finished his caning work. Later, when we come down here, the blind were caning. We didn't want to compete with them so we gave it up. In the early seventies, my wife found an article in the paper asking for people who could cane chairs. There were about twenty-five names on the list and hers was on the bottom, so she was surprised when she got called. People said they had called everybody else, but nobody would do it except for themselves. So that's how we started down here. I keep busy all the time.

One year I went on vacation, and when I got back I took in forty-nine pieces the first day. I don't do any advertising—its just word of mouth. People bring the chairs to me, and I take out the old cane which is usually rotten, and put in new caning. I don't do anything else because it takes longer to try to repair them than it does to put in new. You can buy the caning material and press it in, but I weave it through the holes on the chairs edge. The cane material comes from a vine grown over in the Orient—Malaysia, China, or Singapore. I buy it from New York wholesale. When I'm doing tooling, like I was when you came, I wear an apron so I don't get glue all over my pants. It isn't difficult—it just takes time. It comes out real nice.

Caning is pretty near a lost art now, and there are very few around town. I do it as a hobby. If I get backed up, it might be six weeks before I can get to it. If they don't like it, they can take it somewhere else. I can't help it—I'm only one person with two hands. There's not enough money to do it as a living because you have to charge too much. A rocking chair like that one," George pointed to the chair in his kitchen, "would cost them a couple hundred dollars. People won't pay that—they'll throw the chair away first. I like it, and it gives me something to do. I retired twenty-five years ago and have been caning chairs ever since."

*   *   *   *

"I was born in New York State. We lived in the city, in an upstairs duplex. My aunt and uncle lived downstairs. I had a brother but he died when he was a year old. After my father died, my mother worked and I lived with my aunt and uncle. They didn't have any children of their own. Soon after I moved in with them, my aunt and uncle bought a farm, so we moved there. They were like mother and father to me. My mother came home every other weekend.

I went into the service in February and my aunt died in April. My uncle said, "We've got to get him home," so they went to the Red Cross, and the Red Cross got me home for the funeral. I'm kind of partial to the Red Cross because of this. I got married while in the service, and then went to school. I worked for a company drafting for fifteen years, then I got a job in Green, New York.

Green is a little town, but they have a Labor Day celebration there. They have fireworks and a big party. Not many that we know there anymore. After forty years, most of them have either moved away or died.

We stayed there five years before coming down here with the service. We joined the Lutheran Church down here, and my daughter played the organ. The church had about five hundred people, so we needed to have three services. We were active in the church, but I'm not now. I just sort of dropped out.

Genealogy is a big thing in my life. My wife and I went around the country looking for the Humiston family. We found the original Humiston couple. They came over in 1740. I never could find out the boat they came on. I don't know what happened. My daughter got the weekend off and came with us. There was a plaque on a church floor. My daughter made a rubbing of it.

"We went to the west coast for about four months in the motor home we have here and visited Humistons all the way around. We spent two weeks at the Mormon Library in Salt Lake. We never moved the motor home, and took a bus downtown. That was one of the big things we enjoyed. My daughter was married, and the other one was working so they didn't come on that trip.

We visited Humistons for one weekend in Wichita, Kansas. My favorite part was Bear Country USA. At the exit they had a bunch of cubs in cages. It was all nice country, but I wouldn't want to live out there. No way. Too crowded.

There was one old lady, a Humiston who lived alone. When we called her she said, "I wouldn't know about anything," but when we went to see her, she gave us some of our best information. It was funny.

I went to visit one Humiston in South Dakota. I stopped at the post office and the woman there asked if she could help me. I said I was looking for Mr. Humiston and she said, "I'm Mrs. Humiston." She was the postmistress.

We put all the information together in a book and made a hundred copies. Family members bought them. We sold all one hundred copies, and could have sold another hundred if we had had them. People are still are calling me, and that was back in eighties. I'm still following up on my family genealogy. People call me with information. There are some family stories that I couldn't verify.

I drive the motor home a little bit. I go around town. I go to the grocery store. We get along, don't we, Max?" George addressed the dog. "We have a pool here. We bought this house and put a pool in the backyard. I swim everyday in the summer and I walk the dog twice a day. I eat a lot of vegetables. I love fruit. My daughter and I are going back up to Amish Country this summer. We love it there."

DELORES AND BOB
CLARKE, 80 & 83

Food Pantry
Plainfield, New Jersey

Delores found my advertisement for active people over eighty in the Community Church in Sun City Center. She called me and we arranged an interview a week later, when she had just a few unscheduled hours.

When Delores opened the door of the large, red brick house with a Spanish style roof, I stepped into an entryway and found myself facing an immense Chinese wall painting.

"My daughter painted it," said Delores. "I had a Chinese picture I'd bought, and we couldn't find a picture to match it."

I looked around. The immaculate house was attractively decorated in pink and white. There was a white statue and marble bookends with a religious motif of Jesus and the Virgin Mary. One old chair with a decorative, curved wooden armrest caught my eye.

Doris was wearing a casual yellow dress. She stood upright with perfect posture. The deep wrinkles in her face gave me a hint that she had been a sun worshipper in her younger days.

Bob had a full head of pure white hair and was wearing a navy blue NASA T-shirt. Even with two hearing aids, I had to talk directly to him. Both laughed and joked with each other, and this seemed to be their normal communication style.

"Get out your driver's license, Delores—I want to prove to her that you are eighty years old," Bob said.

"Do you need proof that he's eighty-three?"

"No, I'll take your word for it."

"We've been married sixty-two years," Delores said. "We met going to prison. I'd go to the prison over here in Juvenile Detention, in Hillsborough County. Although the weight of life gets me down sometimes, it's rewarding. They look forward to us coming and visiting.

We were both new here. He was talking about what he wanted to do for the church, and he mentioned a food pantry. I had started a food pantry up in North Carolina, so I told him, "I'd be happy to help you with it."

You don't say that in church because you will end up doing it. It is very successful and has grown tremendously. Last year we took care of 11,162 people. Each year it gets bigger and bigger. I started it over in Lady of Guadalupe, in Wimauma. This is a migrant church but we have a lot of other people, older people, single men, people who are probably on drugs or booze. They have to eat too. We have a lot of single parents and a mix of everybody."

"Do they have to qualify?" I asked

"They have to show ID."

"Do they have to show any proof of income, tax forms or anything?"

"No, this is with the church and if they're there, we hope they're going to be honest. Of course, there are always people who are going to take advantage. They get a set amount of stuff that's pretty well rounded out. They get flour, sugar, pasta, rice, beans, juice, milk, fruit, meats, and vegetables.

I was doing it up in Carolina for fifteen years, and I started this one when I moved here two and a half years ago. I supervise eighty or ninety volunteers. The oldest volunteer is in their late sixties. This is just the one…"

"We had an advantage up there," Bob chimed in. "We had the county check these people out. We have a strange situation here because we can't get backing from the county at all."

"Do you help her with it?"

"Occasionally. I've never carried so many groceries in my life. Nativity Food Bank in Seffner is one of our suppliers, and they get it from Publix warehouse up in Lakeland. We go to Seffner to pick it up. I'm also the yard boy, the houseboy, and the pool boy. I do the plants and flowers, and I do the lawn."

"Do you do the mowing? It's a big yard!" I looked out the window.

"Actually the yard isn't that big," Delores said. "The golf course comes in. I'm thinking of what he had to mow in Carolina. This isn't anywhere near that size."

"I'm active in the Lions Club. You ever hear of that?" asked Bob.

"No, Bob, she's never heard of that." Dolores laughed.

"You want to tell the story?"

"No, you tell it."

"The Lions club sells Christmas trees in the winter time," Bob began. "We managed to pick up between seven and eight thousand dollars. We distribute the money and one of the places is the food pantry. We give them five hundred or so. We also give money to another food pantry down in Ruskin and a seeing-eye leader dog place.

I also belong to the Knights of Columbus in this parish. I'm chairman of the campaign to collect money for the retarded. That's what I'm working on right now. Every March we have a drive. We stand out in front of the Wal-Mart and other stores and hand out tootsie rolls to the people who give money to us. We pick up about six thousand dollars to distribute to six different organizations. I usher in church."

"We're active in the church," Delores said. "I'm a lector. I read the scripture at mass and I give communion to the priest. We've always been close to the church."

"I have to show you all the metals she got. Here is one for outstanding volunteer 1987. I want to show you my metals from the Bishop of St. Petersburg." He showed a picture of himself with the St. Petersburg Bishop. "This was taken last November. The metal was for starting the food pantry, and our hard work."

"Here's a ribbon you can wear around your neck Bob."

"She should wear it even when she's cooking." He laughed.

"There are a lot of people doing things, not just me," Delores said. "I put in a lot of time, that's for sure. I'm down there every day starting early in the morning. You have to give back, that's what this is all about.

We like to play bridge but don't get a lot of time. I go to mass during the week. During lent I go every day. The rest of the year I go three or four times a week. I've been blessed with a high energy level..."

*   *   *   *

"I'm the oldest of three," Delores continued. "I have a younger sister and brother. My father left the family and my mother held it together. My grandmother was her backbone. My mother lived to be ninety-eight and my father was eighty-nine. The grandmothers were eighty-six and ninety-eight. My grandfather was eighty-nine."

"You come from a long-lived family," I said.

"You betcha, and I'm planning on it. I've already told God that I want a hundred and thirty to see all my grandchildren grow-up.

I finished high school. I was supposed to go to college, but we couldn't afford it. Shortly after that we were married. I met Bob in high school. He had graduated and came back for extra credits. He came at a time when money was scarce so he had to get more credits. He returned to high school after graduation to take physics or calculus, and I met him then."

"She may have been in love with him." Bob winked.

Delores laughed. "Not really, we dated a bit and then he went away."

"She was a beautiful girl."

"I believe it," I said. "She's beautiful now."

"I didn't stay young."

"Did you do a lot of sun worshiping?"

"Oh yah. In those days we used to put on oil and stuff to make us burn. When I think of it now, we weren't as smart about health. Nobody knew about it then. We used to go to the shore and we'd lie for hours, rub oil on, and lay on foil to reflect the sun and increase our exposure.

I finished high school, dated a bit, and then married Bob. After I had children, I'd work part time at night to help out. Then there got to be a lot of kids. This is the third house we built. It was a huge house, and after awhile we put on an addition to make it bigger. We've always worked.

"A functional house," Bob stated.

Delores continued. "We could be comfortable in a smaller house. Our kids visit and we wanted to have a place where we could have everybody, but it's so hot in the summer and in the winter there's work and school, and they can't get away. Everyone has jobs that won't allow them to leave in the winter. We have a lot of friends who stop by.

We have fourteen grandchildren and twelve greats. I just finished mailing all the valentines. It gets to be expensive because you have to put something in the envelope that you send with them. There is Valentines, St. Patties, Halloween and Thanksgiving, and then Christmas gifts and birthdays."

"She was a travel agent for fifteen years."

"I worked when the kids were older and in college. I love hearing about traveling, doing it, and every aspect to it. We both like traveling. I traveled a lot when I worked for the travel agency. The boss wanted us to travel so I would know what I was talking about. We've been to Russia, China, Japan, Okinawa, and Asia. We go up to Carolina for a few weeks in the summer. We really love the ocean and miss it very much."

"I grew up in Plainfield, New Jersey, a commuter town near New York." Bob said. "There was just my older brother and I. I'm three years younger. He was spoiled and thought everything belonged to him. That's where we used to get in real arguments. We fought regularly.

I went to a Catholic grade school and the same public high school that Delores went to. There were beautiful girls there. I played football and baseball, although I play golf now. I studied mechanical engineering in college, then went to work for the city of Plainfield surveying in their engineering department. Then I went into engineering for a year or two before the war started. When the war started, we already had two children…"

"I was pregnant with the third."

"…and they decided they wanted to draft me. I was all ready to go into the Marine Corps, and the guy said, "No you're not. You're going to the research center in Cleveland." It was known as the NHPA. I worked primarily on engines."

"The baby was born, and he was about three weeks old when I went out there to join Bob."

"We had to find a place to live together," Bob said. "It was kind of tough finding housing in those days. We ended up in a project area. By 1950, after the war was over, we got everything together and started to build a house in Pay Village on Lake Erie. We raised most of the kids there."

"The rest of the kids were all born there including the ones we lost. I lost five kids through miscarriages, and the last one I went full term but…" Delores lowered her voice and became serious, "…the baby was dead. Mothers and girls have a rough time, but we are close now."

"We went to Ohio during the war," Bob began. "I worked for NASA for thirty-five years. It was an interesting place to work. I was forty-four when I joined. It became NASA in 1968. They had some unusual facilities for testing engines and rocket systems."

"Were you involved in going to the moon?" I asked.

"It took quite an effort. We all had parts in it. I was supervising people in the experiments. We were trying different angles and it was very interesting. We had about five thousand people on that project. At any one time we might have had twelve hundred research experiments going on. There was a bunch of implementation people designing the first capsule.

I left in 1979. They started to contract everything out and didn't use the employees that they had. They were starting to get rid of them, and putting in contractors to do everything. Sometimes they were more concerned about the dollar than doing the project. They had that tragedy when the explorer blew up with the schoolteacher in 1986.

I've been retired twenty-three years now. When I retired, we returned to North Carolina where we'd lived fifty years earlier, and I built a house. We were in a small town called Southern Shores, just above Kitty Hawk. We did a lot of volunteer work and kept the taxes down to the envy of the other towns. There were all sorts of volunteer jobs we could get involved with. I worked for Habitat for Humanity and joined a homeowners association where we built crossovers on the ocean to save the dunes.

"Florida turned out a lot different than they say it is," Delores added. "You can look outside the window and see egrets walking through the backyard. There are millions of them."

"There are an awful lot of con guys down here," Bob said. "You have to be careful."

Delores stated, "Years ago when we lived in Ohio, we could go to New Jersey for two weeks and not lock our door. When we lived on the beach, we couldn't walk down to the water without locking our house. It used to be that when somebody said they would do something for you, their word was good. You didn't need a contract and you didn't need it in black and white or notarized. You believed them and it worked. I think the morality in the country is at a low edge. Companies aren't loyal to the employees and the employees aren't loyal to them.

We don't learn from history. All the big empires and all the big civilizations went down the tubes. Here we're doing the same thing that they all did. September eleventh proved to us that we're not alone on the planet.

I want to get out of Hillsborough County. Too many good old boys. There were good old boys in Carolina, but they are progressive. They can appreciate better ways of doing things and accept them. Florida—boy they're set.....

We voted absentee. In Carolina, we had to go to the polls and show our ID. Here, they sent it in the mail. We could have ordered fifteen of them and they would have sent them. They had no conception of how honest we were or anything."

"We had to verify each other," Bob said.

"We could have verified each other fifteen times," stated Delores." I'm not sure Gore was the one to vote for anyway, but I think the Democrats are more for the poor and underprivileged. Bush wants to drill oil here. Does he think the people are stupid? Talking about the three hundred dollars tax return—what did it do but get us back into debt?"

"Enron," Bob said.

Delores continued. "Its interesting how they dance around it. If it had been Clinton in there, they would have nailed him to the wall over it.

I don't think we should listen to church leaders tell us how to run the country other than morality, but I do think we should be allowed to pray publicly. God's got to have a hand in there somewhere. If I want to put a religious figure in my businesses or if the kids in school want to take a moment of meditation, I think it should be allowed. I remember when I was in school we used to have a psalm read every morning. I think that the Jewish faith, and the Protestant faith, and the Catholic faith have all enjoyed the psalms. I think they should have that right. We go to a lecture series, and we're learning the history of the church.

I have trouble not doing anything. I can't just sit. I write letters, sew, grind coffee or package stuff for the pantry. I get USDA stuff. We get a lot of bulk stuff, so we have to break them down into packages, and grind the beans since the people getting it probably don't have a grinder. I do that at night. I always have to do something.

I make the schedule for people who work for the pantry on the computer. We have several teams that do different things. There are people who work every two hours. And each week it's a different team. Then I have men who drive either to Nativity or Providence, and helpers for each driver."

"That reminds me, I'm supposed to drive tomorrow," Bob added.

Delores ignored the interruption. "Then I have people who come in Monday and Friday morning to package. I'm looking for teams to interview and people to make sure they are under a certain financial level."

Bob lost interest in the conversation and had been looking out the window.

"There's an alligator out there."

"You started this and you're in charge of all of it?" I asked.

"Yes."

"There's alligator over there sitting on the grass," Bob was louder this time.

Delores looked out the window. "There is an alligator over here by the far bank. See him over the hedge?"

"I'll go out and feed him," Bob offered.

"Don't you dare."

"I didn't bring my camera, but it would be interesting having a picture of you both petting the alligator." I laughed. "I remember an alligator handler explaining the way alligators think: You bring food, you are food, and everything is food!"

"Like the little house of horrors." Bob said. "Alligators live in the ponds on the golf course. The golfers hit the balls, hit the tangerine trees, and even the roofs of houses."

"Like those golf balls, we've had our ups and downs," Delores said. "We were blessed that we both are in the same church and have the same faith. I think it's important that you both have a faith. We both believe in God. I think you have to recognize that you have committed yourself, this isn't just playing house. We've been married sixty-two years. Romance is different from when you're newly married. We know each other a lot better. We've had a lot of kids, and our ups and downs, and we're sharing all that. When we were first married it was new and shiny, and there was the physical part. I think as you get older it gets to be deeper.

"She doesn't kiss me enough. I want her to kiss me more."

"Men! As they get older."

"Dirty old men." Bob laughed.

"We both like to pray together," Delores said. "We both like to travel. March first we're going to Rome for a week with two of our daughters. We've been before, but he's never been to Pompeii and Assisi. Of course, no matter how many times you go to Rome, there's always something new to see.

The welfare of our children is important. We're blessed with two kids who live down here. The rest of them are all over the country. We went to Michigan last Christmas to visit them, and we're going to North Carolina for a week.

They keep in touch over the internet. Technology has brought us marvelous things. Christmas time we got a labeler, cell phones, and laminator. We've got all these toys but it doesn't make life any better, and the things that should be changed aren't getting changed."

"What other changes have you seen?" I asked.

"Nylons," Delores said. "When nylons came out, how wonderful, and how hard it was to get a pair. We used to wear them with runs in them because you couldn't get them. Standing in line for coupons, and rolling cigarettes. At that time everyone smoked. We had a little machine you put the papers on. Then there were Big Bands. How wonderful the Big Bands were. And dancing. We still go dancing with the church and different organizations. We go to a dance in Sarasota Saturday nights.

I know Bob complains sometimes that I keep him moving, but it's going to save his life. He's not getting much walking exercises. He has a pacemaker and takes blood pressure medicine, but nothing other than that."

"What is your secret for staying young, Bob?"

"Being married to Delores. I get plenty of walking. The fellow I play golf with is a couple years older than me. We use a cart on the golf course and on one corner I have to pull the cart over the curve. Besides, I lift four to five hundred pounds moving those boxes around for the food pantry."

"Everybody teases me because I have a high energy level and I do a lot, but I make him do too. I think if you sit and think about how old you're getting you will get old. I think part of it is having good genes."

"She always has a project," Bob said. "I'm a big do-it yourselfer. She is a volunteer usher for the Performing Arts Theatre. I take tickets so I don't get to see the plays that much.

She saves money on tolls and goes through route 41, which is a rough neighborhood. I got her a cell phone so I know she's safe. I can also check up on her that she isn't running around some place."

"Yah, I'm sure! I should be so lucky as to run around. Maybe I'll find some wealthy young guy. I've been married sixty-two years and I still don't have him trained. He's not considerate."

"I watch football and baseball."

"I think twenty-four hours of sports is too much. When I talk to him it's "uh, huh." and he doesn't know what I'm saying."

"Does he turn the hearing aids off?" I asked.

"Even before he had hearing aids…"

"I have glasses to read. I can read without them, but my eyes get tired." Bob stated.

"We've both had cataracts removed," added Delores. "It's an easy thing to do, and doctors do it. A lot of things today are different. I wonder how my mom lived so long? She broke all the rules of eating. We eat a lot of fruits and vegetables, but candy is my nemesis. I lost seventeen pounds, and put nine back. He always was very thin. He's not now. He's got about twenty-five pounds to take off.

Thank God my health is very good. I don't take any medicine. I don't smoke, so these are only sun and age wrinkles. I don't have a maid, I do my housework at night, and we are active. I figure this is the way we'll keep going. I read a lot when we travel. I like mysteries and religious books."

"She went to Africa. I stayed home eating cornflakes."

"I went to classes in Nairobi—learning about the country and the natives. He told every neighbor I was gone, so he got invited to dinner just about every night."

"I had to cook," Bob protested.

"You've never cooked in your life. You burn boiling water."

"I cook bacon and eggs.

I traveled with her to Australia, South America, and New Zealand."

"Are your memories still good?" I asked.

"Mine is," said Delores.

"I believe in the "here after." I go someplace and I say "What am I here after?" Its funny, I forget one minute from the next."

"I tell him he's doing the butterfly. Just recently I started telling him to take notes. If someone were to write notes for him, it would be all right, but he doesn't want to do all that work himself."

"Do you have any pets?"

"No, he's enough."

"What do you think of this, Bob?" I asked.

"She doesn't kiss me enough."

"As men get older they get ridiculous. There's no self-discipline."

"That's what happens when you marry a beautiful woman."

Margaret Minere, age 83

Hospital Volunteer
Coldbrook Township, Illinois

I received a call from Margaret and she said she'd like to talk to me. She hadn't attended the Companion or Foster Grandparent meeting as she was home recovering from major surgery related to cancer. A friend who had attended the meeting had brought her one of my fliers.

The subsidized apartment complex for low-income elderly and disabled people was set back from the street. The oak trees and park like atmosphere were a pleasant contrast from the busy street and deteriorating neighborhood. The two-story stucco apartment complex was painted a light beige.

When I entered the room, a dull green parrot screeched her objection. The corner table in the one bedroom apartment was covered with stuffed bears, a homemade Cabbage Patch doll, a stuffed snowman, and alligator. I sat across from Margaret, and her parrot, Jane, in an old, but comfortable, brown Lazy Boy rocker. Although the temperature in the house was turned up to over eighty, Margaret was wearing a warm sweatshirt decorated with candy canes.

"I bought it at the Salvation Army at Christmas time." She began. "I get cold easily. I have a friend who attended the foster grandmother program and told me about you.

She just turned eighty and doesn't want to admit it. We've all lived through a very interesting time.

I haven't driven the car since my surgery, but I'm going out today for the first time. My car must be a mess underneath those trees dropping acorns and branches, and birds flying overhead." Margaret laughed.

"I've been getting meals on wheels for the past ten days and this is my last day. I was sick since September from pneumonia and couldn't get over it. Finally the doctors did some tests, and did a colonostomy. I'm recovering from cancer of the colon.

Dr. McAllister was the surgeon. He kept patting me and saying, "We're so proud of you." He and another doctor were discussing it and said, "We can't believe she's eighty-three." He said he got it all and I should have a full recovery and be all right. They hadn't expected me to have such a quick recovery at my age. I didn't do anything, Mother Nature did it and I just cooperated.

I have a great life. It's been three years since I started at the VA (Veterans Administration Hospital) as a Senior Companion. I like being there, and the nurses have all been so nice to me. I was going five days a week, four hours a day. I hope to do that again, maybe starting the first of next month. It depends on how strong I can get. I visit the patients and they like to tell me their problems. I always get them a fresh pitcher of ice water, a newspaper, or another blanket if they're cold. I pick up their medicine at the pharmacy if they're being discharged. If somebody is restrained, I sit and watch them so they don't hurt themselves.

The Seniors in Service gives us two-fifty an hour. It gives me spending money. I've been a widow for twelve years, and when you lose that second income you go into your savings. When you become sick and need to take blood pressure pills that cost sixty dollars, or other medicine, your money disappears. I'm in a Medicare HMO, but beginning the first of January they will no longer pay for medication. I just called Pfeiffer and they are going to come out with a card so I can buy medicine for fifteen dollars. That doesn't go into effect for a couple more months. I've been on cholesterol, blood pressure, and iron pills. The doctor said that I was anemic from the bleeding.

When my husband and I were together, we lived in a cottage on the Mississippi. I'd fry things in a big iron skillet. I'd cook his breakfast. He liked tomatoes and eggs. We were married over fifty years. We got married in 1938 and he died in 1990. A couple of nights ago I dreamed that I was feeling awful and he came and sat on the bed and put his arms around me. It was a dream, but it made me feel better. You never get used to it."

Looking at her hand, I noticed that Margaret still wears her wedding ring.

"We were busy with our business. We had a good life. When we retired, we went to Texas. We used to go to Acapulco after he retired. We had a travel trailer and we would take out travel insurance for eighty days. In case we had trouble we were prepared. We had good times and traveled a lot. Our last trip was in March and he died in June. We went to Las Vegas. We'd gotten down to a motor home by then, and I was driving. We had a good time."

Margaret showed me an intricate picture of the Virgin Mary. "We went to Mexico and a priest in Mexico City gave this to me. It's made of tiny toothpicks all glued together. I'm a Catholic but I haven't gone to church for a while.

My first trip after he died was with Merry Widow. I took a cruise out of Tampa and you're escorted. I had a good time and met people. I'm still in contact with one person I met on that cruise. I've gone on other cruises since then, but I've gone alone and I didn't mind at all. I always try to have a good time."

The parrot began screaming and Margaret picked up a spray bottle next to the cage.

"Jane's a Patagonian parrot. As soon as I pick the water up she knows and keeps quiet for a while. She likes water in a dish, but she doesn't like it hitting her.

She's a lot of company. I let her out at night when I'm home. She says "Hello," and "What" but she isn't really a talker. She's a dark olive green and has orange feathers between her legs and white circles around her eyes. She puts her beak in her feathers when she wants to ignore you.

She really doesn't like company, because it takes my attention away from her. She has a fit when repairmen come. I've had her about five years and she makes a good watchdog. I had no intention of buying her, but I was at a flea market. She was on the floor and was back as far as she could get in her cage and kids were poking at her. Even adults were putting their fingers in her cage. She was helpless. You know birds in a cage can't go anyplace. I came home and called my daughter. She said "Mom, why don't you buy her." I went back and bought her. I've never been sorry. Once I win the lottery, I'm going to go to all the flea markets and let all the birds out. They don't belong in a cage."

*   *   *   *

"I was born in a farm in Illinois, about thirty-five miles from the Iowa border and one hundred and seventy-five miles south west of Chicago. I graduated from Catholic High School and. I got a two-year degree from the business college in town.

My dad was drafted in World War One. He got typhoid fever and almost died. After the war ended, we went through the depression, which was terrible, and we were very poor. I remember my Dad took a little boat to town, and he came home with just enough money to buy two pairs of school shoes. But you know, we were happy. We played basketball, football and didn't need any money for entertainment. The neighbor kids came over and we didn't need anything. I think just being happy and satisfied with what we have makes a person have a good life.

I had six sisters and two brothers. My brother was the oldest, and I was second. I still have three sisters. One lives in Arizona, and the other two are in Illinois. Of course, I'm the oldest of all of them. They were all worse off than I was, until this happened to me. I was going full speed ahead.

My sister who is five years younger just got hospice to take care of her. She has cancer, emphysema, and heart trouble. I guess she's got everything you can imagine. She hasn't got too much longer to live.

I was up there in Northwest Illinois in '99 to her fiftieth wedding anniversary. I talked to her the other night on the phone. She said, "We're going to have to have another reunion."

"You turn the heat on up there in Illinois and I'll come back." Margaret laughed.

"You like it warm," I stated.

"I'm worse now because of being anemic.

My first job was JC Penny's at twenty-five cents an hour. I worked one day a week and got a dollar ninety-eight. They took two cents for social security. I had two brothers but I had no idea about men's clothes. The first day they put me in the men's department. I had no idea about the neck and sleeve length. Of course it was a country town. Underwear was chest size, and there was long, short and all that. I made so many mistakes that day I didn't think they would keep me. They hired me and another girl, and they had to decide who would be the best person. Her brother fell out of a tree that day and broke his leg, and all his relatives kept coming in and telling her about it. Everytime the manager looked at her, she was talking to somebody, so I got the job because of her bad luck.

I still worked at JC Penny's after I was married, earning twenty-five cents an hour. Seasonal, Easter and Christmas, I worked more. I was paid for eight hours, but I actually worked ten. It was a country town and the farmers came in late, after nine o'clock, so they expected us to stay on the job. After the customers left, they expected us to stock the shelves. But, of course we didn't mind because we were happy to have a job. Jobs were still scarce.

From there I went to a nice department store to work by the week. I got twelve dollars for a week. I said, "That's not much money for a week."

And they said "But look at the prestige you have working in this store."

It was a nice store. Then I left that and went to Grant Company. I got more money and I liked it better. It was faster than the department store. The department store people would come in and try on gloves. But in Grant, people knew what they wanted.

I got married in '38 and he was working on the railroad. They wouldn't let him go to war. They said he was more important on the railroad. At that time they needed people to run the engines.

I started a little grocery store myself, and it kept growing and growing and when the war was over, he quit and we expanded. We had a good-sized grocery store. We were what you call a Mom and Pop store. When the supermarkets came in the neighborhood, we went into packaged liquor. We ended up with two liquor stores, and we did real well. I worked at the stores all the time from early morning to late at night. I kept them clean. I scrubbed the floors and refrigerators. One day a man said to my husband that I shouldn't be doing the floor, so he hired someone to do the floors for me.

Then we moved to Texas and had an eighty-foot mobile home. I was in my seventies. I washed the mobile home once or twice a year. I'd get a big brush, buckets, tubs, and ladders, and do the home and the windows at the same time. I always washed and waxed the car. I think working and keeping busy is the best secret in the world, and being happy with people that you meet. When we retired we thought that we were pretty well off, not rich, but enough to live on.

When I first came to Tampa, I volunteered at University Hospital. I wanted to get out and meet people and visit, but they put me in the Office of Nursing and Administration to file and answer the phone. It was so boring and I wasn't meeting anybody but the girls in the office. They were all young and had their own lives. I stayed there about two years. Then I went to a senior citizens' center, stayed there for a while and made some friends. I left when one of my friends died.

There was an ad in the paper about the Seniors in Service. When I called they said, "How would you like to go to the VA?" So that's where I went and I really enjoy it. I have a good time and have been there almost three years. When I'm at the VA I walk continuously, so I don't need to walk or exercise.

I hope to go back the first of the month if I can get my strength back. I was going to go to Piccadilly's (a local cafeteria) and get liver. I get lunch from the meals and wheels, but I'll put that in the refrigerator and eat it for dinner. I like to eat most everything. I love asparagus. The only thing I don't like is coconut. Right now I have to eat everything soft. This is my last day getting Meals on Wheels. They give you more for the weekend.

I like to keep busy. I've been going through my jewelry, sorting it out and straightening out my desk. There's always something to do at the house. I have several jewelry pieces that I want to give away. I don't go to places where I can wear them.

Last May I went to Las Vegas with a friend for a week. We had a good time. We go to Busch Gardens (a local theme park) together. I belonged to the 1918 club. There are a few men in 1918, but the women are outliving the men. They're all people who were born in 1918. It's an international club. I think keeping busy, staying active and interested in life is important.

I haven't really dated since my husband died. I met a nice man who lives in Milton, Florida. He was in World War II and he was a chemist during his working years. I took him out to the 1918 club and dated him. We went out to eat a few times. I lived in a mobile home before I moved into this complex here, and I took him back to my mobile home a few times to play cards. There wasn't any romance, just friendship. We're still friends.

I had a couple men want to get married, but they weren't bringing anything to the marriage. One was a redneck who worked in a canning factory. He wanted to get married, but he didn't have any money, only his check coming in. I had the mobile home then. He said, "I could just move in with you and we could split the bills."

What would I gain? I'd gain a man to take care of, do his laundry, and look after. He didn't have a car. I think I'm better off alone.

I went to this nursing home and I met this man named John. He had worked as a manager on Wall Street, but he ended up in a nursing home. It's really sad. I visited him everyday. He'd sit in a wheelchair, and when I arrived he'd look up and smile. We were just friends, but I couldn't let go. I had to see him everyday. I was with him the day he died. I tried to tell the nurses the night before that John's a very sick man, but it was like pouring water on a duck's back. I went there about two or three in the afternoon and he was sitting in the wheelchair, fully dressed with a high, high temperature. I talked to the girl and told her, "He has a temperature. He's very sick." She took it but the thermometer was broken. It wouldn't register. So they got somebody else to take his temperature and they put him to bed. He was critical. At seven they finally got the doctor but by seven-thirty he died. The nursing home care was terrible.

I hope to go back to the VA soon. I enjoy working there. I have a lady friend at the VA who likes to travel, so we might take some trips together. I'd like to go back to Acapulco some day, but I don't know if I will. I would like to get up to see my sister in Illinois, but I can't get up there is the winter."

Postscript—Six months after this interview I called Margaret to see how she is doing. She told me that the doctors believe she is cancer free. Although her doctor thought he had gotten it all, she went through chemotherapy just in case the cancer had spread. She is pleased that her hair has grown back now. She is back to work at the VA hospital five days a week.

Russell and Sara, 85 & 81

Caretaker Companions
California & Florida

I was invited to speak about my writing project at a meeting for Senior Companions. Russell attended the meeting and signed the page I passed around. I contacted him and we set up a date to meet. I was confident that I could find his home from the address, but my computer map failed me. After driving around lost for half an hour, I called and Russell met me at a gas station. He lived at the end of several twisting dead-ending streets.

I followed Russell's pick-up truck to his house in a run-down neighborhood. Russell and I walked into the old brick house together. He is nearly six feet tall, lanky, had a day old beard and the heavy wrinkles of a man who has worked hard outdoors all his life. An edging of white hair forms a circle around his smooth head. A large furry dog with a lolling tongue greeted us.

"Usually it's just me and Sara and the dog. He digs holes around the yard, looks like bomb craters. He's a husky. He should be in Alaska pulling sleds. A friend who came down from New York is visiting, and she's giving Sara a permanent."

When we entered the old fashioned kitchen, Sara, who was nearly as tall as Russell, and stick thin, greeted us. She was wearing a housecoat and her friend, a woman several years younger, was rolling her graying hair with large curlers. When she finished curling Sara's hair, she cut a piece of pie for herself and Sara.

Russell took me into the living room. He sat on one of the two Lazy boy rockers and I sat on an old dark brown and green couch. The walls were decorated with photos and a mirror with painted butterflies. The room was dominated by a hospital bed and breathing equipment.

"Sara and I have been together eleven years," Russell began. "We met at the campgrounds. About six years ago she had heart trouble and had to have open heart. Now she had a regular heart attack and just about died. Her heart stopped and she was down to where she wasn't even living. The doctor only gave her two days to live, but she's still here. She's on hospice care and this equipment belongs to hospice. Now she's walking around and doesn't even use a cane.

I put a handrail outside to make it easier. We had a ramp, but she didn't like that. I put new floors in here, right down to the ground. I took everything out, all the beams, and put in new pillars underneath and a new floor joist. I rebuilt the shower in the bathroom because you can't buy that size of a shower base anymore. They're too small so I had to build the shower base. I put in the sidewalk, built the shed, and the driveway so you can walk in without wading in water and put a skirt on around the house. The landlord takes the cost off my rent.

When I was younger, I built houses and swimming pools. There isn't much in the house that I don't know except the electric.

I'm a Senior Companion, but I'm getting paid for staying right here. Sara was in the program first, and she got me into it. She went down and I get my twenty hours a week here in the house caring for her. I bathe her and do whatever is needed. I have regular people I work with, but when she went down I told them I was needed here for now. Those people were still walking around and making it. I've been with Sara all along.

There are three people that I visit. One is near Apollo beach, one in Seffner, and one in Tampa. I get paid mileage, and I get two-fifty an hour. It adds up if I'm busy, about three seventy five to four hundred dollars a month. All I had before was my social security. Bad times and Florida law busted me down.

I was married twenty-seven and a half years. My wife divorced me while I was in the hospital getting a fusion surgery—the vertebrae all grown together. I didn't have no cartilage left. The kids are gone away now. While I was in the hospital, they moved and I don't know where they went. Somewhere up north. The same thing happened with my own family. I just found a brother two years ago that I haven't seen since 1928. The last ten to fifteen years I was in a membership camp and whenever someone would be going out west, I'd ask them to look in the phone book and see if they could find my brother.

I've had a good life and think the best time I've ever had was camping. Membership camp is for people who own a mobile home or camper. You buy a membership and can stay in each campsite for up to two weeks. Then you have to get out for twenty-four hours. We'd get two campgrounds about forty miles apart and go back and forth. We'd do two weeks in this one and then two weeks in that one. We could go and come. If the grass got too tall, all I had to do was move out and go to the other campgrounds.

I'm a good cook and a baker, so we eat well. That's my pie that they're eating out there now. I'm a better cook than most women. I won seven times at the campground when they had a covered dish contest, but the women got complaining about it, so I quit going.

Sara and her husband had a big motor home and I had a big fifth wheel. That's how I met them. We had membership that was world-wide. We could go in and pay five dollars a night to any of the camp-grounds that belonged to the syndicate. Some were nationwide, and some were even in Europe. You could go where you want, or desire to.

I was square dancing before I met Sara, and I'd go to Maine, to nationals, to Rhode Island, Huston, Indianapolis, St. Louis, wherever they were going to hold a national. They only had it one time in Florida. I've been to Canada and all over this country, several times clear around it. I'd go wherever they had the national, Maine, New Hampshire, wherever, with her. It was a pretty nice life but they priced us out of it. They kept raising the membership and the dues and it got to where I couldn't afford it anymore.

Square dancing saved my life. I was about to crap out before I got into square dancing. I hadn't done it since I was a boy and did barn dancing. At that time, they only had about twenty-four different calls. When I got back into it they had about two or three hundred calls in basic dancing, and then in advanced dancing they have another two hundred. When you got to the top, they didn't even have a caller. They just do the moves that are supposed to go with that music. I got into that once in Hudson. It was in a county church basement, and I thought it was just going to be square dancing. The newspaper didn't give the level. By golly, I was good enough that I got through it all right.

Then I said, "I'm going to cop out because I don't want to screw it up for you."

They said, "You're doing all right, hang in here. You just need a little nudge this way or that way."

I left, but I could have stayed in advanced dancing. It was something I enjoyed. At first I went one day a week for lessons, on Friday. I'd forget what I learned from Friday to Friday so I joined two other clubs on different nights. So I was going three nights a week when others were only going one. In three or four months I was in advanced square dancing. I had to give it up. My legs won't let me do it anymore."

*   *   *   *

"I left home when I was about five years old and my grandma took me. My grandma raised and taught me. She believed that a man should do everything that a woman does, except childbirth. She taught me to sew, look at the stars, love nature, and how to live in the world

My dad died when I was eleven. They shipped the kids every which way, and I didn't know where anybody was. I had three brothers and a sister. I just found one brother two years ago, but he died last year. As soon as they sent me his address and phone, I flew out to Denver. We had five days together. He didn't know me, and he didn't look like what I thought he'd look like. I was six foot before the fusion, but he stopped growing. He never grew after fourteen or fifteen years old. I last saw him when I was about thirteen and we were even height back then. I was looking around Denver airport for a guy about my size, and this little guy comes up to me and said, "I think you're looking for me."

He took me around Denver. We went out in the mountains and did some touring. We had a few drinks together, but it wasn't like meeting up with a brother that I hadn't seen in a year. We were total strangers, like two dogs sniffing each other. We wrote a little back and forth.

Now the others, I don't know where they are. My sister is dead, but I don't know about the other two girls. There were five of us, two younger and two older. I was in the middle. I was younger than my sister and when we were real little I used to stand up to her, so I took a lot of beatings. She died when I was down in Panama in 1937. Time I got home she was long gone. Her husband had taken off with the two kids and gone to San Diego.

When I was a kid I lived in California. I was in the Army in San Diego for one year. We would either go from LA down to Mission beach or come up from San Diego to Mission Beach. They had the biggest and best skating rink in the southern part of California. It cost fifty cents.

I was in Panama from 1937 to 1940. I did three years in Hawaii, signed on again and went to Panama. I did three years down there and then quit. When the war started, I went back in and helped train divisions. Then I went overseas with Patton. I was in Overlord, the code name for the Invasion of Normandy, on D-day, June 6,1944, and we went all the way to the Elba River with Patton. That's where the Americans and Russians met.

I traveled during the war. We landed in Scotland. I went over on the Queen Liz. We couldn't land in South Hampton, it wasn't deep enough, so they let us off in Scotland and we went down through England. When they moved us all out, we went to France, Belgium, Holland, then back into Germany. I've been in Mexico, Columbia, Panama. My travels were mostly with the Army. I went to Mexico when I lived in California.

If it wasn't for the VA services, I'd have been dead a long time ago. They've been good to me. They got me my hearing aids. I don't use them because they just magnify whatever else is going on, and I still don't hear what people are saying. If I look at them, I can hear.

I got a flu shot, and needed to get papers from the VA. I have to get health papers every year for Seniors in Service. They don't want us getting anybody sick. While I was there, I got a letter from the doctor saying I'm in good shape. The doctor asked me what medicines I'm on and I said none. Once in a while I take a vitamin C, and I drink orange juice. I juice oranges from my trees. I eat whatever I decide I want, mostly meat and potatoes. I do a lot of baking. If I get enough strawberries, peaches, or apples, I make a batter. I make cakes, and pies, and right now I made a good sweet potato pie. You want a piece?"

If course, it would have been rude for me to have refused. Russell wasn't kidding when he said he is a good cook—the pie was delicious.

"I don't walk enough," Russell continued. "My knees bother me. I tried to walk to Kash and Karry last summer. It was a hot day. I got there okay, but I couldn't make it back. I caught the bus, but I didn't have any change and it cost me a dollar to go two blocks, and I still had to walk from Columbus Avenue.

I've been encouraging Sara to walk. I keep telling her, "Now that you are getting better, walk back and forth in here." Yesterday she was sitting outside and couldn't get out of the chair. I had to help her get up. She's been in bed too long.

I worked outdoors all my life, and I never learned to smoke. I was too stupid to learn how to roll a cigarette. Whenever anybody gave me the makings, I'd make a big hump. When I'd go to light it, it would all fall apart, so I gave that up.

During the war I bought a pipe, and I lost that in the snow one day in the Bulge and I never got around to getting another one. I tried some of those local clay pipes that you could get over there, like the pirates used to use, with a little bowl at the end of them. They were too strong. I couldn't handle it, so I never did smoke.

I did some drinking over there. Everybody did. You had to, to live through it. Anytime we'd find a town, we'd go through the basements and find some cognac or some good booze, and then go onto the next house. I was never a heavy drinker. I used to enjoy beer, but now I won't drink it anymore because it's full of formaldehyde. They don't make real beer anymore.

My uncle used to own a brewery in Indiana. He sent to Germany to get a brewmaster. They were just ready to start a brew when alcohol became illegal. They continued brewing one vat all the dry years. All of the town big shots came out there to drink and play pinnacle all night. There were, doctors, lawyers, the mayor, and my uncle Otto. Grandpa was night watch there. He used to drive the wagon, hauling beer, when it was wet years. Then when the dry years came on, Pa just gave him a job night watching. He'd pull his boxes and then come back and sit in the game, drinking beer. Grandpa died at ninety-six. He was walking his rounds and carrying boxes in the ice and snow. He slid and broke his hip, and died of pneumonia. Grandma said, "I told him if he didn't quit drinking that beer, it would kill him."

My Uncle Otto lived to be about ninety-five. They were big men. Grandpa and my uncle would sit all night drinking those big heavy two-handed schooners of beer, malt and hops, real beer. They never had a headache, none of them. The formaldehyde goes to the brain. It's embalming fluid—its what the undertaker uses. Why the hell should you help the undertaker? Drink beer, embalm your brain, and all he has to do it take it out and put it in a jar. That's why when these rebels down here get two or three beers, they go nutty. I could drink two cans of regular junky beer, and I'd get a head like a balloon and a mouth like a birdcage. It's all those chemicals.

When I brought the moonlight over, buyers came down from Canada. They leased it for ninety-nine years. They gave him such a good price Grandpa couldn't say no. The first thing they did was send the brewmaster back to Germany and brought in their chemists with the white coats, five of them. In five days they shipped thirteen carloads of 3.5% beer to Texas, so it's not aged at all. It's a big brewery. The water comes in through the wells, goes around in cans and bottles and it's gone. Beer should age. Beer should have malts and hops and good stuff in it, not spiked with chemicals. They're making beer today the same way the syndicate made it during the dry years in bathtubs, but it was all phony and it was all spiked. They put in rotten alcohol and colored it with burnt potatoes. It's all chemistry now.

If I go to Wisconsin, I'll stop in a brewery in Madison. They still make real beer, so I'll buy a case or two, or three, and haul them back down. It's been three or four years since I've been to Wisconsin.

I took Sara to the house on the rock in Wisconsin. When my boys were only this big I took them there. We lived there when they were growing up, and I'd go out there whenever I didn't have anything else to do. Now they've added so much it takes you two days to get through the whole thing. Everybody should see once in their lifetime what one kid can do."

Russell bent over to pick up a book about the house on the rock. He is flexible enough to easily touch the floor, although his fingers are stiff and bent from arthritis.

"When they hire the kids and I hear them bitch that the work is too hard, or it's no way to make a living, I say, "You want to see what one kid can do.""

It took Al Jordan eighteen years to build the top part. He had to hoist the materials up on his back, sixty-five feet up onto the rock. When I first went there, back in the fifties, or before that, there wasn't much, but now it takes two days to get through it, and it costs fifteen dollars. They've added and added. They have the streets of yesterday, and the streets of tomorrow, and this infinity thing."

Russell opened the photo album.

"See this thing, my great aunt, the one that had the brewery, had one of these in her house."

"What is it?" I asked regarding the rectangular box with carved designs and a long curved handle.

"It's a record player. That's a big record and here's the crank over here. It will play one record as it comes off the spindle, and comes over here. This is all round with a glass front. It's a beautiful thing.

I used to sit there at my grandma's house, and I'd crank the thing up, sit on the stairs, and listen to it play. I'd tell the kids, "Take the time off, and go look at what one kid can do."

This is infinity, this walkway goes clear off from the house, over to this rock way out there, and over here by the bend is a glass floor. And over there are three big luxury recliner chairs. Beautiful. And over here in front of the chairs, are three stuffed Bengal tigers about seven feet long. Infinity. You go all through your life, through time, until you get to the easy chairs, but still, you have to get past the tigers before you can get to the easy chairs. All the way, you can look out and see the tops of the trees and the deer down below."

"Tell me about romance." I asked. "Are you too old for it?"

"I guess not, but I just give up on it."

"I'm not too old for it," Sara yelled from the kitchen. "He's the one that doesn't want to. He's afraid to have a heart attack."

"She's on me all the time about let's get it back on again. She's had two heart attacks, and I don't want any. More old men die in the saddle than any other way, and I don't want to be the next one."

"I think that would be the best way in the world to get out of here," Sara called.

"But there ain't no sense hurrying it up. I've had my share of romance. I've been all the way around and halfway back. I was married twenty-seven and a half years. We've had ten or eleven years together and we get along fine. When she went down the first time, I was the only one. Now we have the whole family and I get mad at them because they don't know what the heck they're doing."

"So how do you like my curly hair?" Sara called from the kitchen. Her friend had finished the permanent.

"Come and join us," I invited.

✳   ✳   ✳   ✳

"Up until in October I had a very good life," Sara began. "We were both RVer's and we met camping after my husband died. Then we got to be more than just being friends. We've been together, off and on, ten years now.

I had to come back to Tampa against my wishes, but I was working in the Senior Companion program, doing something that I thought was worthwhile. When Russ came down to Tampa, he decided to get into it. We've been doing it together for three years. When I first met Russ, he was a single and living in a small trailer. At first we're just friends. Then we got romantically inclined, like man a wife. About a year and a half ago he became afraid of having sex, thinking it would give him a heart attack. So we're just friends and companions now. I wish he'd get over it. He sleeps in his bedroom, and I sleep in my bedroom. It's hard for people to understand because we make such a good couple.

I had a wonderful life before I met Russ, a happy marriage and a wonderful husband. I have three daughters who live in Tampa. Everything went wonderful until October, when I had that second bad heart attack.

I went out of this world. I really died. They had to pound on me and put me on life support. I made a slow but good recovery. I'm not fully recovered yet, but I forget sometimes what has happened to me. I'm supposed to have a walker, or cane, or something to help support me at all times. But around the house I forget. Yesterday I went out that back door and all the way down the walkway with nothing. My heart got to cutting up pretty bad yesterday. It was just something that happened. We all have good moments and bad moments. It's surprising what the human body can do.

It's surprising what you can do when you think you're on the way out. For as long as the good Lord wants me to be on this earth, I'm going to be a good, normal person. Right now I am with hospice. They have not released me yet, but I'm one of the few people who have survived when the doctor said I had three days to live. You see, doctors don't always know. To begin with it was a touch and go thing. I was in the hospital and I couldn't even turn over without help. I knew what was going on around me and I had the will to live. I didn't want to die. I said, "Lord, I put it in your hands, hold my hand." It sounds foolish to some people, but to me it's very much true. It's really amazing that I'm alive.

There are only two things that I remember from the time my daughter came here in her van and carried me to the hospital. I got to the hospital and I went out. I don't know how long it was until I became conscious again. I have a living will, and if they had read, it they wouldn't have brought me back. God was there, and said, "No, I'm not ready for her yet."

I love Russ very much. He helped me out when my husband first died. He was the best person in the world and everybody just loved him. Since I've been home, Russ takes care of everything. He does all the shopping, washing, and cooking. He has been completely taking care of me. Of course, it's cut him off from some of the activities that he likes to do with the Senior Companions.

I've seen a lot of changes in the past fifty years. My father was the Chief of Police in Clermont, Florida, and that's where I was raised. I must have been about eight years old and we could go to the movies for a dime. I went to a movie called *Just Imagine*. This was sixty-five or seventy years ago and there were so many things in the future that I have seen actually take place. For example—zippers. We only had button-holes when I was a child. One thing that stuck in my mind was this woman who was at work. She had a suit on at work, but that night she was going to go out. She took those zippers and made it into an evening gown. People didn't take excessive vitamins for food, and people didn't live in high-rise buildings, and airplanes weren't flying all over the place like they do now. People adopted babies because the mother didn't want to go through childbirth. That movie—*Just Imagine*—so much of it has come through in my lifetime."

"We went from a gas light to electricity," Russell said. "I remember when we would light Christmas tree candles at the end of the branches. Everybody would stand around the tree with a bucket of water, and my dad lit the candles. We'd ooh, and aah, and then quickly blow them out. That was a quicky. They were little candles like on a cake. We made our own toys, wooden tops and yoyo's."

"We've had a good life," Sara said. "He gets upset sometimes since I've been sick. I'm just now able get out and go. I don't see anything in my future other than just living. I don't have any plans to go back to being a Senior in Service now. I'm on hospice care. I'm just taking one day at a time. Everyday is valuable. I'm proof that the doctors ain't always right. I'm thankful for what they did, but there is a higher power.

I've traveled around the United States, but I've never been out of the States. There are still a lot of places I'd like to go, but I know that I have to slow down. I used to want to go to New Orleans to the Mardi Gras."

"You don't want to go," Russ interjected. "Its' a big drunken party. It's only fun if you go at the beginning and get involved.

In 1972, I was in New Orleans and talking to the postman. He said that he'd worked in the Mardi Gras but he's not doing it again because it's too much work. So I volunteered.

I said, "I'm just lying on the beach and not doing anything. I'm a good cook, so I'll give you a hand."

I got in it. The theme was *Sailors Through The Ages*. I was in the King's Court. Every night we'd have a dress ball in the county church. I'd cook chicken and oysters in a big vat about this high." He brought his hand shoulder high to demonstrate.

"You're making me hungry," Sara said.

"The vats blew up when they'd load them with grease, and there'd be grease all over the kitchen. So they put me outside with a spider, a plumber's tool. It was cold, about thirty-two degrees. Every fifteen minutes the priest came out to bring me a CC and water.

He'd say, "It's cold, I don't want you to freeze to death out here."

He'd bring a big four-foot platter. I scooped the chicken and oysters. After dinner we'd clean the tables and move them out. Then came the balls and the orchestra and music. We'd dance. I think that was the most fun I had in my senior year.

If you want to volunteer, you have to go a couple of months ahead, when they start getting the crews together. What you do is you get a group of friends together, and you run for a crew. I'll be a Queen and the husband will be the King. You get your crew together and you go out raising money for the Catholic Church. The one who raises the most gets to be in Marti Gras. Each time we met there was a big food spread because they were trying to figure out what they were going to have for the ball. That was two to three months of some of the finest eating in the history of the world. Oysters, seafood, chicken, everything. We were all meeting together the last night. It was like waiting for an election. You get all the money together and you wait for the priest to count it up. You're waiting for the priest to come out and deliver the word who wins. It was about three in the morning and he said, "You guys win". We had a hundred and seventy-eight thousand dollars. They printed books. You can go and look for 1972 books in the Chamber of Congress. They put me in a picture with a lady from the Chamber of Congress. I was the only Yankee ever to be in the King's Court in Marti Gras."

MILDRED BRISKER,
AGE 86

Foster Grandmother
Columbus, Ohio

When I spoke at the Foster Grandparents meeting, several staff pointed out Mildred to me, and said, "She's the one you HAVE to talk to." They were righ; this diminutive, African-American woman was a powerhouse of energy and enthusiasm.

I had no trouble finding the white mobile home with brown trim in the mobile home park. Mildred's directions had been exact. Her car had a handicapped sticker and an "Arrest drunk drivers," license plate. There was a motorized cart on the cluttered back porch.

The house was equally cluttered inside. There were many pictures, awards, and thank-you plaques on the wall relating to Mildred's volunteer work. She had artificial flowers in vases throughout the room. Although it was clean, the small, one bedroom mobile home was overrun with craft projects.

Mildred walked slowly and used a cane when outside the house. She was wearing a shabby, stripped, blue cotton shirt and clashing green pants, but there was nothing shabby about her welcoming smile or her long fingernails painted gold with a red vertical stripe. Mildred had dark gray hair, and a nice complexion. She was a few pounds, but not seriously overweight.

The couch was filled with various craft projects, and I couldn't find a place to sit.

"Move the pillow over. My kitty sits on that." Mildred pointed to the space I could clear to sit down. "I have a black and white cat. I leave the door open and she comes in. She's a lap cat. I like dogs, but regardless of the weather you have to take them for a walk. Cats are no trouble. She won't go any further than that porch.

I'm a Foster Grandmother. They needed people to help out with the children, and who better to fill those shoes than seniors. A lot of them are home and don't want to be sitting doing nothing, so they get out and help in the community. When I first started out, I was with physically impaired children at another school.

I go there five days a week, four hours a day. This is an afterschool program with normal children, kindergarten through fifth grade. They're divided into three groups. We call them the blue group, the green group, and the red group. The blue group is the little ones, kindergarten and first grade, green group is second and third grade, and the red group is fourth and fifth. We rotate. While one group is doing their homework, another is outside, or doing a special project with the leader.

Doing their homework is a must. The parents expect them to have their homework done. There are no excuses. They have time.

I'm there for the children. I help them with their work, comfort them if they have problems, and cheer them when they're sad. They entertain me with plays and talks. They get a snack when they first come in from class. It's all part of the school program.

I started a nursing course when I was in my fifties and worked until I retired. Any job where there are people working, they need volunteers. I learned that when I was nursing. When you walked onto the floor and you saw that you had a volunteer, you knew that you had someone who was willing to help you. When I retired I wanted to help people who were working.

Saturday is usually my day to go to the mall and walk around, not just to shop, but also to walk. On Sundays I volunteer at the Henry B. Plant museum down at the University of Tampa. The museum couldn't exist without the volunteers being there.

I'm a member of the sheriff's department. I'm a volunteer member of the parking enforcement team. We help the sheriff out. He has too many other things to do other than watch parking spaces and fire lanes, but he knows we're there, and if we need backup he's right there.

It's countywide. I check the handicapped parking places and the fire lanes. We go in malls, or wherever they need us. If you are in a fire lane we ask you to move, and if you don't move we give a ticket. It's the same way with the handicapped spots. We have a good record. People in Florida are aware that if they don't get their car out of there they will be fined anywhere from one to two hundred dollars. They don't take chances anymore. I like it because it gives me contact with people and I get outside in the fresh air.

Once, years ago when I first started, one guy thought he was being smart and tore up the ticket. We had copies and the sheriff took it to him. I think I'd rather get it in the mall than have the sheriff come to my door and hand it to me. That's the only one. Usually they thank us.

I'm eighty-six last month. I've been working since 1990. They're glad we're there. The people who first lobbied to have parking enforcement made trips up to Tallahassee and fought hard to get that. I've had people come up to us and thank me."

*   *   *   *

"I had it easy growing up. I guess the children have it hard now because there are so many things outside to influence them. Hey, I went to school and I came home. I didn't hangout because there were no malls. When I went some place, I had a purpose. I didn't go any farther than the corner store and back home unless I was with my parents. I don't know about other people, but that was my life. I lived in the city, but I spent the summertime in the country with relatives on the farm, learning about farm life. We did things on the farm.

I was an only child. I lost my father when I was ten years old. My mother lived to a hundred, but she kept her age a secret. My aunt lived to a hundred and six.

I became a cosmologist. I had my own shop that I sold. I have a manicurist and still get my nails done. That's part of life. I had them done before the holidays, and my next appointment is Saturday.

The *Tampa Tribune* took a picture the other week. I'm getting gray, but I can't worry about that. I don't have time to worry about my hair.

I volunteer at the clubhouse once a week. They have a system up there where you call in to say you're all right. Someone picks up the messages. If you don't call, then they call you. If you don't answer, then they go down and check if your car is there. If your car is gone, then they know you are out.

I had my WEB TV on. I got an e-mail from my youngest boy. I talk to my children long distance and read the news on it. I read about things that are happening in the world.

There was a volcano in South Africa yesterday morning. They don't know how many are dead. The lava went straight through the city in one little town, and they are in trouble. They have no food, no water, nothing, just what they've got on their back—that's it.

I never have time to read the paper, that's why I like WEB TV. I can get what's important. E-mail is a part of life now. You've got to have that—it's part of learning something new. In life, you're supposed to learn something every day. If you've gone through the day and haven't learned something, you've wasted that day. That's another reason I have e-mail on.

I like sports on television and the wheel of fortune, but I gave up my cable. I decided that I could get sports on another station. I don't watch much T.V.

I love to travel, and when my father was living we traveled. As an adult I do a lot of traveling. I'm planning to go to Los Angeles now. I'm going to fly out, and take Amtrak coming back, because I want to ride the Sunset Limited from Los Angeles back to Florida. Sunset Limited started in '94, and goes from Florida to the west coast. It's the extreme Southern route. You can catch it in Miami and go all the way out to Los Angeles. I've been on all the other routes except the Sunset Limited. I've been on the northern and the middle, going back and forth. You get to see different parts of the country. You don't get to see anything when you fly.

When I was driving back and forth to Ohio, I used to stop all the time to see points of interest. My husband and I went out of the country in '67. We went to Madrid, Mexico, and the Islands.

We were married forty-three years when he passed. It's hard. He died in 1996. It's still hard. When you're used to doing things with somebody, and all of a sudden they're not there, you have to do things by yourself. That's the reason I volunteer. It fills that void. I can't just sit around doing nothing. I lost him in January and I became a foster grandmother in February. The children don't give you a chance to grieve. They keep you going and give you something to think about."

"Have you dated since your husband died?" I asked.

"Who wants a boyfriend? They all got complaints. They need more care, and I don't have time to care for them. They want to be bossy, and I can't be bossed. They tell you what to do and when to do it, and you have to fix what they want. My husband let me have a free life. I could travel or do volunteer work. He used to always say, "You'd make a good tour guide." I know he liked me working at the museum.

I use a cane because I had back surgery. They want to do surgery on my leg, but I don't want to. I use the cane here because it helps me to be safe. I can do pretty good. I have a walker I use when I walk in the mall and at school. My walker has a seat, so I can sit down if I want to. It makes me independent. When I go to a buffet, I can put my tray on the seat and don't have to depend on other people to help me.

I eat anything except chicken. I can't eat chicken. I'm allergic to it. I can eat anything, and then I drink Slim Fast everyday for the vitamins, and I eat fruits and vegetables. I don't take the time to sit down and cook a meal. Thank goodness for takeouts—you can get something and you don't have to cook. Now they have these new meals that sit on the shelf. You don't even have to keep them in the freezer. All you've got to do is open them, put them in the microwave, and they're ready in five minutes. Now, why would I cook if I can get that kind of food? I waste too much just cooking for myself. It's hard to cook small enough amounts, so I end up throwing away a lot of stuff. If I can buy frozen or packaged foods, it's easy, just one meal, so I don't have lots of waste.

I'm going to a dinner tonight. They're cooking spaghetti, and I'm going to enjoy it. We have little parties and they serve dinner once a month to people over seventy-five. And they have lunch. That's fun because I get to see other people in the trailer park.

I'm by myself but I am fortunate that I have lots of friends. I lost two friends this year.

I lost one of my best girlfriends. We were friends since 1957. I was with them on their fiftieth anniversary, and I wanted to be with them on their sixty-fourth anniversary last year. This year she's not here. That was hard, losing a very good friend like that. I'm used to calling her and asking, "What do you think?"

She was ten years younger than me, and she was very special and very wise. While I'm an only child, and spoiled, she had sisters and brothers. She wasn't spoiled, and she was used to sharing. As an only child you don't have to share with anybody. Everything is yours.

I've got a couple of great-great-great-grandchildren on the way. I'm crocheting blankets for them. I crochet baby blankets for newborn babies in the hospital. We did red and white caps at Christmas time for the babies. They all went home with Santa Claus caps.

We drew names and there was a man in a wheelchair, I crocheted him a lap robe. I don't know who he is, but I spoke to someone who knows him, and she said he was so excited. It was the first time anyone had given him anything in a long time. It made me feel so good. I'm now working on one for someone else. It's going to be a full-length afghan.

Here is a collage I made. These are all pictures of me, from age eleven months until in my eighties. I put all these pictures together. I need a maid, but I get done what I can. What gets done gets done. I keep busy, and I keep my mind busy. Don't be dormant.

Those I bought ready to glaze," Mildred showed me several ceramic figurines, "and they go into a kiln. Being a senior, that's one advantage, you can get it done at school free. I took classes in ceramics and art. I've had about four semesters at Hillsborough Community College and a Community College in Cleveland.

Keep busy and don't let yourself do nothing. Younger people are lazy. All they want to do is play video games, watch TV, and hang out at the mall. Once they reach a certain age, they will wake up to the fact that they need to learn to live a little longer. They need to use their minds. I think TV and video games ruin people.

I read a lot. I just finished a book. I love to read tour books. It's just like being on the highway—they're fun to read. Looking at the tour books and the maps is my hobby. You look at that book and see the mountains and the scenery. I don't go anyplace that I don't learn about first. I look things up in the Florida tour guide. My Grandson moved to Davie, and I sent him an e-mail telling him everything I found out about Davie. I might one day drive over there. It's in Fort Lauderdale, about a five-hour drive. The drive is fun. Just take your time and let everybody else fly by you. I have nothing to do but take my time. People who are rushing can go ahead and rush.

I went away for Christmas to Columbus, Ohio, to see cousins. My father's people live up there. I'm the oldest member of the family. I went up to Bushnell to the cemetery when my niece died.

A couple months back, a girlfriend and I went to Punta Gorda. We stopped on the way back at a church retreat. It was a religious thing. I belong to an Episcopal Church. We had our lunch at the retreat. By five o'clock we were back in the city. It was an interesting day.

You know I made the newspaper. Here's a copy. It's a picture of me wearing a hat. I thought he did a good job on the picture. I had some copies made. I got this plaque the other day. That was nice. I was giving a speech a few weeks ago. I talked on three subjects, the Negro baseball league, black women in church hats, and braids. I had a group of seventy-five or eighty and three people came up and told me that they enjoyed it, so it must have been all right.

I got interested in the Negro baseball league because my husband used to be in that, so I have a book about it. I purchased that book about black women in church hats, and it was very interesting.

Braids was the hardest subject to find. The library didn't have a book, so I called the main branch, and they got back to me with a name, but they didn't have it. So then I called the company, and it's not in print any longer. I called Amazon.com, but I ran into difficulty there. I found out I could get it, but I didn't know how to order it. I'm not sure if they got the order or not. It is a book that I'd like to have a copy of.

It upsets me that they would stop printing something as interesting as Black history. The modern stuff I don't care about, but the history of braiding goes all the way back to Egypt. It talked about the men braiding. The braids were long, and they had real gold threads in them. And it explained the religious reason why they shaved the child's head completely. Then the girls' hairstyles included braiding and ornaments as they began to develop. Their thinking is it takes a girl eight years to become marriageable. As her body changes, her hairstyle changes. When I first saw people begin braiding recently, I thought it was silly. I thought it was just a fad, but then I found out there was a purpose behind all of it."

Photo—Swimmers

FRANK TILLOTSON, AGE 87

Swimmer
New London, Connecticut

Frank came to me as a referral from a friend of a friend. I was invited to a swim meet and talked to him briefly. He said he was leaving for another swim meet the next day. He asked me to call him back in a month, as he would be home for one week between meets.

F rank lives in a singlewide mobile home. The homes are parked close together in rows, and his is distinctive from other mobile homes only by a banana tree growing in the front yard.

Frank is a tall thin man with a full head of thin, but not balding, hair. The salt and pepper color is distinctive in that there are separate black and white areas. He has a short beard and a mustache. Frank was wearing a brown and green-checkered flannel shirt and faded blue jeans. He has a severe tremor in his hands and head but this doesn't seem to impair him or slow him down at all.

The mobile home is crowded with a table, two chairs, a computer, and fax machine. There is a large bookshelf with a collection of antique books and variety of other interesting objects, including a huge lobster claw over a foot across.

Frank began talking about his travels immediately, and kept me enthralled for the next three hours. Some of his story seemed so amazing that I might not have believed he'd been to so many exotic places if he hadn't shown me photographs and objects collected during his adventures.

"I went out of town yesterday and picked up a young lad, a son of Romanian friends," Frank began. "We went to Homosassa, to some beach. I got up at five-thirty and got back at about eight-thirty. It was a two hundred mile trip. It took about fifteen hours, but otherwise he'd never get to see it. We had a good day.

He's twenty-four and graduated from college. Kids graduate from college in Romania and can't get a job. People work for as low as thirty dollars a month—a dollar a day. Graduate pharmacists with a Master's degree get a dollar an hour, two hundred a month. You live in the Sahara desert, you live on I don't know what. Things are not all cheap, but they don't pay anything for medical or dental care, or school.

I did okay in the last swim meet until I pulled a muscle and had to quit. There's nobody else in my age group eighty-five to ninety, so it's just a matter of doing what I can. They gave me an underwater camera. Everybody who won their age group got one.

The doctor says I'm going to live to be a hundred. I've got an essential tremor. Either one or both of my hands shakes, or my head shakes. It has no connection with Alzheimer's or Parkinson's what-so-ever. The drugs they use for Parkinson's does nothing for it. They don't know what causes an essential tremor, and they don't know what will cure it. I've had it thirty-five years. I didn't even know I had it until a doctor friend told me. It doesn't bother me unless I get nervous. They have a pacemaker for a part of your brain. The technology's about a year old and it seems to be working fairly well. You have an implant here, and wires, and another implant in your head. I don't need that because it doesn't bother me that much."

*   *   *   *

"I was born in Connecticut. I had a younger brother and half-brother. My father was a tugboat captain in New London, Connecticut. He died when I was four years and a month old, but I can still remember him. We lived in New London. I was married and divorced twice and have two boys. One lives on Long Island and the other lives down in Naples. I make it a point every time I go up north to stay with my half-brother, and see my younger son. I get along with him all right. He was down here a while ago.

I ran the farm with my stepfather for two years after I got out of college, and then I ran it two years on my own. I did various things after that. I had a delicatessen. It started out with nothing but people kept asking for stuff, so we kept adding.

I did a year of law school, went to real estate school, insurance school. Had a New York State Insurance broker's license. I never got a real estate broker's licence because the person I was working for said I didn't need it.

I worked for a fellow who ran a real estate business. He said, "I'm going to run for supervisor of the town. I need someone to run this business for a year. Will you do it?"

I said, "No, I'm too busy farming."

He finally talked me into it and I ran it for a year for him. He suggested I go to Philadelphia and take the North America Insurance course, so I did. When I finished, I applied for a New York State broker's license.

After that, a couple small companies that were for sale contacted me. I bought them and wrote automobile and fire insurance. Nothing much. I liked the money income, but it got more than I could handle alone, and I couldn't afford to hire somebody else. I gave it up a few years ago."

*   *   *   *

"I swam the backstroke three years in college. I swam all summer in the bay. That was 1939. I didn't swim again until 1973. Out of curiosity, I went over to this big pool and took a look. I got into the water and swam a lap or two.

A guy came up to me and said, "You ought to join Masters."

"What's that?"

The United States Masters Swimming Incorporated is a membership organization. It was a new program when I started and had a thousand members. Now it has over fifty thousand. It's nationwide, including Alaska and Hawaii. We swim competition everywhere, locally in Orlando, Jacksonville, in Georgia and every other state. We swim National Championship in the U.S. and International Championship. I've been swimming essentially every day since 1973.

Normally I swim five or six days a week, but right now I've got all I can do organizing this project. We're doing an international postal meet, where everybody swims in their own location under certain regulations and with certain people. Then they mail them all into a central point. Our little club of fifty people is the central point this year. There is a woman and her husband and me doing this. We've been working on it everyday for about two weeks. There are about two thousand entries. The entries were mailed in. Sunday was the deadline. Out of the entire two thousand, there was only one mailed a day late. I think we decided to accept the entry because there's no mail on Sunday. I forgot to ask them what day he swum the contest.

There was one that was interesting. The paper itself had been wet and was written in black pencil. It said, "I'm an old guy and I dropped my watch in the water."

Now according to my rules, you can't do it alone. You have to have somebody counting, because you have to keep record of how far you swim and how long it takes you. You have an hour, and each fifty yards is recorded as you go along. He had nobody to record and he'd written down 2,110 yards. I said to Margie, "Do you want to accept that?" She said, "Ya, I'll accept it." Except we couldn't because there was no check and no address.

Some papers come in where they had obviously been dropped in the water, and they were all crinkled up. We can hardly read them. Some sent in checks for the wrong amount. All sorts of little things.

Then there are relays. Our age group is eighty-five to ninety. We have one ninety-year-old, eighty-seven, eighty-five, and myself. Normally relays are four people. Either four men, or two men and two women, but this one is three men and one woman. I encouraged the ninety year old to swim it.

He swam 1,600 yards, and the fellow from South Dakota—he's the other eighty-seven year old—swam 1,700. I swam 2,035. We're the only people in the world in that age group who swam that event. I was eighty-five then. I'm the youngest. We swam two relays, a two hundred yard medley relay and a two hundred yard freestyle, which was the first time ever in swimming history that four people had swum those relays. We got a big write-up in a national magazine with our pictures. If we keep this up we'll get famous. It takes a lot of stamina to swim an hour. I estimated that I could do two thousand and I beat it by thirty-five. I was pleased.

The epitome is to get to go to Olympic trials. I personally know only two people who have ever been. I look in the mirror and see one of them. I was picked to officiate, to judge the best swimmers in the world, and to make sure they do things properly.

It was in 1990. Not the Olympics, but the trials. They're generally held in Indianapolis. They've got a good set-up there. The most interesting thing was the security. Once I got an officials ID, I could go anywhere, anytime, except at the Olympic trial where they wouldn't let us sit in the stands. I wandered around and if I saw a swimmer I knew by name—I could talk to them. I could talk to anybody. It's a one shot deal. They never let you do it again.

Swimming is what started me traveling. We have a good travel agent in Jacksonville. If he can get twenty people, you get everything but the kitchen sink. I have to pay. You don't get anything for anything.

Next weekend it's four days in Orlando. There's a National Swimming Certification, a Local Certification, and the National Championship Certification for officials. Most people never get to National because they don't know about it. It doesn't get you anywhere."

"Have you been traveling to other countries?" I asked.

"Have I?" Frank handed me a hand written page. "If there is one particular country you want to know about, I'm known to be a story teller. I thought I'd give you a list of where I've been."

I read the list, "Canada, Mexico, Bahamas, Virgin Island, Puerto Rico, Peru, Brazil, Bolivia, Tahiti, New Zealand three times, Australia, South Africa, Tasmania three times, Indonesia, Hungary, Germany three times."

"My friends are Romanian, but I have to go to Budapest to get to get there."

"Romania, three times," I continued reading, "Bulgaria, Turkey, India, Singapore, East Malaysia, West Malaysia, Penang Island, Thailand, Thuket Island."

"That's a beautiful place."

"Hong Kong, China, Taiwan, South Korea, all Provinces in Canada, fifteen US States including Alaska. Indonesia, Bali. Cebu, Satarua, Ambon."

"Those last three are the Spice Islands." Frank explained.

"Alaska is interesting. You really need a lot of money if you're going to travel up there, or else you need good friends. I drove there in about 1985. After that I flew.

I ran into a swimming meet. I went around the fifteenth of February, when they had their state swimming meet. I set most of the records
while I was up there." Frank laughed.

"One man asked me, "Where are you staying?"

I told him and he said, "You don't stay there anymore, you stay in
my house."

So I did everytime I visited there. I've been up there eight or nine
times.

Once I went to a carnival in February. There was a Ferris wheel,
rides, games, the whole works. There were big blocks of ice rolling
around in the river. It seemed too cold to me.

This last trip up, the teenaged son was using his college money to
fly. He's going to aviation school. When he turned seventeen he got a
private pilot's license. You have to have about two hundred hours of
actual flying to get that. He was getting his instruction time. He flew to
Seward with his instructor and me. We flew over that country in the
winter, no tracks on the ground. Then we flew from Anchorage to Mt.
McKinley to look at the mountain. We flew up, looked at the mountain, and then flew back.

Two days later we flew to Fairbanks. That was the most spectacular
flight I ever made. We were flying between two canyons. They
couldn't have been more than five hundred feet wide and a thousand
feet deep. Everything buried in snow. Were flying along at 125 miles in
this narrow canyon, with walls closer than the house next door. Of
course, you don't fly high because there's no point in it. Those small
planes don't benefit like jets do.

Jets don't go very fast near the ground, except for fighter jets. Big
jets burn fuel unmercifully near the ground. When you get up, they
don't burn much fuel. That's why the airline flights fly about thirty
thousand feet and can get up to forty two thousand.

People don't realize that if you want to go to Japan, you don't go
directly to Japan. You fly up to Alaska, across the Aleutian Islands, and
then Japan. It's shorter going over the top of the earth than going in a

straight line. It's a great circle. You can't imagine the freighter planes that fly over Anchorage, Alaska on their way to Japan or the Asian countries.

I am the only one who has ever bought an around-the-world ticket from Delta Office downtown. I bought the ticket, no reservations, just got on the airplane, went to Germany, and on around to Turkey. I took about a week in Turkey. I was alone. I would have gone with somebody else if I had somebody to go with who was compatible. You can't find anybody who wants to make a trip like that. This wasn't related to swimming, I just decided that I would go around the world. I had saved up enough to do it.

I went to India and met two fellows coming home to India on the plane. One asked, "Where are you going to stay when you get there?"

"I don't know."

"There's a man meeting us. When we get there, you follow us and we'll take you to a place to stay. Make sure you follow me so we get through baggage."

Two 747's came in at once, and Bombay isn't equipped to handle two 747's. We went ahead of everybody else.

I followed the guys, and at one point someone said, "You can't go."

"He's with me," my new friend said.

"Okay, go ahead."

We went right on through.

I have no idea why they got such special treatment. One was a doctor, and I don't know what the other one was.

A guy met us with a broken down old car. They took me to a place that was two hundred dollars a night.

I said, "I can't do this. It's too expensive," so they took me to another place.

The next morning a man sitting in his taxi came over to me. He asked, "Are you taking a tour today?"

"No."

"Is there somewhere you'd like to go today?"

"I certainly would. There are a number of places I'd like to go."

"You can have me and my cab for twenty five dollars for the day."

"Good, when do we start?"

"As soon as I tell my wife I'm going for the day."

He came right back and we went. He took me for three days. On the second day he said we're going to the Buddhist caves. He brought his ten-year-old son who had never seen the caves.

The Buddhists dug the caves into the mountain. They were tremendous caves, maybe ten feet high. Of course, once you got into them it was quite dark. There were some minimal electric lights inside. They had huge statues, maybe eight feet high. No gold, but what took me the most was that all around the cave were reliefs. As opposed to carvings, which go in, these stood out. They had all kinds of farm scenes, people, animals, and crops.

India was filthy. Bombay, I wouldn't go back.

I became friends with the man sitting next to me on a plane. He said, "I guess we're getting close enough that we can smell Bombay."

At five thousand feet, the odor of Bombay is so strong that it gets into the plane, and you can smell it. The odor was from garbage and trash in the streets. Big white cattle wonder around the city dumping on the street all the time. Nobody cleans it up.

We saw the Queen's gate. When Queen Elizabeth went to Bombay way back, they built an immense hotel, five or six stories high, and they built a huge gateway. It wasn't a gate for a person but for fourteen teams of horses to go through side by side. It was on a dock, right where the Queen got off the boat. While we were there we took a boat ride around the harbor and military base and looked at the ships.

I took a lot of pictures of markets with food being dried. In India, there were sea cucumbers, shark fins, and little fish drying on racks with birds sitting on the top.

We had eaten a few times in tourist places, but one day I said to my friend, "Lets eat where you would eat."

This was a mistake. We went to this place, and it looked like all the rest that I had seen, and everything was fine, but two days later I began having stomach problems.

That's how I ended up in a hospital in Thailand. First I went to a public hospital and the doctor told me what to take. I got the prescription but it didn't help. My friend in the next room in the hotel, who had a little motorcycle, one hundred cc, but big enough for two, said, "You should go to my hospital." So we hopped on this thing and we're firing up the road and we get to the hospital. I had insurance so I got the best room. I had a nurse who dressed in business clothes, like the doctors, and she was in and out all the time. I was there two and a half days, and the bill was three hundred dollars for doctors, nurses, food, the whole works.

The nurse asked me if I liked the food, I said, "The food is fine, a little spicy."

So she asked, "What do you like?"

So foolishly, I told her what I like and she said, "I have to go do something—I'll be back."

She came back in five minutes and said nothing. The next meal came and it was everything I like. She had sent somebody to the market to buy these items.

Everything I say leads to something else, such as talking about food. There was a friend of mine living in Chincoteague Island, on the Eastern shore of Virginia, who said, "Why don't we write a cookbook?"

I said "Good, where are we going to get the recipes?"

"Well, I'll get my mother's and mine. I'll make sure we've tried every one to make sure they work. Then you can do it."

"So that's what I did. They cook a lot of good stuff. That cookbook was the only thing I ever wrote. We printed about a thousand, and gave most of them away. The recipes go back so far that there aren't processed foods, only things like lard and fresh fish or oysters.

I used to raise oysters in the bay in the fifties with a guy from New York City. We never made any money at it. We had fifty thousand dollars sitting on the bottom and in two weeks they were all dead. A hurricane came close and we had about three days of heavy rain. When it went by, it sucked all that water into the Gulf of Mexico, which was heated to about ninety degrees. When the water came back in, it was so hot it killed all the oysters.

They have stony sand bars in Chincoteague, and oysters grow on them to beat hell. They get leases for them. One guy in the landscaping business had oysters as a sideline. He went to his lease one day, and he saw a man harvesting his oysters. He found out where this guy lived, went over to this guy's house with a machine and truck, and took two yards of topsoil from the front lawn. The guy found out where his front lawn went, and he came and raised hell. The guy said, "You stole my oysters. I just took some soil." They're full of stories like that.

When you're traveling, contacts with people is the most important thing. You don't have to be worried about English. I don't know of anyplace where somebody didn't speak English, even in China.

China was so crowded that you had to have a permit to drive in the city, so people used bicycles. They have apartment houses twenty stories high, and they're building them as fast as they can. They no longer give the unmarried people free houses. The unmarried used to live in big dormitories free, but now they have to have their own quarters and pay for them. Here is a picture of a school in China where they trained the little bitty kids to dance. They used the kids as an exhibition for tourists. It really wasn't very impressive.

Here is a photo of a Buddhist Temple in Thailand with dragons decorating the entrance. People bring in gifts, food, and candles, and leave them in the front of Temple."

The phone rang and Frank picked it up on the speakerphone.

"Don't worry, we will get money up for Frank's bail. He will be free," the speaker began. Frank laughed, and conversed briefly with his friend.

"I was in Chiang Rai, Thailand," Frank resumed. "That's the furthest north city of *any* importance. It's the third biggest city. Bangkok is the biggest city, but don't go there.

I was staying at a little hotel. I was going to lunch and some man sees me and assumes I'm a traveler. He asked me "Where are you staying?" so I told him.

He said, "You don't want to stay there. When you leave here go to the end of the block, and turn left and go one block and turn right and go until you see Boon Bun Dan guesthouse."

I said, "Okay," so I did. They showed me a room in a little hotel. There was a window looking out, and there was a little courtyard. There were ducks, chickens, and roosters who talked in the morning and woke everybody up. Everything was clean. I had my own bathroom. Rooms with an Oriental design were eight dollars a day. Here's a photo of the dragon along the stairs. Here's a boat. They're big and clumsy, and very heavy wood. Looks like a little house in the center. They use it to go fishing for several days at a time. These boats have little automobile engines and they have long tails that go out in any direction. If you want to turn, you turn the whole boat.

East Malaysia is a dry rainforest. This seems to be a contradiction of terms. I went on a one-day trip there. Natives use the leaves or blossoms from the trees. They cook them up and use them as contraceptives, and it works. And it reverses when they stop.

People in Malaysia lived in shacks, under umbrellas, and in cardboard boxes. In this picture you can see the sleeping man's foot sticking out of the hut. People have little boats that carry one or two people.

I went Kuala Lumpur to Singapore on a first class train. They're narrow. All the country has narrow track railroad, not the wide stuff. The train had two seats on one side and one on the other side. There were captain's chairs, very nice, comfortable. Every one of them was on a one hundred percent swivel, so if you wanted to talk to the person next to you, or across the aisle, you just turned and had a little space between the aisle. You could do the same thing with the guy ahead of you. They brought you lunch, a good lunch, and dinner. It was never mentioned ahead of time, nobody ever said anything about it.

Two Mormons accosted me at the ticket booth. I knew they were Mormons because they all dress the same, black pants, white shirts, black ties, real nice looking guys. They spoke to me and I spoke to them for some length. They told me stuff I might want to see, and asked if they could send somebody to talk to me. I said, "Sure if you want, but it won't do you any good." I'm old enough that I don't need to go to church.

You never think of Singapore as a big city. There are only forty to fifty acres. It's tiny. They have a big park that I didn't get to see because I didn't have enough time, but I did go through the town, and it's spic and span. If you blow an automobile horn without a good excuse, you're arrested. They don't want the noise.

Frank gave me a personalized pen, which he uses instead of business cards. "I've got to order more before I go to Romania so I can take some with me. I'm going next month."

"You'll be swimming there?"

"You're damn right I'll be swimming. I raised a little money to build a pool in Romania. We still have an account in the bank here, and I asked our newsletter writer to put a note in that the pool was about done, but we still needed money. All we got was one fifty dollar check. Then it went in the next newsletter, which was more wide spread. I still have about eleven thousand dollars that I have to get to the Romanian people for the pool.

This is an entry form for a swimming meet [written in Romanian]. I thought maybe when I get there I'd run over to that meet, but the entry won't reach them in time. They're having a Masters swim meet in March in Reykjavík, Iceland, and I'm going to go to that one.

I swam in South Africa and had a hell of a good time there. Unbelievable. I won all the races I swam, and broke some records.

I had bought two cokes and had given one away. There was a man with a dust broom in his hand sweeping the dirt road. I stopped and spoke to him and he looked at my coke. It was open, but I had only taken one sip from it.

I said, "Would you like a coke?"

"You're going to give it to me?"

"Yes."

He thanked me three or four times.

I saw the driver in the hotel the next morning and he said, "That man came to me and told me about you giving him the coke. Nobody had ever treated him like that."

It was a hot day. They were doing well if they could go to a spigot and get water. They couldn't get electricity. They couldn't pay, and the government wouldn't pay.

I have some close friends in Australia. These folks wrote me a note and said, "When you're at the meet in New Zealand come over and go to the Australian National Champion." So I went to Darwin on the North Coast of Australia.

I stopped in Tahiti during my first trip to New Zealand. New Zealand is beautiful. The South Island is beautiful. They have a few million sheep. More sheep than they have people. It's economically and custom-wise, forty years behind the United States, and twenty years behind Australia. When I was there they were delivering milk to the front door and put the bill under the bottle when it was due. If you wanted food in New Zealand you could go to a store to buy it. If you wanted meat, you went to a meat market. If you wanted chicken, you went to a chicken market. If you want milk, you go to a dairy market. If you want vegetables, you go to a vegetable market, and if you want groceries, you go to a grocery market. They were organized, but that was the way they did it. I understand now they have big supermarkets. I haven't been there in eight years.

A cyclone destroyed Darwin in 1965. Here we have hurricanes, down there they have cyclones. Same wind but turned the other way. It destroyed everything in the city but one building. They had to rebuild the entire city. People moved away and buried the dead.

It's a very nice city with all modern buildings, huge white medians and huge white streets. That was a nice trip.

I stayed in Indonesia for about a week, and that is when I went to those little islands, Ambon, Satarua, and Cebu. I went on a boat tour. It was just my guide and me with two other people and two outboard motors. He took us to Satarua, which is about a two hour run wide open. On the way we stopped at a little island.

I asked the guide "Why are we stopping here?"

"This is where you have a nice swim."

"Okay."

I took all my clothes off and had a swim. You couldn't see anybody and the water was nice.

We went on this island. It was quite a big island, and we went to the mountain where they bury people. This big mountain was made of limestone. They just dug a hole, put the body in, and walked away. They left it open. I was walking along the mountain, noticed a big crevice, and I looked in. It was piled high with human remains, skulls, legs, and arms.

Nobody goes to these places because the tours can't make any money going there. They like to take you places where someone is selling something.

Then we went on to Satarua and I found out they had cancelled my flight. I headed back to Northern Australia. I had to leave a day early and I missed a day in Satarua, which probably has a population of five hundred people.

In Satarua they make brown sugar out of palm trees back in the rainforest. It's interesting because you can hear the wild birds back in there. I followed a path about half a mile into the jungle and there were a bunch of these palms the right size. They cut them in chunks about three feet long, quartered them, and then rubbed them against a spindle with spikes sticking out. They used to do it by hand, but now they have a washing machine motor using gasoline. They grind out the center of the palm, put it in a long trough and bail water from the stream.

I don't know who's living upstream. It's a very small place, so the water may be all right. I don't know. They put this stuff in and let it soak until it absorbs all the water. Then they take it out, dry it, and it turns brown and makes brown sugar.

The rubber trees are like sugar trees but you get sap. They scale them and put spigots in the trees. You have to take it out of the bucket every four hours or it will harden. They lay it out in sheets and dry it with a machine. It looks like the backside of a sheepskin. You see a guy on a motorcycle going along and on the back they have a pile of these long rubber sheets to sell. Much of the rubber is produced by people who do it as a sideline, but they aren't doing it anymore. I don't know what effect it's going to make on the supply of rubber. It's very gradual, as these people get older and don't want to do it.

Phuket is an interesting place. I always go to the big national markets, the outdoor markets, with just a roof over them. They have meat, fish, vegetables, bananas, and everything you can think of, like a supermarket. I saw elephants plowing.

I went in the hospital with a stomach infection in Chiang Rai. The head nurse had lived in the United States for about twenty years and had gone to nursing school in Kansas.

She said to me "Will you go visit my sister in Phuket Island?"

I said, "Sure." I had no idea who her sister was but I found her. She was thirty-eight years old and had a brand new Mitsubishi pick-up with a diesel engine. I told her I want a place to stay near the water where I can swim, where there's a decent beach. She got me a hotel room, a former high-class resort with a big beach, and picked me up at the airport. I registered and went up to the room to make sure everything was all right. There were a few students playing cards outside.

I said to her, "Don't you think we should get out of here? Somebody might be wondering what we're doing up here."

She said, "I don't care what they think. I'll pick you up at eight in the morning."

"You will?"

"Yes, I'll take care of you for a couple of days."

She took me everywhere, including a big fancy resort. We walked in like we owned it. She took me to see little boats where they had tanks with blue crabs, vivid blue fish, and huge shrimp kicking around. The prices were as high as they are here.

I bought lobsters sometimes. This huge claw on my bookshelf had two and a quarter pounds of meat in it. It's fourteen inches long and the lobster weighed fifteen pounds. This breed of lobster only has one claw.

That's a real swordfish sword up there, one that I harpooned. I was in the fishing business as well as the food business. I had a trawler and a couple of lobster boats. We used to sell these things—hand carved.

Here are bellows, they still work, and there's a bed warmer here somewhere. I don't have the handle because it broke off."

Frank pulled a large metal pan with a cover out from behind several boxes in the corner.

"This comes from somewhere in the 1700's and is brass or bronze. You put charcoal in it, and move it around the bed to warm it up. The handle splintered, but I shouldn't have taken it out.

This model ship was made about 1865 in Sag Harbor, Long Island. It's a model of an early slip-rigged whaler. Most of them are square rigged. I bought that for ten dollars and Robert Montgomery told me that it was worth five hundred.

You've heard of Robert Montgomery—he was a famous actor. Heck of a nice guy and a good friend of ours. He invited my wife and I to go to his house in Maine and stay for a couple of weeks. My wife wouldn't go. I damn near divorced her then. I did later anyway.

It would be nice if I had a girlfriend who would travel and pay her own way. I don't have money to pay for a girlfriend. I wouldn't be here right now if I had money enough to be somewhere else. I'm committed to work at meets, and I'm committed to swim in a meet in April. I'm going to Romania next week. Which way you travel depends on which day you go. You gain or lose a day.

Six years ago I did a parachute jump. There was a lady about three years younger than I was, a fellow swimmer from Orlando who invited me to jump with her. I picked her up and we went to a private airport in Tampa. They showed me an instructional movie and then showed me the plane. It was an old Alaskan bush plane, a two motor job with high wings. There was my friend, myself, and of course the trainers. They packed my parachute, but after people learn, they have to pack their own parachutes.

While we were still on the ground, they explained, "You go like this doing baby steps: step, step, step—step, step, step, and when you get to the door, and I stay step, you just step out. We were up 12,700 feet, at the end of the oxygen level. Over twelve thousand, you're supposed to have oxygen in the plane. The plane is going over a hundred miles an hour ahead of you, and you're under the wing. The tail is high, so if you hesitate, and can't get out, or if you catch your foot, there's no possibility that the plane will come along and hit you. You're safe from that point of view. Okay, we walked over to the door, and I stepped out. I felt sure as hell I'd fallen forty feet onto a concrete floor— WHAM! That air hits you. You fall alone 118 miles an hour. I just looked around. It was a clear blue sky, little puffy white clouds, not clouds you pull into or anything. Pretty quickly my trainer says to me, "Put your arms out." You're supposed to have your arms out and your legs spread, so I did. We're falling, and I was wondering how far we'd fall. Afterwards he said to me, we dropped eight thousand feet—whish. When he opened the shoot, he said, "If you want to change directions, you pull on that rope, and pull on the other rope if you want to go the other way." We landed

This is the saddest thing. Before we went, there was a young girl from England who was skydiving. She told us how wonderful "old people like you" would dare to take a trip and go sky jumping. I was just over eighty. A couple days later I read in the paper that a young woman from England had made a parachute jump, the chute didn't open, and she was killed. She was such a lovely person, to think that she was wiped out because of a mistake of hers, or somebody else in packing the parachute.

Swimming is the secret to my health. If you swim, you live longer. Because of swimming, I have traveled on everything you can travel on. The only thing I haven't had a chance to do is make a balloon ride. I've traveled on every kind of boat there is, trains, and airplanes.

I read an article and the survey showed that people who sleep less live longer. I've never in my life slept more than seven hours. I get seven hours and am wide-awake. What's the point of sleeping any longer? Sometimes I get tired in the afternoon.

I asked my doctor, "What do you think of that?" and he said, "Take a nap."

Good doctor.

The other day we were working on those two thousand entries, and I said "Margie, I'm getting tired." She said, "Take a rest." So I did. I laid down.

LEE DE ANGELO, AGE 88

Sun City Center Board of Directors
Chicago, Illinois

I left my flyer with the woman in charge of Continuing Adult Education classes in Sun City Center. She gave Lee the information and he called me.

The Spanish style home with a red tile roof was elaborately land-scaped with white stones, red mulch, and bushes trimmed into a circle. The driveway was white cement with an elaborate leafy green design. Lee opened the door as soon as I stepped into the screened front porch in front of the house.

Lee, a tall, slightly balding, thin man, smiling and bursting with energy, greeted me with "Can you have lunch with us?

Let me explain. Us is Phil and his wife Irene. Phil has been conducting something called *Issues and Ideas*. He has a program every Monday. I've done several with him. When I told him about you, it created a firestone. He wanted to give you the names of thirty people who are over eighty years old, secondly, he wants to have lunch, and thirdly, he wants you to conduct one of his programs.

That's the Us. If you can join us, it's at Lake Towers. I'll take you there at noon.

I'm on the Board of Directors. Our city has no mayor. There are nine of us who run the city and we meet constantly. We're like any city with a legislator and a mayor. The Board of Directors elects a president. We do it all. We're all volunteers and nobody gets paid. We have offices at Pebble Beach, and a little library there. People come to us with problems. We have all the opportunities and problems inherent in a city of over ten thousand people. We charge a hundred and eighty dollars a year to live here, and we have a budget of $1,800,000.

I'm very busy doing an endless number of things. I do the programs for Phil. I'm writing a second joke book. I'm the president of a club called the Laugh-a-Lot. We have an endless number of clubs. We have a paleontology club, a garden club, and a tropical fish farm. We have an unlimited number of things. Anything you can think of, we have a club. If we don't have, and somebody says, "Why don't you have that?" We say, "Why don't you start one?" Like me, I started the Laugh-a-Lot club. I have a talent to make people laugh. I try to make people laugh in the first five minutes I meet them.

The Laugh-a-Lot club meets once a month. The dues are that you've got to bring a joke and tell it. If you don't bring a joke, you have to read one from my book titled *Do Not Take Internally, A Complete Book of Utter Nonsense.* If you don't get a laugh from it, it's because you're a lousy joke teller. If you do get a laugh, it's because I write brilliant jokes. That's that."

*   *   *   *

"My grandfather was an only child, my father was an only child, and I was an only child. The whole line stops with me. I was the one and only, spoiled. I graduated from the American Academy of Arts. My dad wanted me to be a commercial artist and sent me to the Academy of Art. I had absolutely no talent in art, but I could write. During the depression I worked in Chicago. I was twenty-six years old and worked for General Electric Supply Corporation who also sold Hotpoint appliances.

My mom said, "If you don't like cold weather, go to California." That's how I ended up being an advertising writer in Los Angeles, California.

When I was with Hotpoint, I was often in charge of taking dealers to different countries. I spent a lot of time in Cuba, when Cuba was available to us. I got to meet a lot of people in LA because I was in the shows that Hotpoint had for its dealers. I met Carol Brunette, and a lot of wonderful people. Here's a picture, that's me with Bing Crosby.

I went to war and became a sergeant. While I was in Japan, my first wife ran off with someone and divorced me. Her dad was a forest ranger, so she knew a lot about horses. She was a bareback circus rider. She'd been in the circus when I met her, and when I joined the Army she went back to the circus. When I was in Japan, I got a Dear John letter from her.

When I got back home, I met that lady," Lee pointed to a picture on the refrigerator, "and her daughter. Her daughter was three years old. I married Lil when her daughter was ten. She's the one I spent forty-nine years with. If she could have lasted one more year, we'd have been married fifty years, but her lungs gave out.

I met a lot of people in California. I was doing such an incredible job promoting Hotpoint appliances that Hotpoint transferred me, and guess where their city was? Chicago. So here I am, back in Chicago. I hate Chicago. It's so cold.

I quit Hotpoint and started my own advertising agency. I had a lot of wonderful clients. In 1972, my agency was in Chicago and we lived in Oak Park, a little suburb in the west side of Chicago. All of my clients were in the loop, so there was no need for me to have a car there. I took the El to the office. The El went through an ethnic neighborhood that was getting more dangerous everyday and never would you go at night. If you were lucky, they just took your money. If you weren't lucky, they killed you.

Anyhow, I told Lil, "I want to stay alive awhile longer, so lets get out of here."

We went to California and looked, but land was too expensive out there, so we came to Florida and ended up buying a house in St. Pete. Lil and I had a lovely home with a pool in St. Petersburg. We lived there from '72 to '95.

One day my wife said, "There's a doctor calling you. Are you ill?"

I said, "No. I've never heard of that doctor."

He was a minister of a downtown church in St. Pete. The church was failing because St. Pete was failing. Like so many towns, St. Pete was a disaster. Anyhow, we tried to save the church but were unable to. It closed its doors. The pastor got a job here at the Sun City Center First Community Church. He called me and said, "Please come and visit us."

We had three grandchildren, boys, who came down and visit. But they grew up and the house was too big. Lil and I looked at each other and said, "Lets move." A month later we were in this house in Sun City Center.

The month I moved in, the very first addition of the Sun City Center News hit. I wrote them a nonsense letter and got a call from the editor, "Lee, we would like you to join our staff."

So I became a member of their staff, working with and playing golf once a week with John, the man who founded it. Because my background is in advertising, I knew how to do this. I was getting quite familiar with it when I got a phone call from his wife, "John's in the hospital. Will you take the paper over?"

I did it for four and a half years. Then, all of a sudden there was a resignation from someone on the Board of Directors. I knew the president quite well, so I asked him, "What do you think of me being on the Board of Directors?" He knew me and knew my talents. The board did not have someone familiar with the area of communication, which has been my area of competence since God knows when. The next day I was on it. I got on the board five years ago, and three years ago I was reelected.

I've had a marvelous life. It's been so fascinating and I've been around a lot. My parents didn't live long enough. My mom died of a stroke in her forties and my dad died of cancer in his sixties. I'm eighty-eight and fairly healthy. The brain still works, the body, more or less. I can't sleep in a bed because my back hurts, so I sleep in that chair. I'm having trouble breathing."

"Did you smoke?" I asked.

"Endlessly. In advertising a man does two things, smokes and drinks martinis. That's mandatory. Both Lil and I smoked. She didn't inhale. I inhaled all the way down to my toes. About thirty years ago we both quit cold turkey. I have never smoked since.

I've been fairly healthy, except three or four years ago when I had an aortic aneurysm. I had just lost my wife so I tried to die. But I had enough friends who helped pulled me through, them and the Lord, I guess.

Then I started working for the city. I've met so many marvelous people, had a lot of fun. I made enough money so I can live till 2020 and not have to work. It's been enjoyable. I have three offices, this one, the one in there with two computers, and the one in the dining room. Luckily, I have enough fond memories that I don't mope. I just go back to some fond memories that I can relive. That's pretty much me.

Lil has one daughter, no sons. The daughter has three sons who are now married and living in the Chicago area. They have seven children and one on the way. Here are pictures of three grandchildren. I see the boy quite often. That's the picture of him with me at Disney. The oldest grandson I don't see, but the middle grandson is a great guy. His wife is a real doll. They come down often. They have two kids that I can't stand. They cry all the time. I really don't care for crying children, and when you're eighty-eight you don't have to listen to crying children."

In spite of his protests that he doesn't care for the children, Lee went on to talk about how cute his grandchildren are.

"I refer to my daughter, my granddaughter, and great-granddaughter as the *three chicks*. There's a picture of the *three chicks* and me on a ride in Bush Garden called the plume. When I went on it, I thought I was going to die. I had a lot of fun. I'm enjoying myself, but I wish I felt a little better. My breath is a little short.

I spend a lot of money entertaining. I like to eat out. I don't necessarily have to go to a posh place. I used to drink a lot as an ad man, but I don't drink much anymore because I've lost the taste for it. I throw a lot of parties. I have parties whenever friends or my kids show up. I have a lot of friends that I made through the newspaper. When I joined, the staff had twenty-four people, so I immediately had twenty-four friends. The best person I met on the newspaper is this man you're going to meet for lunch. Phil took a liking to me, and carted me all over the neighborhood, showing me the amenities. I'm delighted that you can join us for lunch.

I'm a member of a church. I support it financially, and go twice a year, Easter and Christmas. I'm friendly with the pastor and about a year ago he said, "Lee, why don't you come to one of our single parties." So I went. I'm a member of a big church with a great hall. There were four men and over eighty women. Most of them white-haired, tottering. I'm not looking for a lady. Nobody can compare to that lady [Lil]. I haven't looked for anyone. I'm totally happy with my memories.

How did I get to be eighty-eight, as active and as mentally alert as I am? I can't answer that. The Lord. I cook for myself. I eat healthily. I eat a lot of vegetables. I've never exercised in my life. I've taken a lot of cruises, mostly in the Caribbean. I just got back from one. I just took my kids on a seven-day cruise in the Eastern Caribbean.

I don't have any plans for the future. It's in the Lord's hands. I go from day to day and do my job at the office. I'm expanding my book. It varies how many hours I work, depending on the week. Every Monday we meet for a couple of hours. I'll probably have my son and daughter-in-law, and the *three chicks* come down."

A month after this interview I spoke about publishing to Issues and Ideas, the Senior Continuing Education group in Sun City Center. Lee's friend, Phil, greeted me. He told me that Lee's doctor had found a large colon tumor and operated. Lee had had a difficult time with the surgery and passed away.

Rufus Purify, age 88

Head Counter
Douglas, Georgia

When I was interviewing Wertha, I asked her if she knew any African-American men over eighty who were still active. This is a population that I was having trouble locating. Wertha didn't know any, but contacted the pastor of her church, who called me. Several phone calls later, I spoke to Rufus, who invited me to meet him at the church.

Rufus was sitting near the entrance, inside the First Baptist Church of College Hills, which is located in a ghetto area of Tampa. Rufus was wearing a white sweatshirt with black pants and had a brown tweed sports cap covering his graying hair. He wears glasses, is overweight, and uses a walker. He greeted everyone as they came in with a smile or a joke.

"How are you doing for an old lady?" Rufus laughed when I introduced myself.

"I thought I was the young one." I responded.

"I'm the young one."

"You're a young eighty-eight year old. Tell me what you're doing here."

"I'm a member here. I've been here sixty-one years and I'm a trustee. I keep the books straight and see how they spend the money." Rufus laughed. "We work, pray, whatever there is that needs to be done. There is a first chair lady, a second chair lady, and a board. The church has a board. I've seen all that here. I volunteer whenever they're open, five days a week. I stay here and take a count of the people coming in to eat. We're serving lunch to the homeless, but it's for anybody who wants a meal. It's slow the first and the last of the month, fifty or sixty, but other wise we have a hundred to 125 people. Mostly we see ninety something to a hundred. I just sit here until I'm ready to go home, and then my daughter picks me up.

I live with my daughter. I can drive, but I don't drive. She do most of the driving.

"Hey, sugar, how you doing?" Rufus greeted an elderly woman with a loud laugh. "That's the cook right there. She want to be called Deacon. We have a good crew. We share meals every day except holidays and funerals."

A middle-aged woman greeted me, "Hello, Alma Purify is my name."

"Nice to meet you. Is this your dad?"

"No, she's my sister," Rufus laughed and winked at his daughter. "There's a good friend of mine too. Hi." He waved to a man who had just arrived.

"All these people help me live my life. My wife be dead eight years the eighth of this month. She was a big part of my life. I've got two daughters.

"Hello," someone else greeted Rufus. He is clearly well known and liked.

"That's one of my friends too."

"Lets find a quieter place." I said. People talking and activity in the kitchen was making conversation difficult.

Rufus walked slowly using a walker. "After my wife died I fell, so my daughter bought me this walker. I tell her, "You know what, if it wasn't for arthritis in my knees I wouldn't be sticking around home." That's the only thing keeping me down.

You know, they don't want me to drive either. In an emergency I can drive, but my daughters don't like to have me drive."

We got settled into a back room, away from other people and noise."

*   *   *   *

"I come from a family with seven brothers and three sisters," Rufus began. "I was the oldest boy, and the third oldest. My sisters would have been ninety and ninety-two, but they're dead. I go to a family reunion every year. It's been in Atlanta, Georgia one time, Douglas, Georgia, New Jersey, Virginia Beach, and Orlando.

I grew up in Douglas, Georgia, in the country. I went to tenth grade. The reason I quit school was I couldn't find out the reason that they made numbers out of the alphabet—algebra. I had a teacher who said you had to get it. His name was Greyboy. If you didn't get it, you were in trouble. I stayed out of trouble because I didn't go back. That's been a long time ago.

My Grandfather worked on Davis Island and half of the time the man didn't pay him. At first his rent was fifty cents, then it went up to a dollar and then a dollar fifty a week. He lost his place after it went up. He worked seven days, and they didn't pay him. Then the man stuck an eviction sign on the door because he didn't pay for rent.

I worked and took care of my family, my mother and father, during the depression. I was seven or eight years old. This fellow gave me a job and food and gave me fifty cents or a dollar a week. I was bagging groceries. In that time sugar used to come in hundred pound bags, rice came loose, bananas in a huge bunch, and lard came in big jars. Potatoes used to come in a hundred and fifty pound bags. I'd bag them up in small bags. They taught me how to weigh the potatoes. I lived in a wood frame house with a hall, front porch, and back porch. It was a Spanish area. I knew Spanish, but now I've forgotten. It goes from you. When I left the grocery store, I left the Spanish area.

We walked until I was nineteen, and then I used the company truck. I worked Sunday. I worked everyday. I stayed upstairs until I built a home.

I got married and bought a house. It cost twelve hundred dollars. I paid twelve dollars a month. It was nice. I sold the house and bought two lots, and later on I built a home and a store. After I built the house, I moved and lived there. I still had the store for a while. It wasn't a commercial plot—it was residential. That worried me a lot. Someone came out and said, "You have to tear it down." They sent me a letter and said I had to tear it down, or they would tear it down.

Then I went with Crenshaw Seed store. I hauled seed and fertilizer, driving a truck.

I came to Tampa in '29, got a job working in another grocery store and was there nineteen years until they closed the store, so I went into business for myself. I owned a grocery store. There was a Citizen's Bank...you remember, oh, you weren't born yet. The bank went broke. They lost a lot of money and closed up.

I was married in 1933. She was seventeen and I was nineteen when we got married. She taught elementary kids. She tried to mold their mind and teach them wrong from right. She taught the older kids in high school, and boy, let me tell you, after molding their mind she taught them how to use it and respect it. She taught them how to speak direct and meet the public. She would have been eighty-six this year. I was married sixty-one years.

"That must have been hard having her gone after all that time." I stated

"No, it was nice. She was the one married." He laughed. "Life is just a bowl of cherries if you make it that way. I have the two girls. I had a boy but he was dead at birth. It makes a difference, but life has to go on.

I had a house built in 1946 and then I sold that one and bought another house. I worked on a dock for three or four years, got a job as a salesman for a couple of years, and finally worked as a truck driver until I retired at sixty-three.

After I retired, I got a job delivering Meals-On-Wheels for the county. That's where I retired the second time. My wife and I did that for about eight years. She died in 1994 and I still delivered meals until I got hurt.

I have a friend Arthur Ritis and because of him I fell off a stool and sprained a hip. The main point is during that time I suffered from arthritis.

A few years ago we built two churches. First we had a little white church. We tore that down and built a brick church."

"Did you help build it?" I asked.

"Ya."

"Physically you put bricks in?"

"I ordered material. They tore down some buildings downtown and had the bricks for sale. I was working for a driver back then and I used his lift truck to get the materials.

Then we built this church. I brought cool drinks and coffee to the people who were working. We built that room over there, and paid off the mortgage. This church is debt free and we have," Rufus dropped his voice into a whisper, "money in the bank.

The former preacher from the first church died, then we had another preacher and he resigned, so we had to get another one. The young fellow we got, Abe, now is about seventy-five. He does a good job and people like and respect him. He's over the prison ministry and renders services to the prisoners. He's been there for years and years.

After we built the church and dining room, he decided he would feed the people. It was for the needy, but the greedy came too." Rufus laughed. "It was where anybody could eat, but we have to have a count, and that's when I got into counting. There was another man counting with me but he died four or five years ago and I've been doing it myself ever since. When they come in the door I count the people. Anybody that wants a meal is free to come in. They leave a donation, some of them, and some do not. We let the Lord take care of it. We have some that come for lunch everyday. Some have a job and some don't. We get a few who give donations. And here we are.

Florida changed a lot over my lifetime. When I first came here they had white water and colored water. We had to go to the window in a restaurant. We couldn't go inside to eat. Then Martin Luther King came through and things changed. People went to sit down and they throwed them out. I didn't know that wasn't right, but other people did. Finally they said, "We got to go eat inside."

On the road, the buses and streetcars, we had to sit in the back. There was a little sign that said, "For colored only." We did that for years, and then it changed. We got rid of the streetcars. When integration was declared, we could sit anywhere we want on the streetcars.

What worries me now is the arthritis. Thank God I haven't had a stroke. I eat anything and everything. I eat food. I got a flu shot. I hear fine, but I've got cataracts."

"Are they going to be removed?" I asked.

"I told the doctor "No. The cataracts have been there too long." Up until a year ago, I could read without glasses. About twenty years ago the doctor said, "If they don't worry you, don't bother them." About three years ago I was told they're not bad enough to come out, but that new young boy wants to operate.

I didn't used to have any wrinkles, but they fell off."

"Fell off?"

Lost weight, so I have a few wrinkles. I was weighing 262 and now I'm 240. I'm 5'7. That's what they tell me. I have to take medicine to keep the blood pressure down.

Indirectly, I've had a girlfriend for about three years. We just communicate by telephone. She's seventy and lives in Michigan. I'll bet I haven't seen her more than four or five times in the past two years. It's just friendship. We won't get married, she's too young. After sixty years that's enough. I've got a lot of women friends. They all think I've got money, but I don't. I've got my own teeth so I can bite them." Rufus laughed.

"Another thing, I haven't stopped looking. I'm still looking. When you stop looking, you're dead. I'll tell you, life is just a bowl of cherries. I'm just living my life as I live it, one day at a time. This summer my daughters and I are going to Orlando for a family reunion, and we're probably going down to Miami for a vacation.

The important things in life are eating, sleeping, and girls. What's more important than girls? I have a nice time. I have a lot of fun and I have friends.

The secret to a long life is pretty girls. Don't worry, be satisfied, love the Lord, and treat others like you want to be treated. Don't get mad with others opinions because everybody has one. Think before you speak and do, and always keep a smile on your face. Satisfaction is the key to a long life."

Hubert and Kathryn McHargue, 86 & 89

Married 70 years
Indianapolis, Indiana

Kathryn and Hubert celebrated their seventieth wedding anniversary with a large party that received newspaper coverage. I saw the article and called them. We set up a meeting in their home.

K atherine and Hubert live in a white doublewide mobile home in an upscale retirement village. As I walked past their red midsize car parked in the driveway, I saw that the screen door was open and they were waiting for me. I glanced around inside and noticed African violets, a flower that I find difficult to grow, flowering in pots on the windowsill. The furniture was Early American and I commented on the unique cane rocking chair in their living room.

"This is a Lincoln rocker," Katherine said. "My grandma's half sister had it delivered in a horse and buggy with the mail. It dates back to the early 1900, possibly before."

Both Herbert and Katherine wore glasses. He was wearing beige shorts and suspenders, and had a potbelly and a large double chin. She was thin and wore a pink shirt with blue trim, pink shorts, and black tennis shoes. Both had nice completions, although Katherine had a few fine wrinkles. Both had white hair, and Hubert requested that I not say he's "bald-headed," but instead, to describe his hair as a bit thin on top. Katherine had trouble hearing but didn't use a hearing aid. We sat outdoors around the patio table on the screened porch and began talking about their seventieth wedding party.

"We had two parties," Hubert began, "one at the church and one up here at the clubhouse. We had to go through the cake ceremony again. We got a call from Jay Leno in Los Angeles, but we weren't interested in going, even though it was all expenses paid. We've been to LA before and don't want to fool around with it.

We've been to Hawaii a few times. We like the big island better. The only three states we haven't been in are Alaska, Washington, and Oregon. We have a standing reservation in Canada for fishing in July, but we will also go to Alaska. We want to get those other three states. We'll fly up and bring the inland waterway back, which will get us to Alaska, Washington, and Oregon. That will make every state. We've been in Eastern Canada in Nova Scotia and New Brunswick, then on the other side we went up to Lake Louise and the Queens highway.

Our son and his wife in Indianapolis were going with us, but they had a wreck so they had to cancel it out. Our deposit is still up there, so we are going to go. Oh yes, our son thinks they have to tour us, but we get separated. I can drive to Atlanta and Nashville without any problems. Katherine hasn't driven since getting stuck in a deep snowdrift a few years back.

We stay active. The Lord has been kind to us, and we've had good health. That helps. I don't know how it happened, but we still have our teeth." He laughed." I guess there's something to genetics. I had a great aunt who was 102. All my great uncles have lived from ninety-six to 102. Maybe I'll be lucky on that end of it."

"My dad was a coal miner, and he had slate fall on him." Katherine said. "He only lived seven years after that and I lost him at forty-nine. My mother and her sister Nanny both died at eighty-three." Katherine got up to get her family pictures.

"We enjoy going to the beach over John's pass, eating shrimp, and stuff like that," Hubert continued. "We travel with our son and daughter and all take turns driving.

We're going back to Sumter in March. We have two great granddaughters out there and we are going to have another one soon. At Christmas we went over to South Carolina to visit our granddaughter. The year before we went to Colorado Springs. We got in that big blizzard out there and had to travel all the way to El Paso to hit route 10 to get to Florida, about a thousand miles out of the way.

We spend quite a bit of time together in the evening. We enjoy the TV news and I read a lot. I subscribe to the National Geographic and also U.S. News and World Report. Kathryn does work on—show her your work you've been doing getting ready for the strawberry festival." Katherine got up again to get several crocheted quilts.

"We go back up North in summer. We live half a year here and half a year up north in Indiana." Hubert explained. "In our county we have a Bridge Festival. It's well known all over the United States. We still have thirty-four covered wooden bridges in our county, crossing rivers and creeks. People sell crafts. They have a carnival atmosphere and stands. Kathryn also sells a lot of her stuff at a Civic Center. She enters the Strawberry Festival down here. She has won just about every year. She also judges.

Katherine showed me two blankets, one knitted and one crocheted.

"I do a lot of fishing, and I've done a little bit of writing," Hubert stated. "I keep busy with flowers, with yard mowing. We stay active. She does most of the landscaping."

"He's doing all the talking, but telling me everything you do," I said to Katherine.

"I love flowers. I don't know where my pictures are..." She got up to look for her garden pictures.

"She doesn't sit still long does she?" I said to Hubert.

"Oh no, no. She's very active."

We spent some time looking at garden pictures, which I enjoyed. The giant sunflowers were particularly impressive.

"Tell me about your judging." I addressed Katherine.

"I've done it for about fifty years. I judge knitting, crocheting, and quilting. I do not judge sewing because I don't sew. I couldn't judge baking because I don't do that much baking. A lot of judges do judge things that they don't know anything about. Last year I made a baby afghan but the judge in the baby accessories section wouldn't judge it.

I started quilting right around the war. The principal's wife lived across the street from us and came over and said, "They are having knitting and crocheting across from the library. Would you like to go?"

I said. "I don't think so."

She said, "I don't want to go by myself—won't you please come."

She finally talked me into it and there was a big crowd there. By the time the instructor got around to us, it was time to go home. She had us make a chain. When she got to mine, she said, "Well, I tell ya, I think you'd better rip it out and do it again."

That started my interest. I did quilting before that because my mother and my aunts all quilted, but I'd never crocheted or knitted.

I've done it ever since. Then I started getting into judging in the fairs. The first time I judged it was hot, so they let Hubert sit inside the building. I looked at him and he approved of what I picked out."

"It is fun," he said. "I've become interested in it, too. It helps to enjoy the fairs. I just observe, though."

*   *   *   *

"There were four boys in my family and I was the youngest" Hubert began. "Katherine is an only child.

We have two sons. We had a girl, but we lost her to cancer. My older son has a master's degree in mathematics. My younger son went the other way. He's a machinist. We're real pleased with them. We have these great grandchildren, who are a blessing.

We were high school sweethearts. I went to another school my first two years and came to her school when I was a junior. I looked the girls over and picked her out. We started dating. She was sixteen and I was eighteen when we married.

I'm a product of a one-room school with a big old pot bellied stove. Children came in as first graders—we called them primers then—and sat next to the stove. As they graduated each year, they were moved toward the north windows.

I remember I got kicked out of the school one day. I was near a big haystack, and there was a skunk under there. I went out there about five thirty, while it was still dark. That's when skunks sold for good money. I found a star skunk, which was rare and worth more. I caught and banged it on the head, but I didn't know I got squirted a little bit. I didn't know until I got to school and warmed up next to that potbellied stove, and the stink came out. The teacher said, "You've got to go home."

Katherine began, "I started school when I was five. It was a small school and it wasn't crowded, so why make me wait a year? I went to a city school, and then to the country. The town had a grade school and a high school. The first year in the country the Klu Klux Klan burnt the school buildings. One Saturday night they burnt one building and the next Saturday night they burnt the other.

The KKK was active in that section of Indiana and blacks were not allowed to be there after dark. Nobody ever knew why they picked those two schools to burn, as there weren't any black children in those schools. The guy that did it had two children in my class. He went to prison. They said he was hired and was just the guy that lit the match. The others who planned it were higher up."

"I almost got kicked out of my high school senior year." Hubert said. "I skipped school to see the national air when they stopped in a little town in Terre Haute. I got see Jacquelyn Cochran, Amelia Earhart and Frank Hawks just about as close as from here to that flag. Never regretted it. But that particular day our English teacher had given a test on Shakespeare. I can tell you I got a lot more out of seeing those people than Hamlet, although I nearly got kicked out of school. Being the president of the class, they said that's a poor example, but I'd do it over.

I was in World War II in the Philippines. I didn't get scratched, but I got malaria so I couldn't fight. I had three recurrences. It occurred about the same time every year, in the fall around the beginning of school, and I took quinine to get rid of it. I haven't had it for thirty years. My health is okay. We have a few minor things. I've been battling a tooth problem but so far we've still got our choppers. I hope they last a few more years, but if they don't, we'll just get them replaced, of course.

I had an unusual experience with a dentist overseas in the Philippines. There was a corporal who pedaled to run the drill. When he slowed down, the drill slowed down."

Katherine added, "My mother went to the dentist to have a tooth filled, and the dentist pulled every one of them. That night she almost died from losing all her teeth at the same time. They didn't think anything about it, but now they try to save them."

"We were married in January 1932, right in the heart of the depression," Hubert said. "Thank goodness our people were farm people at that time, or we'd have starved to death.

I had a wonderful experience in college. At that time it was on a quarterly basis. I did my doctorate work in 1957, in education at Indiana University. My first tuition was twelve dollars and fifty cents, and I took a full course of subjects. I did that to get a teaching certificate, which was on a two-year basis.

My first job was in 1935. A hundred dollars a month, and I got a big pay raise that year, two fifty a month. I was a grade school principal and also did coaching. I went into school administration in 1948 and stayed in that until 1967, when I went back into straight teaching, which was one of the best moves I ever made. I moved back to Indianapolis High School and taught psychology and sociology to college-prep seniors. It was a wonderful experience, and I think I taught them something, too.

They've taken several things out of the schools. I think today I would be in trouble. I would use the old-fashioned method and they would have me jailed the first day. One of the things that I think is really important in schools is discipline. You can't touch the kids anymore. If they are writing, you can't even show them how to hold the pencil or pen. Can't touch them, can't correct them. I don't believe in beating up on children, don't misunderstand me, but I think there are cases where you have to use the paddle once in a while. You may not agree with that.

They took the flag out in a lot of the situations, and they took God out. You can't teach religion in the schools anymore and prayer is out. I think the smaller schools had something over the consolidations, and consequently, a lot of schools are in trouble. I'd say most of them are. I couldn't go back into…naturally, I won't."

"We had this one case in our home town school," Katherine added. "This boy had gone through all eight years and had all women teachers. His papers were unreadable. So Hubert paddled him one day because he knew the boy had good brains. The other three women teachers said, "Oh, Mr. McHargue, you shouldn't have done that. His dad will come and really jump all over you."

Hubert said, "That's fine, let him come. I kept his papers."

So the next morning Papa showed up in his work clothes. He showed him the paper, and the father agreed with him that the boy wasn't trying.

Later, the boy said, "You know for eight years I hated school, until Mr. McHargue gave me a going over." He graduated with honors. That one little paddling done it."

"Were you in teaching too?" I asked Katherine.

"No, I was a secretary for eight years. I wrote a lot of high school papers and corrected them."

"She was a secretary, lollygagging around in the office, you see." Hubert laughed. "She typed my thesis for me.

I taught seventh and eighth grade. There was a boy who was sixteen years old and couldn't write. The only thing you could read on the paper was his name. Anyhow, I said to the Trustee and to the School Board, "I'm going to give this boy a diploma." I knew he wasn't going to go any further. So he went into the military and got a battlefield commission in France, and then retired in Huntsville, Alabama as a major."

"You seem to keep in touch with a lot of your students," I commented.

"Show her the stack of cards you have from our anniversary party," Hubert commanded.

"She doesn't need to jump up again," I stated.

Katherine sat back down. "I imagine that we have close to a 130 cards. Most of them are from his students."

"What about romance? After seventy years you must be over the hill. Is that right?"

"Over the hill?" Hubert laughed. "No, we're not over the hill. Of course, it changes around a little, you know. No, were not over the hill."

"There's a lot of people," Katherine said, "who sleep in separate beds. To me, when you sleep in the same bed there's…well you can feel over there. A few nights ago I couldn't feel him next to me so I took my foot and hit his leg. Well, I knew he was still there. Sometimes we get up to go to the bathroom and we stagger around. I thought, "Oh dear, if he's not in bed, maybe he's on the floor." But I felt him so I knew he was in bed and went back to sleep. We know a couple who sleep in separate rooms. They're missing so much being together."

"I think one of the things that is important for any marriage is to have the same interests, same kind of background," Hubert said. "And it's all right if you have the same religious beliefs, and politics…and meanness."

"His family is all strong Republicans. I'd ask them, 'Are you sure that's the right guy to vote for?' His dad would ask, 'Are you sure she's a Republican?'" Katherine laughed.

Hubert added, "We're not that strong Republicans, really. I think on the local level, you have to vote for the person who's going to do the job, regardless of politics. We become Republican on the national level."

"I found I was mixed," Katherine said. "It was nothing that was talked about."

"A strong family background and being the same religion is important," Hubert added. "We're both Southern Baptist and go to church. Yep, and we had our reception at the church."

Katherine added, "We spent time with older people. We visited the parents of the children that he taught. I think they had an influence on us by being older, and we saw how they got along. I think that helped us a lot."

"Common interest in the home helps," Hubert said. "When we went out, we liked to dance. If we can find a place where we could find an old fashioned square dance, we'd try it again. There are two types, one is Western and the other is the old fashioned hoedown. When we were young folks, we'd go to someone's house. They'd move the furniture and we'd use the front room. Believe it or not, doing things together helps to keep people together. We'd square dance and do taffy pulls. Young married people got together and made candy."

Everett Wilson, Age 89

Retired Mink Farmer
Connecticut

*Everett came to me as a referral from another man I inter-
viewed for this book. He had spoken to me on the phone about
refurnishing an old car.*

E verett is a tall, spindly man with slightly rounded shoulders and a
pleasant personality. He is thin and spidery, all arms and legs. He's
quite bald, with just a tease of white hair forming a semi-circle. He has
thick glasses but not thick enough to hide the tears when he talks about
his wife.

His pink house located in an elite retirement neighborhood is big
enough for a large family, and cluttered enough for me to believe one
lives there. Everett had about a hundred projects going all at once. He
cleared a spot on the blue striped couch for me to sit down.

"I lost my wife," he apologized for the clutter. "I don't even try to
keep track of it, maybe as much as six years ago. She lived in this house

only one year. She upholstered the chairs and curtains so everything matches. This house has three bathrooms and three bedrooms. My dear one built it to have the children feel welcome. The house is as large as they allow you to do, and they let us have a couple of extra feet."

Beside me was a large book, and on the floor was a box, speaker, and a variety of wires and miscellaneous odds and ends. I asked Everett what they were.

"I just haven't taken it back together, the cartridge was stuck in the VCR. I was looking up something. These wooden cabinets sound good." Everett pointed to large speakers set on the floor. "These are all fifty years old. There are eighteen speakers in each one. There's two base ones in the bottom, a couple of middles, and then up above. It isn't just coming from one row each. That's a dictionary of music terms," he paged through the book for several minutes.

"I have a violin. I went sixty years without even looking at it, but now I'm enjoying it. I'm in the Sun City Center Community Church Orchestra. We practice on Mondays, although there's been some difficulty. One lady kept the orchestra together, but something happened to her, and one of the dancers has been sick. My other group meets in the church where we practice in the basement.

I have an old car. It's the only thing I chose to ride in because if someone hits you, you're not going to be the one to get your neck broken as readily as somebody in a lighter car. I think cars are going back to being heavy. There was a time when the frames would just crunch. I'd see them where they got hit on the side. So that's why I have such an old car.

It's a swell car for me, very powerful, too, a 6-liter engine. It's much preferable to me than the best of the new cars, and I was fortunate to get it. My wife's sister left it. It's an '81 Cadillac, 8 cylinders. It's a very complex engine. If you're not demanding power, it drops down to 4 cylinders. It runs so cheaply I hardly ever put gas in it. The dial shows how many miles per gallon you're getting.

There's more to it than that. I'm not rebuilding it, but there's something I need to do to make it look all right because it was plastic. I have some aluminum sheeting to put in, and then paint it. I've been very slow getting around to it, so it looks a little strange. It's the accomplishment of running a piece of machinery, the pleasure of letting it do its maximum work. I'm fixing my car so it looks all right. I don't want it drawing attention looking yucky because it's an unusual car."

*   *   *   *

"I'm handy. That comes from being a farmer, born and raised on the farm. I remember my mother having fifteen or twenty hens and gathering eggs. They laid eggs and she sold whatever we didn't use at the table. By gones, that was everything.

We were just over the state line between Springfield, Massachusetts, and Connecticut. We didn't worry about the surveyors being off by three miles way back in Washington's time. They corrected that.

I have a sister over in Texas eight years younger, and my wife was nine years younger. My mother was the disciplinarian, and my father would say, "Give them the benefit of the doubt," when we did something wrong.

I was twenty-seven when we were married, and she was…I shut her out so much of my mind for survival. I guess she's been gone six years. It's stressful for me to think about. We built houses on the farm and we had a good family. That was a long time ago. I don't know now how many years we were married, but it was a long time. I was twenty-seven." Everett wiped his eyes.

Life is life, and you go on. My traveling was usually by degree. I'd go from one family to another. There are nine grandchildren, and a couple of great grandchildren. I fly now-a-days. The amount of the miles I'm flying is like going to the moon every so often.

Your automobile is the most dangerous thing you have anything to do with. My wife never had an accident, and up to now I've never had an accident. My creation must *never* have an accident. That means you need to drive looking out for others. If there is a big accident, you can train yourself to be a second of two faster than you would be. When I taught kids driving, it was always important to do it. If they had an accident, I don't think they'd ever tell me.

We have five daughters, and a boy. He lives far away. His wife is strange and doesn't let him come see us, so he's lost in that way. There's no point into going into that. That's the way life is. The daughters are New England people. They're up in the snow country. Deep snow. We have a camp up there at 1,400-foot elevation. There's a lake called Moose Look Magantic. I go up there in the summer. It's been in the family maybe forty-six years. We're very fortunate nothing has changed around there. There's nothing surrounding it. Some wealthy woman bought it and gave it to the state. Nothing can ever be changed. Can't even cut a tree for a campfire. That's welcome for us as a family. The mountains will always be an unsullied bygone.

There were times in my younger years when we could shovel off snow and skate. The children were all young, and together as a family. Now they're widely spread. The ice is two to four foot thick. When that's thawing, the power of it from the drifting wind, piles the ice up thick, and it sounds like thunder.

Those were the days, sliding down hill on sleds on the way to school. We walked to school. There weren't buses. No matter if it was two miles, or three miles, you walked to grade school. There was another school, in another county. We weren't supposed to go there, but we would look in the windows and they had benches. We had individual seats with a desk built in.

My mother was a New York Brooklyn girl. She graduated from the Julliard School of music. She wished that I would be a musician and earn my money playing the violin. In those days violinists made good money, even in a small town. Mom liked music and sang a lot, so she had me take lessons. I didn't care a thing about it back then. I didn't practice, but I went on through two or three different teachers as I improved. One said there wasn't anything more he could do, and recommended another man who gave lessons. I'd watch these men earning their money at the musicians' park. There'd be an orchestra and I'd sit nearby and watch them playing. I enjoyed that. I didn't even see a violin for sixty years after that time.

We have a lot more population now than in the open country that used to be. There was a big hotel on the lake just outside of Chicago. After trolleys there were rails. They were fast electric cars. They didn't protect these cars and the ground was hot. It was dangerous. People used to fall and get electrocuted when they touched the ground. The rail would be two or three hundred volts, so you were supposed to stay away from the tracks.

I'll always remember my mother talking about what happened to her. This was way back She was very young girl, maybe eight years old. In the north, blacks kept to themselves, but nobody ever talked disparagingly about them. There was a colored man, and he had his pride. She was taunting him and she said "nigger, nigger, black shiny eyes..." That is all I can remember. Anyway, she said this to a black man, and he took it seriously and started to run for her. They were not respected, as they should be, for a long time. After she said that, he started for her, and she ran across these open rails to get away from him. She got away because he knew enough not to go over those things. She said, "I never again did such a thing in my life."

I left school because of the mink. I went a year and a half, and had physics. That was everything I needed to know. My education came out of the Springfield, Massachusetts, library. That's how I learned the things I needed to know, which in this case was refrigeration.

Ammonia, used in refrigeration, is terrible. Three parts per million and your eyes start burning. The first I ever knew of ammonia was from the Colony Club in Springfield, Massachusetts. That's where the elite people went.

Harry G. Fiske, who also made Fiske tires, owned the farm I was on. Somebody was at the head of the dairy, and there was an agricultural part raising crops, and there was a poultry department, which was my father's area. We raised popcorn and sold it to entertainment people. They had those things that they'd carry to the fairgrounds or in a park. You've seen them. They have a big window, and scoop up the popcorn and sell it to you. He also taught me the value of a nice car.

Fiske visited the place in a Packard car. In those days they turned cars in after one or two years, and that car sold very cheaply. When my turn came and I had enough money, I went up to the place and kept track of cars coming in. When a Packard came in, I bought the car for something like fifteen hundred dollars. It was an 8 cylinder, big heavy car with big wheels. The rubber was no good on it, but we rarely heard of a tire blowing up. When I first was underway a car didn't even have a heater to it, so you put a soapstone in a burlap bag down at your feet.

In those days the most expensive mink in the wild came from northern New England. They were small mink, very fine textured. They weren't plentiful either. Mostly in those days you were either very wealthy, or you didn't have any money. If you worked for somebody, you were only paid as much as necessary to keep you from going to somebody else. We did very well on the Fiske farm. They didn't seem to mind me feeding the mink chicken heads and stuff.

Then as mink became commercial they developed disease. Each state has its agricultural college and when one disease came under control by the experimental station, they would get something else. At first we didn't know how to feed them. Back then, we bought hamburger for eight to ten cents a pound. I bought it and fed it to the mink.

I didn't sell many at first. We just got good mink. Wisconsin people in the Milwaukee area developed the superior Eastern mink. The farm was a mink ranch in Connecticut.

My wife, Esther, designed and oversaw the building of the houses for the men who worked for us on the mink farm. We had a loyal crew. We could go off, children and all, and not worry. I would call up Harry every night to check on things. He was religious and strict, but the men would put up with him because they were working for me in the mink farm. Some were with me as long as twenty-four years.

We had telephones all over the place and big bells. Car horns in some places. Every man had his own number so they could call without having to walk a long distance. It might be two or three rings, or a long and a short, or a short and a long. They would go to the nearest telephone and answer it. We had our own wire system with only two wires, one to the ground.

We had other farms that raised mink, too. It's much better if you have a little refrigeration to store the pelts. I did it about twenty years, and then we went out because there were too many. I seen what happened to the silver fox people. They stored the pelts in cold storage and when they brought them out of cold storage, it spoiled the scarcity.

Milwaukee had a national mink show. My ability to judge mink was based on what I got in New York. The most I ever got was two hundred and fifty dollars a pelt. I didn't have much fur of that quality and only a few would make it, but I still had the most mink in that bundle. The price didn't stay that high long.

As soon as the maids were wearing mink jackets, that was the end of the mink business. It was too common. For a long time they only raised mink in this country. They never raised them in Europe. Then somebody came over and got some mink. By the time that happened, we were increasing our production. It's all passé because everything is different. We had a splendid operation in the mink business, but for me there wasn't another business. My children were young, and I'd already learned what to do with money to keep it coming.

My children are very independent. One son joined the National Guard. He had a very small amount of money, but he lived carefully with that. He rose up through the ranks of the National Guard. He just retired, and is at the top of the country in real estate. He is the best example I can think of a self-made man. He rose up from the bottom. He has a nice family, and a big house with basement close to Washington, D.C.

He wasn't too close to what happened there on September 11th. How can anybody that smart do such a thing? This was caused by religion and hatred.

I was never any good at religion. I believe in the principles and the Ten Commandments, all of that absolutely. I suppose I'm a heathen, but there are other religions that are much larger than the Christian religion that we base all our good living on.

They're still finding out new things as earthquakes and other things uncover fossils from the ground. There are people who find where people were living thousands of years ago. The earliest of us were somewhere down in Africa, in the west area there. You have to go even back past that to get to the originals. The family was what you were. After a while the family grew and you had a tribe. Then tribes had intermarriages. That's the natural thing. But they kept the sour pusses mixed in there, and they had a fight.

Now the Taliban are reviving diseases by putting them in envelopes. When I was young there was talk about a cow dying of anthrax. They carefully buried the cow. It doesn't kill the germs, but it got rid of it. I don't know what they do now. There are different strains of this. There were killing viruses. The flu killed adults. They have different strains coming from the Orient. With the traveling, we get viruses right away. Vaccinations help.

My mind is busy all the time. My health is excellent, with no concern in any area that you can't correct. My parents lived into the early nineties. That's the most important thing about the probability of staying around, if you were fortunate enough to survive the diseases. I haven't had a change in glasses for years now. Sometimes I think I need it, but I find I need to clean my glasses. I maybe don't hear as minute sounds as I used to.

I run. I choose bad ground to walk on so I have strong ankles. My father taught me how to get up on your toes and then back down to have strong ankles. There's a mile from that street and back. I'll maybe run half the way, and then walk back. If it isn't wet, I walk on uneven ground. I don't miss too many days, but it's not a religion with me.

I eat apple, pineapples, oranges, and fruits for breakfast. I like a variety. I take that seriously because I grew up on the benefits of diets in animals. You have herbivorous, carnivorous. Omnivorous, that's us."

THEODORE & FRIEDA
BROD, 89 & 85

Rabbi and wife
Europe

A friend who has studied with him referred Rabbi Brod to me. When I called it was the week before Passover. As busy as he was, the Rabbi suggested I come right over. We spoke briefly, as he was preparing a large Passover dinner for the Jewish community.

The small house is located in a wealthy area of town and appears professionally landscaped, with a flowering magnolia tree in front and neatly trimmed flowers and bushes. Inside, the house is overflowing with books neatly arranged in shelves along most walls. There is a collection of menorahs in the window and numerous Jewish symbols throughout the house, including a design of lions and the Ten Commandments. Mezuzahs are posted on every door, and people were coming in and out, waiting for their lessons.

The Rabbi was not dressed when I arrived but was wearing a bath-robe. He was sitting behind a card table covered with books and papers, intently concentrating on a Hebrew text. He looked aged.

"I am a Rabbi," he began. "I was born and raised in Europe, first in Austria and then in Poland. I got my early lessons in Judaism there. In those days this meant that you spent from eight in the morning until four in the evening studying. I started at three years of age.

Then we came to America, to Philadelphia. I finished studying for Rabbinic and became a Rabbi at the Yeshiva in Philadelphia. I was ordained at age twenty. I was the youngest of the Orthodox Rabbis. When I was about thirty, the head of Yeshiva, the Rabbinical School, went to Jerusalem to visit his parents and he passed away there. So, I took his place and became the head of the Rabbinical School in Phila-delphia. I also had a Synagogue in Philadelphia, the only one of that kind, the Lubavitch, which is the ultra Orthodox.

I've been in Tampa fifty-six years. We came here because my wife had two children and was pregnant with the third. She caught a very bad cold and it affected her. Three doctors said we must go south.

They said, "We can only save one, either the baby, or my wife."

So we left on a Sunday. We had two children, my wife, my mother-in-law, and myself in the car. My mother-in-law, may she rest in peace, came with her daughter. We got into the car and drove south. I was in contact with a physician over the telephone in St. Pete, but we never made St. Pete because she got very sick. I came into Tampa on Hillsborough Avenue, and we stopped at some cabins.

The man who was in charge of renting these cabins had a Jewish owner. He thought that anybody who wears a yarmulke must be a Rabbi. So he called his boss and said, "I think a Rabbi has come to rent, and he has a very sick wife."

The owner came within a half hour after he called him and quickly called a doctor. With God's help, the doctor was successful in curing her. At that time, penicillin had just come out. By using penicillin with oxygen they cured her and the baby was born all right.

The man who got the doctor and owned the cabins needed a principal for the school. Since I was principal of the Rabbinical School in Philadelphia, I would be the man for it. So in two to three days the board voted and I became principal at the Rodolph Shalom Synagogue, which is a Conservative Synagogue still in existence.

So I settled down in Tampa instead of going any further in St Pete. A couple years later they made me Scholar in Residence at the Synagogue. I taught the new Rabbi that they hired. He had graduated in a new Rabbinical School in Philadelphia where you only needed three years to become a Rabbi. He was short, so I taught him the difference at his home.

An Orthodox Synagogue here in town was closing, so I took it over. They were in a small wooden building. It was too successful and the board decided we needed a larger building. They wanted a new building that was Conservative. They decided they didn't want to be Orthodox, so they looked around and brought a Conservative Rabbi in from somewhere. Rabbis my age don't have their own congregation." His voice sounded bitter.

"What else can I tell you? I remained here close to fifty-six years, and thank God the children grew up here. I've got one girl and two boys. The girl is a doctor of psychology and has written twenty-one books. The shelf behind me is full of her books. They have been translated in eleven different languages. The latest has been North Korean. It's used in first year medical. My oldest boy is a lawyer here in Tampa, and the third one is a medical doctor.

I've been Rabbi for fifty-six years, a long time. I take care of divorces, both Conservative and Orthodox, which in Hebrew is called a *get*. Even if you have a divorce from the state, you couldn't get remarried unless you were divorced in Hebrew. It's still the same rule for both the Conservative and the Orthodox. In Philadelphia I learned how to make these divorce papers, which has to be done with a goose feather and special ink. You can't use a pen, and it's written in Babylonian. I did that quite a bit. There was no one in the area who knew how to do a *get* so they would send it to me. Even the Reform now and then would send me one, although they don't believe in a Hebrew divorce.

I do what I always did. People come every day with their problems. Usually family problems. They sometimes hesitate to go to their Rabbi—the Rabbi's now-a-days are very young and they feel like they are talking to their own children, and they have children problems. So they look for an older man. I get a lot of people.

I teach Hebrew. Private students come to my home. I charge so much an hour, and I teach Babylonian, because I teach Talmud. Talmud is written in Babylonian. I also teach Kabala, which is mysticism. I have quite a few who like to delve into mysticism.

Sunday I teach three classes over at the Jewish Community Center. They have high school children who take Sunday lessons.

That's about all I can tell you about myself. I've been married for sixty-five years to the same lady, and thank God, everything's been very good.

I'm going to the Hyatt this Wednesday and Thursday night. We have 205 people who have paid thirty dollars a piece for their meal, which is going to be strictly kosher. I will read a book called the Haggadah. I've got to get some work done now."

*   *   *   *

The Rabbi's wife, Frieda, came in from shopping while we were talking. She was wearing a navy blue dress and looked younger than her husband, but certainly in her eighties.

"His problem is that everyday he worries because he's been working thirty or forty years on a couple of books, and he never has time to work on them." She began. "There were eight sisters, and only one younger brother, who died in the Second World War. He was the oldest boy.

There are ten in his family and I'm an only child. I was brought up in Philadelphia and my parents were very Orthodox. It was not an Orthodox area, so I was pretty isolated. I was happy, but I really knew very little about the world, so I went to college because I wanted to learn more. I learned what a big world it was and how much there is to learn, and I was barely, barely, like a pebble in the ocean. I majored in English and journalism.

My father was a Rabbi and my husband a teacher. Back in those days a taxi wasn't a big deal so neither my husband nor my father drove. My mother preferred it that way because my father's mind was always elsewhere. She was afraid he would kill somebody if he drove.

I love traveling, but my husband hates it. He wants his own bed. I've gotten around a little bit thanks to my daughter.

As you grow older, things get lower and lower." She laughed and pointed to her breasts. "I've got my share of stress, but I live with it. I'm healthy. Except for his diabetes, he's in good health. The worse of it is that it went into his legs and he can't walk. Mostly he eats fruits and cereals, so his diabetic diet isn't a big problem.

Right now is a very busy time. I'm moving out the *chometz* [every-day foods] and in the *Pesach* [special holiday foods and dishes]. This whole week I've been working on how many tables, with how many children, and what they're going to eat. I'm not computer savvy and have it all organized on these 3 x 5 cards and files. Thank you very much for coming. Maybe you can come back after the holidays. There's so much to do now, I've got to get back to work."

MILDRED ROBERTS, AGE 90

Amazing Mildred
St. Joe, Missouri

I spotted an active senior in the grocery store and got in the checkout line behind her. We walked out of the store together and by the time we reached her car in the parking lot, we'd exchanged names and phone numbers.

Mildred lives in a white, doublewide mobile home in a retirement park. There is a religious cross in the window and a station wagon in the driveway. She is average height, has a nice figure, and looked good in her blue jean vest over a matching shirt and jeans, and blue tennis shoes. Her hair is pure white, and she was wearing light makeup on her cheeks and lips. Her wide smile showed her own sparkling white teeth. She wears glasses and has some kyphosis, rounding in the back, but walks easily without any problem. During the interview she got up repeatedly to show me yet another picture, something her husband, or grandchild had made, to answer the phone, or to demonstrate her exercises. Sitting still wasn't something Mildred did very long.

Inside there is a green carpet, and an identical pattern with green leaves and red cherries on her couches, drapes, and even oven mitts.

"I love this little house. It's just right for me. When we came down here, my daughter had this house all ready for us. We did some things, but not a lot. When we came down here, we had a sale and sold most everything except some sentimental things we wanted to take along. I spent a lot of time talking to my daughter on the phone, and she had everything ready when we arrived. She bought all the furniture and had the drapes and valences made to match. We came, and she had the refrigerator all stocked."

Photo magnets of her family covered much of her refrigerator. There was a ceramic chicken collection with chickens throughout the house.

"My mother started the collection for me. Everytime my father traveled, he'd bring me back a chicken. I had a big collection when I was in St. Joe.

My daughter has lived in Tampa twenty-five years. I've been here five years. We came after that terrible ice storm in Missouri. My husband passed away last September, five months ago. Archie was ninety-three and we were married sixty-eight years. It's hard, but the Lord has been with me every day. When I get up in the morning I say, "Thank you for another day, Lord."

I'm doing real well. Of course, I have my bad times too. I have two children, my daughter lives nearby and my son lives in Denver. They're both very, very supportive. I call on them when something comes up, and I need help or a drive. After sixty-eight years, life will never be the same without Archie, but I have to keep going and the Lord sees me through. My daughter's husband passed away three years ago. He was Pastor of the Emmanuel Lutheran Church. We really enjoy being down here, and being close to them. My daughter comes over every Tuesday to do things in the yard and help with things that need to be done. I have a good family, and they're all very supportive.

My husband was an entrepreneur. We were in and out of a lot of businesses. We were always doing something. My husband would have an idea that he was sure would make him a millionaire. I always went along with him, and we didn't end up wealthy, but there's enough to see us through.

I'm a pretty cheerful person. I don't believe in being grumpy. I'm contented if I'm here alone. I don't have the energy that I had ten years ago, but I painted my cupboard not too long ago on the bottom. I didn't want to get on a ladder to paint higher. With two hips having been broken, I don't take any chances.

At ninety, I'm not interested in doing a lot of activity. I have good health for my age, but I don't have the energy I used to have. I keep busy. I love to read mysteries. We have a library in the Activity Center and they have a whole wall of mystery books.

When I get up in the morning, first thing I do is say my prayers. Then I exercise for forty-five minutes to an hour. I had to do a lot of therapy, and I still do those exercises that they gave me for my broken hips. I do yoga exercises and stretching. I have a little routine all worked out that I do that every morning. I use hand weights but I don't go into aerobics. What I do gets my heart going. Then I have my breakfast.

I sew quite a bit. I buy a lot of clothes at Goodwill. I have for years. I'm pretty good about altering them or doing little things. I don't usually make anything from scratch. If they have short sleeves, I lengthen them, or whatever needs to be done. Naturally, my arms aren't very pretty anymore. I enjoy sewing. I can still thread my needles and thread my machine. I figure that I'm going to be all right as long as I can thread the needles.

I have a routine for doing my housework. I drive, and go grocery shopping. I go to Wal-Mart, and I like to go to Joanne Fabrics. On Sunday I like to go to the Lutheran Church because it's close for me.

It's about twenty minutes. Sometimes on the way home from church I'll stop at the Wal-Mart in Plant city. They have a great big Good Will store in Plant City that's open on Sunday. If there's anytime left, I rest a little bit.

This is my family from both sides." Mildred opened a photo album. "The grandchildren have heard me talk so much that the oldest child wrote a book about my life with Archie, and called it *Amazing Mildred*. She did it on the computer."

✳   ✳   ✳   ✳

"I was born in 1911, and everything's happened since then. They barely had automobiles then. The model T Ford was new. We had radio, but not television or air travel. This has been a good time to live because so much has happened. I just wonder what more could happen. Computers are taking over the world, but I'm not interested in learning computers. I'm happy the way my life is.

I grew up in a very good Christian home. My mother and dad were active in the Lutheran Church so I had a good grounding in my faith at home. I had the one sister, and I had a brother who died at birth, sad to say. My parents were very outgoing people. My dad was a salesman. He called on people to repair their leather shoes. My mother was a wonderful homemaker, cook, and housekeeper. She taught us girls to do things the way we should.

They were sociable people and we had a lot of company, especially for meals. They always had open house at Christmas. We had our family dinner at noon, and then at four our open house started. They invited friends and my dad's customers.

I had high school and business college. I graduated with a two-year degree. I graduated from high school when I was only fifteen years old. I went to a parochial school. It was like one of the old country schools with one room. All the grades were in the same room. I'd get my work done, and I'd listen to the next grade up. Before long I'd be doing their work, and I'd get promoted. I graduated from eighth grade when I was eleven, and went onto high school.

I met my husband the summer after I graduated. He had graduated the same year from another high school. At that time all the high schools came together for their graduation ceremony, so we graduated together, but we didn't know each other until later. Because we had graduated the same year, he didn't know how young I was. He always said if he'd known how young I was when he met me, he wouldn't have gone with me. By the time he found it out, I guess he was already hooked.

When I got married in 1933, we lived in St. Joe. My husband started out being secretary of the fire department in St. Joe. He did that for the first nine years that we were married.

There was a large animal pharmaceutical company that made drugs for cattle and so forth. I worked for them. I worked for years. I worked before we were married, and after we were married. I was home with the kids after the children were born. I didn't work until they were getting ready for high school, and then I went back with the pharmaceutical company. When I retired in 1976, I was traffic manager for the company. I was the head of shipping. Everything had to be routed and shipped properly.

We've always had a station wagon. This is our third. We fixed it up so one could rest in the back. Our children lived away all their adult life. Mack has been in Denver twenty-five years, and Donna was down here, so we always traveled to see our kids. Donna moved quite a bit and we saw quite a bit of the country visiting her. We flew once but we liked driving better. I don't think I'll make any car trips on my own. I don't know if I'll fly to Denver, but we'll see. There is a lot more confusion in the airports. I'm contented at home.

Both of my hips have been broken. I broke this one while I was still in St. Joe. I was having lunch at McDonalds, and there was a buster chair. I didn't realize it was there, tripped over it, and broke the first hip there. So I had to have an ambulance take me. It doesn't have a replacement, it has a pin and a plate.

I broke the other one after I came down here. My husband did a lot of woodworking and we used to go to Builders Square. We were walking down the aisle, and there was a man standing in front of the desk with a big carton in his hands. He turned and knocked me down with the carton.

I can't walk real well anymore. I have too much pain from arthritis. I was very, very active in my church in St. Joe, and I had two really, really good friends in St. Joe that I miss. We would go out together and have lunch and do things. I still talk to them on the phone. I've got family here but I haven't had the opportunity to make friends while caring for Archie. What I did, I did with him and with my family.

My son calls once or twice a week from Denver. He came down when Archie was diagnosed with bladder cancer. We were still in Missouri then.

His health wasn't good after we came down here. The last year of his life we were lucky to have hospice care. I wanted to keep him home if I possibly could. Hospice care was such a blessing for us. At first they came once a week, and then later on they came twice. For the first few months hospice was here, he liked to get out, and I took him with me wherever I went. I took him to the grocery store, and he sat up there in front while I shopped. He liked to get up and go, but it got to where I wasn't able to get him into the car anymore. When he was sick, we got a lot of nourishment for our faith by watching church on television.

He fell several times. I made him crawl to the couch and I helped him get up on it. The Lord gave me the strength and stamina, and also the help of hospice. I couldn't leave him. If I had to leave, my daughter would come over so I could go to the store. Someone had to take care of him. At the end he couldn't dress himself. I had to give him his shower and feed him.

Archie was quite a care for me. He was only bed-fast about ten days. The nurses would come in and check all his vital signs and make sure he had the medication he should have. The doctor also came to the house occasionally, maybe three or four times all together. Of course, the nurses kept in close contact with him. I also had a homemaker at the end. We moved all the furniture out onto the porch and they brought in a hospital bed for him. At that time, they brought in a home health nurse. They became like daughters to me. They still call me and one just called and said they're going to take me out to dinner. They've done that a couple times. That is such a wonderful organization. It's a blessed work. That was the last year of his life. Now I'm adjusting to being alone.

The Lord was good to us. He made it possible for him to stay at home. When we saw that he wouldn't be here much longer, my son came from Denver. He stayed a week before Archie died, and a week after. That was a great, great help for me to have him. I was so thankful that the Lord let me have Archie at home. He would have been so disoriented if he had...

We knew this was imminent, and we made all the plans ahead of time. In a way it was a relief, but of course I miss him a lot. He was buried in the Florida National Cemetery. It's a beautiful place. I'll be buried with him. He was in the military. The wife can be buried with her husband. We've gone ahead and made all the arrangements.

I'm doing real well. I've always enjoyed being alone. It never bothered me. I have several tapes of hymns that he enjoyed, and I still play those. I put on a hymn tape every morning when I finish with my prayers and exercises, and am fixing my breakfast. I enjoy it.

I eat different things, usually fruit and cereal in the morning. I have eggs several times a week. When he was able, my husband cooked breakfast every Saturday morning. He always made pancakes. We did that for years. Then when he couldn't do that anymore, we had frozen waffles. I still do that. On Saturday morning I have frozen waffles, and sometimes I'll have sausages. I eat everything. For lunch I like yogurt with fruit, and sometimes I'll put wheat germ in it. If my daughter cooks something, she brings me over some and I freeze it. I have some stew. When I bake biscuits, I put them in the freezer. I used to bake them from scratch but I don't anymore. I'll bake a can, and then I'll always have something in the freezer. I eat well and try to have a good diet.

People say I don't look ninety. My health is very good, except a little discomfort from osteoporosis. Since Archie's been gone, my blood pressure has been a little high, but I have good health insurance coverage. I've used face cream for years. I don't know if that helped.

My dad passed away when he was only sixty-seven. My mother lived to be ninety-seven but she mentally wasn't very good. She stayed in her home until she was ninety-three. I helped her in her home, did her laundry and cleaned, and left food for her. She was able to stay at home until then with my help. I kept her with me for a while, but it was hard and Archie said it would make me sick. She had a private room in a nursing home. She was happy to go there.

I keep busy. There's always something around here that I want to do. If I do have a little time, I enjoy reading my book. I want to give a good witness to my faith. That's important to me. I go to church every Sunday. I only joined here after Archie passed away. My faith means so much to me. It's a stabilizing influence and a great comfort. I enjoy seeing my great-grandkids growing up, and I want to be a good example to them, and the opportunity to teach them whatever wisdom I have."

Photo—Softball
Game

PAT REILLY, AGE 90

Softball Player
Pennsylvania

The Kids and Kubs is a Seniors Softball team that plays in St. Petersburg, Florida three times a week. I learned about them through a newspaper article. At ninety, Pat could have boasted being among the oldest members on the team.

P at was playing when I arrived, but as soon as the last inning completed, he took a few minutes to talk with me. We found an empty picnic table in the St. Petersburg Park and sat under the oak trees, watching squirrels and green Australian parrots looking for seeds. The parrots are not native to Florida and are only found in this one city, where flocks have become common.

"Originally they had those green parrots in Sunken Gardens, and they got out somehow. My gosh, they're everywhere now." Pat began.

"Seems as though softball is my whole life now. I play ball six times a week. Summer time I play three times a week here at the Kids and Kubs. I'm on another team, Woodlong. They have four teams. I play on the over sixty. Those guys can play ball. I can keep up with the slow ones. I played down there until I was seventy-four, and then I joined this club here.

My oldest brother joined first here, and then I joined. They meet once a month and vote for people. I wasn't seventy-four until the next day, but they met and voted me in, so I didn't lose any time until the next meeting. I only missed a game or so.

We travel in tournaments for the ball games. We might go to California or Iowa to play with an over eighty team. We won the first time in Chicago. We have a family reunion the third Sunday in July every year. I said to another team in Pennsylvania, "If you guys can get up a team, we'd come up and play you." So we did.

I live in a mobile home park and I take care of people's homes there when they go north for the summer. When tomatoes are in season I pick tomatoes and sell them to people in the mobile home park and the ballpark. I don't make much money at it, but it's something I like to do."

*   *   *   *

"I grew up in Pennsylvania. There were six boys and two girls. I was number two. We lived out in the country and everybody was poorer then. We had to walk.

In the country everybody went barefooted in the summer time, although it got too cold in the winter. We went to school barefooted. I used to dread the day I would have to get a job and wear shoes all day.

I got through eighth grade in a country school, a one room, you know. One teacher taught the whole eight classes. When I was old enough, I got a job in a candy factory making candy for twenty cents an hour. Work was cheap then. I got a job for a dollar a day working on cars. I paid three hundred and fifty dollars for my first car and it was a good one. If you got five dollars worth of groceries at the store, you had enough for a week.

I left there and went to Western Union for a year or two. Then I worked in silk mills up around there and made a little more money. They wouldn't let us work in the silk mills too long, the depression and all that. The men stopped buying the silk shirts, so I had to go into some other yarn. I worked the silk mill for about fifteen years.

My wife worked at a snack bar for a man who owns his own ice cream. One day he told her he was going to open up a few more of these little restaurants/ice cream stores where they served coffee and sandwiches. And he says to my wife, "Do you want half of them?" She came and told me.

Well, silk mills were pretty well done, so I said, "Let's go. What can we lose?" They put us in a snack bar, and we sold ice cream and sandwiches. Most of the people who came in there were kids. We had a music box and they played that in the evening. We were there about a year and a half, and the guy paid us each fifteen dollars a week. After a year and a half, he come in there one day and said, "I'm going to move to Canada, and I'm going to sell these places. Do you want one?"

I said, "Heck ya, I'll take one." So he said, "Take inventory and send them to the house."

I put in two pinball machines in the front. You know how kids are with the pinball machines. We made enough off them to pay the rent.

We stayed there until the war came on. Then things got so scarce we couldn't get the ice cream and stuff. After four years we went out of business, just closed it up. I worked in the defense plant then.

After the war was over, one of my brothers bought a beer joint and wanted me to go in and partner with him. The place needed a lot of fixing up, and he had run out of money. We were there for four years and he sold it. We made money on it.

After that, my wife and I went back into the snack bar business across from a small college, Millersville. The students used to come over for coffee and sandwiches, especially Friday nights. Everybody came over Friday nights for supper. We had three boys and they helped us with the snack bar. We stayed there ten years before we got tired of it, so we sold it.

Our neighbor said to my wife, "Why don't you go down to St. Petersburg Florida and work at the dog tracks? The girls out there make pretty good money."

She come home and told me that. I said, "Let's go." In about four days we left. We got here New Years Eve, '62. That's how I got to Florida. I got a job in Web City. It was a big store, but it's not here any more. I worked there until they closed, and that's when I retired. I was serving double dip ice cream cones for nine cents or a dollar for all you can eat. My brother would come down, and he always had two ice cream cones. The store was a block long. They had eight cashiers on one side, and twelve on the other side. In them days they didn't have the automatic stuff. We had to stamp the prices on things.

My wife died about eleven years ago. We were married fifty-three and a half years and you couldn't get a better wife than she was. If we were going away, she would have my bags packed. We went out west one year, and one son was out there in Wyoming. We toured around for about a month and then went home. I'm glad we came to Florida—that's one thing I owe to my wife. I don't mind the heat. I stay all summer, except when we go away to play ball.

I used to live with a gal. She was a millionaire. She had cancer and died. A couple months later her stepdaughter called me on the phone and said, "Jane left me the two mobile homes, and she didn't leave you nothing."

I said, "I don't care."

It didn't make me mad. The mobile home just sat there for five months. She called me one day and said she's coming down and selling the mobile homes. I had one of my own, so I moved back into mine. She came down and sold both, and she gave me six hundred dollars!

I kind of like things the way they are today. Everybody knows everybody in the mobile home park. Every afternoon we have a little beer party and sit out in the sun and have a few beers.

I never made much money. I live on six hundred and fifty dollars a month and don't worry about the future. I pick tomatoes, pack them up and sell them for a dollar each. I don't make much money, but it makes a lot of people happy. Some buy two bags and give one to their neighbor. That's nice and it helps me out. I have to cross the skyway bridge to pick them.

I help people with their lawns in the mobile home park, and they pay me. I only charge about five dollars and work all day. I like it in the mobile home park. People are friendly there. The only time I don't save money is twice a year when I have to pay my insurance, which takes the whole social security, and Christmas time. I send all my relatives money, and that takes the whole check. It don't cost me much for groceries. Sometimes I eat at my girlfriend's.

I think running around with women is the secret to staying healthy. I have two girlfriends right now. One is not too good. She had an operation last year and she has cancer. The other girl lives on the beaches, and I go out there. I just came from her place to here. They know each other a little bit, not too much. I alternate spending time with them. That's my night work. I guess they do mind a little, but what's a guy to do?"

Photo—Archie with
his snails & bottles

Archie Jones, age 91

Snailer
Palatka, Florida

A friend who collects snails contacted me and suggested I call Archie and interview him. I spoke to Archie for a while over the phone and arranged to meet him at his house in South Miami. This was a five-hour trip each way for me. Although the trip was long, I was not disappointed, as I found Archie as fascinating as my friend had promised.

The entryway in Archie's large Florida style home contains two huge bookshelves. Antique books with gold bindings fill the shelves and books overflow onto the floor. Six large pieces of driftwood are set on top of the bookshelves, and an exercise rowing machine and weights are on the floor next to the books. The inlaid wooden floor and red Oriental rug accentuates the large room's luxurious appearance.

"Driftwood is a hobby of mine," Archie said when he saw me admiring it. "My wife and I used to collect driftwood. You'll see it around the house."

The walls were covered with photos, as well as oil and pencil draw-ings of the beach, birds, butterflies, and colorfully striped tree snails. A hand carved, foot-long wooden shell from the Philippines, an Oriental lamp with a blue and brown leaf design, and silver candlesticks were set on another bookcase. I sat on his Early American couch, and he sat on chair next to the couch. Due to Archie's poor hearing, I sat close and spoke loudly.

Archie is a thin man of average height. He was wearing black pants, an undershirt, and a red-checkered flannel shirt. He appeared to see well without glasses. His tight, wrinkle free skin was ruddy and appeared scared or burned.

"I was an accountant," Archie began, "and then I was a drug execu-tive of a wholesale drug company for twenty-five years until I retired.

I was born in Palatka, Florida, in 1910. Miami didn't exist when I first appeared on the scene. My brother was born on a houseboat when my parents were on a vacation. We're all alive and kicking. My parents were both drowned in accidents in their forties. I was almost eighteen when my father passed away. Mom lost her life in '37 in an accident. That was at the bottom of the big depression. I finished the tenth grade. That's as far as I got with formal education, but I studied with tutors and took some adult education courses, and read a lot. I love to read and do my reading late at night. I read everything except modern stuff. I like philosophy, malacology, biology, paleontology, history. You name it.

I was out making a living for the family at eighteen. I started out at a sewing machine company, and then I went to work at E.B.Elliot, an advertising company, and then I left him for a better job at Sherwin Williams, a paint store on Miami Beach.

My sister married a naval academy graduate who flew with Pan American. When they moved to California, my sister said there would be a lot more opportunities out there, so my wife and I moved there in 1938. We got there just in time for a strike. I finally [knocks on wooden table] found a job with the Doctors' Business Bureau in San

Francisco. Then I went to the Marco National Valve Company in Berkley and remained with them until I was drafted into the big war.

We didn't get in until '44. I spent a little more than two years in the army, and then I decided that if I was ever going to come back to Florida, I'd better do it then. My wife and son were living with her parents in a little town called Madison, Indiana, down the river from Cincinnati. We came back to Miami and have been here ever since. I was married a little over sixty-five years, and she passed away sixteen months ago.

She had shingles for eighteen years before she died. She had a few small strokes and then developed Alzheimer's. She didn't last very long after that. She had a rough life those last eighteen years. I took care of her the whole time. I hope nobody ever has to go through that.

I drive, but I gave up my car when I turned eighty-five. My ophthalmologist told me I couldn't get a driver's license.

I changed ophthalmologists to a lady doctor who said, "Nothing is the matter and there is no reason why you can't get your driver's licence."

She gave me a note but I didn't need it because when my license came up for renewal, they sent me a notice in the mail. I had three options: one, I could go down and pick it up at one of the offices in town, or by mail, or by having five dollars added to my bill, I could get it by telephone. I called Tallahassee and two days later I got my driver's licence. They don't know whether I'm blind, one armed, or what. I still have that license, but I gave up my car when this ophthalmologist told me I couldn't get a driver's licence. Sometimes I get a taxi, or if I need a car for all day, I'll rent one.

I rented a car and drove up to St. Augustine last year for a family reunion. This reunion was my mother's side of the family. There were 154 of us. The Canova house is one of the oldest in St. Augustine.

I have two boys. You just met Kenneth. Kenneth is a fisherman and hunter, but doesn't go out snailing. He is living with me and helps with the driving. My other son lives in the Panhandle.

In 1934, I was a hunter and fisherman, and I heard from hunters about these beautiful snails that were lurking way in the depths of the Everglades. One day in April, during the dry season, a friend of mine, Dan, and I were out hunting tropical fish in Pinecrest, an area fifty miles west of Miami. Pinecrest had nothing in its village but a school-house, postoffice, hotel, and homes for the families. It was a place for the people who were building the Tamiami trail to live. Scattered around they had some hammocks, so Dan and I were collecting these beautiful tropical fish. While eating lunch we sat on a big limb dangling our feet in the water. I looked around up in the tree and there was a tree snail. I quit hunting, quit fishing, and concentrated on snails. I've been collecting them ever since. The technical terminology is malacologist, but I call myself a snailer.

Liguus are mixtures of colors; you get blue, deep oranges, reds (which fade very rapidly), browns, yellows, green, and all colors in-between. They have a variety of stripes and vertical flares or longitudinal stripes and bands. I think they're the most beautiful land snails in the world. Some of the Cuban Polimeta's are more bold and striking, but I don't think they have the beauty of the Florida tree snails. Incidentally, all of the tree snails of color and beauty are found in the tropics and subtropics. The largest ones in Florida get to be 80–82 millimeters, but that's like a seven and a half foot man. They're about six or seven millimeters long when hatched, and a large snail is sixty millimeters. Seventy-five is about as big as you're going to get. There's a nice article that appeared in the March 1965 *National Geographic*. It told a little bit about the park project I work on.

The snails came over from Cuba after the last ice age, which happened fifteen thousand years ago. They'll mate with any other snail. Cold weather kills them. Even the cold weather that we have down here will kill all the snails in the hammock. But the eggs laid in the ground, where it's warmer, survive and hatch. This doesn't happen often because the temperature is always a little warmer in the hammock than outside the hammock. So unless you have two straight years of freezing weather, the snails will not become extinct in that particular area, but if in the first year all the snails above ground are killed, and the second year all the young are killed, that's the end of that particular population. They can't come back unless they're introduced. By and large, the hammocks are isolated, but the snails find a way of getting from one to the other. I'm talking about the Everglades National Park now—if the burning isn't accurate, the vegetation grows up between hammocks, and they use that as a highway. Or a limb in a storm can be blown several hundred yards from one hammock to another, and might happen to have a snail or two on it.

All forms of life have ups and downs, increased population, and decreased population. They might be considered threatened now, but it's through the introduction of fire ants, or something like that. The collectors pose no problem, never did, because…I used to take some of the shell clubs out hunting these things when you could hunt them. We would have anywhere from a dozen people up to thirty-five or forty people. Invariably, someone would ask me, "Archie, how many snails can I take?" and I would shock them by saying, "Take all you want."

They were conservationists, most of them, and that was a horrible thing to hear. I would have to explain to them, like all forms of life, they reproduce faster than the food supply, and the more snails they took out of the hammock, the healthier the colony would be. For instance, in the literature on Liguus tree snails, the authorities said that the snails lay from eight to a dozen eggs apiece. When I raised my snails in the back yard, they had plenty of food and my snails had over forty and sometimes over fifty eggs in a clutch. My snails were two or three times as large as the ones out in the hammock, simply because of a food supply. When they eat all the food up, the population is very thin, hanging by a thread."

"So what was the reason for making it illegal to collect them?" I asked.

"A bunch of nonsense and people not knowing what they're doing. It's *in* now to be a conservationist. Half of them don't know what conservation is, but it's a good way to make a name for themselves and they feel good about it. If you protect the land, the snails will protect themselves. Ninety percent of snails now live in municipal, state, or federal lands where you can't collect them anymore.

I've been working on this tree snail project with the park since 1957. The park was formed in 1947 and ten years later I was part of a group that began this program. Ralph Humes, a dear friend of mine who is an excellent sculptor, and Dan Beard, who was the first superintendent of the Everglades National Park, decided we needed to be protecting these snails. At the time they didn't need protecting but in the future they would. Dan thought it would be a good idea and Chris Van Fossen, Ralph, and myself headed up the project. We worked with a park ranger named Erwin Winte. He was incidentally, the first ranger in the park, and a tree snail collector. We had to first find some hammocks that were suitable to introduce the Liguus into. We looked for hammocks that had the flora and fauna that the tree snails needed and didn't have any other snails. For the next twenty years we introduced quite a few varieties in the hammocks that we found. Most of them are extinct now except those we introduced into the protected areas.

Now I'm monitoring the colonies—or what's left of them. In May of 1989, a severe fire destroyed not only the hammocks, but also the snails. About eighty-five percent of the hammocks that we introduced these forms into were destroyed. Then we had a freeze about Christmas time that same year. Then in 1992, we had hurricane Andrew, which blew over a lot of the trees that were still standing.

So we've been monitoring the snails. When we can find them, we've been putting them together to mate during the mating season. One snail might be isolated in one section of the hammock, and another, in another area, but they could never get together because there were not trees. I have also been taking out snails that don't belong, that were blown in there by the hurricane or maybe a limb blown into the hammock, that sort of thing.

To get to the snails in the Everglades, you have to walk out there. The only other means is a helicopter, and we don't have those available. It's the roughest country in the world. There are pinnacle rock and pits. In the dry season there's no water there at all, but I was walking a few weeks ago and in places the water was up to my crotch. We never got onto dry land. When the rains begin each spring around May, the mosquitoes become very bad. I try to get out every weekend, but I don't always make it. I go out perhaps thirty-five to forty times a year.

I grew them in my yard in Coconut Grove years ago and I watched them. The snails are *hermaphroditic*. Each snail has both male and female sex organs, but they need to mate in order to reproduce. It's a complicated situation. I'd say around forty percent of the time the two would mate, exchange roles, and then mate again. Mating begins around August 15th for the mainland snails, and a month later on the Florida Keys. Approximately a month later they crawl onto the ground and dig holes into the leaf mold at the base of a tree. They'll dig a hole about the depth of a shell. A three-inch shell would dig a hole about three inches deep, and so forth. They bury their eggs about September in the mainland snails and early October in the Key shells. The eggs remain there until the rain comes next season.

During the week I work on snails. I'm always doing something to them, rearranging the cabinets, looking up some data on certain shells that people ask me questions about. This, that, and the other thing. I have quite a large collection and people come by and talk shells. I don't like to look at them too often in my cabinets, because I don't want the thrill to wear off.

I was talking to a fellow snailer the other day. He married a girl from Switzerland on the base of the Matterhorn.

I said, "Which is the hardest to get through, climbing the mountain or walking through the Everglades?"

He said, "In the summer, the Everglades is harder than the mountain. It's a tough territory."

I've got a bottle collection that I found in the Keys and on the
shoreline."

Archie spent some time showing me his antique bottles, including
one with round bumps on the outside. It was a poison bottle used
before there were electric lights, and the bumps were a warning so people wouldn't mistake it for medicine in the dark."

*   *   *   *

"We took a break from snail talk, and I joined Archie in his kitchen
where he made us both a cup of coffee.

"I'm happy as long as I've got my marbles, and I'm in pretty good
health. I'm happy to be around. There's no secret about staying
healthy; the good die young, so there wasn't any problem for me. I'm
getting along in years."

"Were you burned on your face? It's very smooth."

"No, that's Rosacea. I didn't put my beauty cream on today. There's
no cure for it. It's an anti-immune disease. One part of the body affects
another one. It doesn't affect my health, but people think I'm sun-
burned.

I use dark sugar, which is a lightly refined sugar. It's a lot better for
you than white sugar. I don't have a microwave. My sister's been after
me for years to get one but I won't. It gets too hot and destroys all the
nutrients and enzymes in the food. My Mom had a pacemaker, and she
was afraid to use it. She wasn't comfortable with it, and neither am I."

Archie had around fifty bottles of herbal vitamins in his kitchen and
dining room. I asked him about them.

"I have vitamins for my eyes. My doctor is a little perplexed because
my macro degeneration has stopped dead in its tracks. My cataracts
have stopped dead in their tracks. They told me seven or eight years
ago they couldn't do anything more for me, that I'd have to have cata-

ract surgery. I had chelation and then went to my doctor, but didn't tell him what I'd done.

When the doctor finished examining me and didn't have much to tell me, I asked, "What about my cataracts?"

He said, "Oh, they're incipient—they're just beginning. Don't worry about them, they're no problem at all." Archie laughed.

"If I can give you one piece of advice, take care of yourself. The doctors aren't going to do it. You have to take the bull by the horns and take care of yourself. Only go to them when you absolutely have to have their services. I have prostate problems and I take medicine, but I don't take it the day before I go out because it takes my equilibrium away. It's tough enough getting over those rocks.

I don't take anything else. I took synthetic vitamins for years, and they didn't help. Now I take all natural vitamins. They're made from whole foods, so you get the whole food complex in the vitamins. I'm treating my whole body. I eat a lot of fat. You need to eat a lot of fat if you want to stay alive and thin. You need to eat the right kind of fat— red meat fat, butter, you name it. You get a lot of the omega 6, but you get very little of the omega 3. I get my omega 3 out of flaxseed. I don't have high blood pressure.

One doctor told me, "I know some men forty years old who would like to have your arteries."

I eat eggs. Eggs are the best food you can eat, the finest most complete food. I don't like cooked vegetables. I have a blender, which I use with carrots, spinach, celery, whatever's in the market. I blend it all together, freeze it, and eat about a ten ounce glass of that a day, plus whatever vegetables I cook up.

Drink your whiskey, drink your coffee. I don't drink very much. I take three-fourth of an ounce with apple juice or coke-a-cola. I drink one or two of those. If I go out I'll have three or four. I drink coffee, whiskey in moderation, and a beer after mowing the lawn or a snail hunt in the summer time. I don't like it in the winter. I gave up smoking after I got out of the army. All I got out of it was a cough. One day

I said, "I'll give up smoking," and I did. I had no problems with it at all. My son has been trying to give it up, but he can't. They say two cups of coffee a day are good for you but I went for years without taking any."

Alex Goldman, 92

Psychologist
Brooklyn, New York

A couple of months had passed since I had left fliers in Sun City Center when Alex found a left over one and called me. Although I had planned to stop interviewing, Alex sounded so interesting that I decided to "do just one more."

There had been a Florida thunderstorm that morning, and I noticed the golf cart in the garage was wet. Alex had told me he planned to golf that morning, but he had been rained out.

The house was moderate sized and comfortable for Alex and his son without being extravagant. There were numerous pictures of cities, but not many of people. He displayed numerous figures, vases, and pots that had been collected throughout years of travel. He also had antiques such as a water pitcher, an English pushcart, and sign saying Coca Cola .5 cents. Alex showed me a pair of French provincial chairs that he had recently had repaired.

Alex is a thin, aged looking man who has lost height to time. He was wearing a peach colored T-shirt, beige shorts, and a lifeline alert box on his wrist. His smooth skin is interrupted with heavy, deep wrinkles around his jaw and mouth and his gray hair is sparse. Alex has a warm, welcoming smile and expressive hands. As he spoke, he regularly removed his glasses and used them to gesture.

"There was a rainstorm. I came home soaking wet from the golf course," Alex began. "I was outside wiping off the golf cart. Yard maintenance goes with the house—the only yard work I do is the flowers along the walk. I'm in favor of not doing any yard work that doesn't need doing. I trim the bush on this side because I don't want it growing into the flagpole.

I'm a psychologist. Two professional organizations I belong to have sections relating to aging. The *American Medical Association* has a section on geriatrics and the *American Psychological Association* has a division on aging.

The *Human Factors of Ergonomics* has a section on aging consisting of people who don't know what they're talking about. I taught ergonomics. It's exactly what the word means, the measurement of work and the energy that goes into work. It's the human factor.

Most of the technological advances that affect economics in the history of civilization are late nineteenth and twentieth century. This includes the automobile, transcontinental railroads, telephone, airplanes, computers, and even industrial uses for electricity. The industrial revolution was still labor intensive, but at that time we had become, to me distressingly, concerned about wealth.

I write an occasional letter to the Tribune or St. Pete Times. I went up to New Jersey to talk to an editor who wanted me to write a column. But it turns out he wants me to write what *he* wants me to write, so I decided to start a web page, and put in it what I want."

*   *   *   *

"My great grandfather worked for one company for seventy-two years. Then they told him that he'd have to retire when he was eighty-nine years old. When he came home, he said, "You know, my father told me when I took that job it would be temporary."

My mother lived to be seventy-two. She was one of ten children, most of whom I knew. I never knew her mother, who was dead long before I was born. Her father was a building contractor in Europe. My father was born in Hungary. He came here alone, to Baltimore, when he was nine years old. It's a long story.

I was born in Brooklyn, and lived there until I graduated from high school. I had one brother who was ten years older.

I've outlived two wives. I met the first one when I was a graduate student. She was a schoolteacher. We had two children, one of whom died five years ago.

In 1939 my father was sick. I was living in Baltimore and working in Washington. My mother was frantic. She wanted me home, so I quit my job and came home. By then my wife had died.

I came up to New York and got a job. I shared an office with a social worker. She was a lawyer but was working as a social worker. Then the war broke out. I was a reserve officer and got called to duty. In the course of time we got married. Sometime during the war we had a child.

I had no personal contact with the Holocaust, but I had two occasions to talk about relating to it. Sometime in the late thirties my parents used to spend Rosh Hashanah and Yom Kipper time in a resort in New Jersey in the Orange Mountains. I came along once, in about 1940. This little town was almost entirely populated by Hungarian Jewish immigrants. They even published the paper in Hungarian. I only know two Hungarian words: Goulash and paprika. There were two occupations in that little place, one of them was eating and the other was playing pinochle.

One man who played pinochle was there recovering from a treatment at Mayo Clinic. He was Jewish and an officer in the Hungarian Army. We got talking and he said he was going into New York tomorrow to arrange passage.

I said, "Aren't you a little crazy?"

"What do you mean?"

"You're a Hungarian. You're a Jew. You know that Hitler is running and has already invaded Hungary."

He said. "I'm an army officer. Hitler authorized and sent me to the United States for the Mayo clinic. They're paying my bills. I'm expected to go back."

My other contact was earlier than that. I was visiting my Alma Mater and the dean asked to see me.

He said, "We have a request to nominate somebody for a graduate scholarship at Frankfurt, and we sent in your name. Every indication is that you're going to be offered the scholarship. You can get a PhD and actually get paid for it."

I said "Dr. Kent, are either you or the regents at Frankfurt unaware that I'm Jewish?"

That was something that they should have recognized and considered. In those days it wasn't really anti-Semitism in the way we think of it today, but Jews were unwelcome in American professional schools just because they were Jewish. That's why so many doctors of my generation, and especially my father's, are graduates of foreign medical schools.

"There was no competition," he said. "If you go to Frankfurt, you're considered an American." He said to me, "You ought to change your name."

I didn't go to medical school. Later I was to find out that was a stupid thing. I spent just as much time and I got my doctorate degree from a medical school, but it was in psychology, not in medicine.

When I visited Israel, I went to see someone who might have been a relative of my wife. We got his name from a fourteenth cousin by marriage. When we got to Israel we went to visit him. As a matter of fact, we stayed with him for two nights when we were going south, and a night coming back. He was a survivor of the Holocaust and much perturbed over the fact that his two sons, after serving their two years in the reserves, had stayed in the military. He wouldn't have a gun in the house, and guns are all over in Israel. Violence is never the answer to anything.

I spent six years with the Office of Naval Research supervising grants and aids to research universities. I covered the United States east of the Mississippi. When I left there, I went to work for an Air Force contractor. I visited Air Force bases around the world working on contracts and conferences. When my daughter was in England, I'd go to France and Holland and then England to visit her.

In 1978, I was on staff at the Veterans hospital in New York City, and one day I was reading the New York Times. There was an add for a faculty position in Australia. I wrote an application for it and, low and behold, over the course of time they offered me the job. So I resigned from the VA.

The chief said, "You're crazy. Everybody knows you'll never stop working."

I said "Charlie, we have a written policy that says you'll retire at sixty-five."

"You're more than sixty-five and nobody is asking you to retire. If they do, all I have to do is write one short note asking for an exemption and it will be granted. It won't even have to go to Washington."

"I'm leaving, anyhow."

"Now tell me why."

"I'm going to Australia to teach. I had no intention of quitting work."

I was in Australia with my wife for a little less than three years. In Australia education is free. That includes, college, graduate school, and professional schools. I lived close to the desert in Australia, not in it, but close to it. It was an area that knew almost no crime. I remember one time when I locked my car up, someone said, "What are you doing that for?"

"Because the insurance says."

He laughed. "Suppose they sold the car, where are they going to go? They'd run out of fuel before they got to the next petrol station.

Things have changed. Anyplace I've ever been, they've changed. Including Afghanistan, where I've never been.

When I came back from Australia, I had two offers waiting for me. Before long I was teaching and then I went into consulting.

You have to know something about expert consultants. An expert is somebody who has a briefcase and is at least fifty miles from home. Somebody once asked me, "How is it I run into you in Singapore or Arizona when you live in New York? Nobody from New York ever called me. They get somebody from Australia.

This is true. I got to Florida that way. I was called on a case. I said, "Tell me what you're after."

He told me and I said, "I know at least three people in Florida who can do that for you."

He said, "I know six, but I want *you*."

"Okay, I'll come down. Since it's more than two hundred miles, I fly first class, and you need to buy tickets for two because I'm bringing my wife with me. Make sure you make a reservation in a hotel that has a swimming pool."

Anyway, I got here and I ended up staying.

Then, for a ten-year period when my wife was ill and required attention, I turned down all sorts of jobs. I had a housekeeper who said, "That's silly, I'm here. You can go."

I wouldn't leave my wife and finally I said, "Oh, to hell with it. I'm not going to do it anymore."

Once, after my wife died, I was loading the motor home to go away. I said to my son, "Since you're coming with me, I want to make the twin beds." I gave him the sheet but he couldn't see what I was handing him. It was Friday. I called my doctor and got some nonsense to take him to the hospital because it was after five. I ended up rushing him to Brandon. He was there seven hours with the story that they couldn't do anything, or find anybody who could.

They gave me a number, and said, "At eight tomorrow morning you call this guy."

"Tomorrow is Saturday."

They said, "He'll answer the telephone."

Well, at eight in the morning he called me and he said, "Get him over here."

It ended up he couldn't do it, and he sent me to a young woman in Tampa. Anyway, he had surgery three times. In the process, everybody kept saying, "You can't let him live alone."

I had a big house. He could have lived with me, but we decided to go into an assisted living place together. I went to the best one I knew, but we both hated it so I bought this house.

There's an old saying, "If you give a man a fish, he eats for a day. If you teach him how to fish, he'll spend his time in a rowboat with a six-pack of beer fishing." Seriously though, I'm critical of failure to recognize that I am my brother's keeper. I contribute to charities.

If I'm going to give the money away, I want to decide where it's going. What I want to do is form a charity of my own for two purposes. I make my contributions to Jewish organizations. I'm touched by the Holocaust museum of which I'm a charter member.

I have an obligation. I have a son who is disabled, and he doesn't earn any money. I guess twenty years ago he could have gone back to work, but he doesn't really want to. I don't believe that you have to earn your bread by the sweat of your brow. I have to see that he's taken care of.

I won't spend money to get contributions. I got a brochure, an annual report from somebody I gave a thousand dollars. But I added up all the numbers. I'm assuming that it all went for a good cause but last year they spent $349,000 and their expenses were $613,000. I'm not saying that's bad—I'm just saying it's a shame. I'm going to form a charity that makes sure it doesn't spend all that money.

Some circumstances are entirely unmet. There are cases where social agencies meet part of a need, but by their rules, there's an unmet part.

Here is an illustration. There's a woman who's a paraplegic and an agency will pay for a scooter, a motorized wheelchair, but not a ramp to get into the house. When I bought a scooter for my wife, medicare paid for it, but I had to build a ramp, which was not covered.

The other kind of situation that concerns me is not at all infrequent. If someone has to vacate their house today because it's unlivable, there are organizations that will pay for temporary housing. But they have to go in and apply, and a social worker has to visit. They need help immediately, or they will end up being homeless.

I used to volunteer for the community. We have an ambulance service that is better than the paid one. Until fairly recently we had a volunteer fire department. There are volunteers at the hospital and organizations that tutor children for whom English is a second language. They have all the volunteers they need. They stopped calling on me way back when my wife was sick.

Seniors in Sun City Center flood the education opportunities. We have two great lecture series going, staffed by professional people. I still teach classes on occasion.

In 1950 I got diagnosed with diabetes. I saw the internist whose office was next to mine. He gave me two books to read.

I said, "Vinny, you read those? You're the specialist."

"Every word."

"Okay, just tell me what's in them."

I did what the book said, I bought a scale and I weighed everything for about two weeks. Every single meal should consist of one-third vegetables, one-third protein, and one-third carbohydrates. After a couple weeks, we went out to lunch together.

I said, "I'm doing what the book says. The problem is, I'm hungry all the time."

"So eat more."

"Wait a minute, you said three ounces."

"Make it the same proportion, make it four. I say this in very specific terms because I expect people to cheat a little, but you took me so literally that you're not getting enough."

The truth of the matter is that in six months I lost fifty-six pounds and I've never put a pound of it back on. It still says that I'm diabetic and insulin dependant on my doctors' records, but I've stopped taking the medicine.

During that session in the nursing home, they pumped more and more and more insulin into me, even though I screamed at them that you don't know what you're doing. If pushing insulin pushes the numbers up, maybe you should take less insulin.

Except for that period, I haven't actually taken it, even though they give me a bottle to carry around. It gets thrown out because it's two years expired. When I go back to have it filled, they can't refill it so I go back to the doctor and he writes me a new prescription. I never use it, but he the law says I can't have the other things unless I take it. It's there if I need it. I measure my blood sugar faithfully. Every once in a while it's high enough to take insulin. I wait until tomorrow morning and if it's still up, then I'll take the insulin.

From time to time I was taking medicine, but when I went up to New Jersey I stopped taking it. I never felt better, especially stopping the painkillers. When they prescribe pain medicine, I try to point something out to them. "I'm not asking you to stop the pain, I'm asking for a diagnosis of what causes the pain, so I can get at it."

I substituted herbal medicine for it—not that I trust herbal medicine in this country. You never know what's in the bottle. I had surgery, had some plumbing redistributed. I'm not as young as I used to be, but then I never was.

I follow the common rules, don't eat pork, don't eat a lot of beef, and don't eat fried foods. If I go into Brandon, I'm as likely as not to eat at Sweet Tomatoes. I eat vegetables and low fat foods. Remember, stick with the gardening.

I used to hear patients say they can't exercise. I say, "Push a vacuum cleaner." I swim and I play golf, and I look at the Thai Chi video and do some of it. And I walk. I travel, visit, eat, play golf, swim, and read. I used to spend my vacations, and still do to some extent, at Elder Hospice.

The good old days, they're different. I'm not sure if they're better or worse. It's true that in other societies, and even some sub cultures in our country, we still support extended families rather than depend on social security. As an individual ages, he's going to have some functions deteriorate. My vision certainly isn't what it was thirty years ago. My hearing isn't even what it was two years ago. My health is fine.

I'm going to Toronto next week. I'm going myself because my son doesn't want to go. I'll be visiting some distant relatives of my wife. We correspond. I'm driving because I hate public transportation of any kind. Not because of September 11th. Public transportation has become a nuisance. I can't stand the scheduling, I can't stand having to get from here to the airport, or having to get a hotel. I took the motor home to New Jersey last month."

JULIE DEANE, AGE 93

Working Out
Queens, New York

Julie had found a flyer I had left in the Kings Point Community Center gym. She brought it home but didn't contact me until a month later when her daughter Blanch, who was visiting, saw the flyer and encouraged her to call.

J ulie's home has tan brick with matching stucco. There are large hibiscus plants and oak trees in the yard. The home is moderately sized and kept immaculate. The couch and chairs have a flowered design with green leaves, and silk plants match the furniture. There are religious icons, photos of old houses, and a pelican picture on the wall.

Julie is a short woman who stands straight. She has only a hint of wrinkles around her mouth. She hears well, and doesn't wear glasses. Soon after I arrived, she showed me the small diamond ring that she still wears and told me she'd been widowed twenty-three years.

"I have no interest in dating what so ever—are you interested?" She laughed. "I'm not alone. I have the most wonderful neighbors. They are so caring. If they don't see a light on, they ask me, "Are you all right?" They watch out for me because I go out by myself. I like to go shopping and roam around the stores.

I have an article that was in the paper about me," she said in a distinct New York accent. "It's titled *Julie Deane's 87 Reasons to Work Out*. If possible I work out everyday for forty-five minutes to an hour. I do it religiously. I like to do it and I feel it does something for me.

I get up in the morning and I like a good breakfast. One morning I'll have my eggs, my toast, my fruit and my vitamin. Then the next day I'll have my cereal, oatmeal, my fruit, and my vitamin.

I've been a vitamin person ever since the forties when we had a nutritionist, Carlton Fredricks, up in New York. He was very good, and spoke about what good foods you should eat. I've always followed it. He said to take wheat germ, which is very healthy.

Carlton Fredricks was a smoker and he could never stop smoking. He died of lung cancer—he was so addicted to it. I never smoked. I remember one time when I put a cigarette in my mouth and I wondered how could people have that taste in their mouth? Some people crave it I guess.

I always have fruit. I eat about two in the afternoon. I eat a salad every day. In the morning I have barley greens. You have to send away for it. It prevents you from getting any illness. My daughter had leukemia so she started taking it. I have that every morning. Then at night, if I feel like it, I have half a sandwich or fruit.

I enjoy cooking. I cook everything. I made Swedish meatballs. I grated potatoes and onion in it. I put egg and a little flour. I put a little nutmeg in it, and allspice, and salt. Then I took a beef bullion cube and thickened it to make gravy. I never made that recipe before. I didn't know what to make for dinner, so I thought I'd try something a little different. We're going to go out today for fish. When I go out to eat, I prefer a fish dinner, but I do like beef and prime ribs.

I go to bed early. I require about nine hours sleep. I'm working out in the mornings because my daughter is here, but I usually go up about four-thirty so I won't interrupt the day. I started doing this after my husband passed away. I always stay the same weight. I get on the scale and I'm 124. I went on a scale and the nurse said I'm five feet. I lost my two inches. I need them.

I'm healthy. When you exercise, you get more muscles instead of flabby. I do sixty sit-ups, twenty each time. I pull the weights down, the rowing machine, bike, and treadmill. There are so many things you can do.

I take a thyroid pill, but otherwise I'm in good health. I have no illness and don't take any other medication. I have macular degeneration in this eye, but I've got 20/20 vision in the other eye. The lid is beginning to droop and I'm going to have eye surgery on this eye. The doctor is going to lift it up. It isn't noticeable, but my vision is blocked. I have arthritis but it doesn't bother me. I never have pain.

I drive. I shop. I love to read. I could read all day. I read newsletters and everything that comes in the mail, but I don't have time to read books. I do my housework. The day goes so fast.

I like the radio better than TV. I like the news, and talk shows, and learning people's opinions, don't you? I listen to CNN and people talking about politics. I love to hear the controversies when different people call. They talk about the trouble in Israel. When people can't get along and be peaceful, it's sad.

Religion is a very difficult...politics and religion; you can get into more trouble. I'm Catholic and go to church on Sunday. I have the blessed Mother on my necklace, the mother of God.

I love living in Kings Point. We go on bus trips, too. I have a cousin who goes with me. We go to flea markets, Sarasota Arts Center. We go out and have lunch and the bus trip. While my daughter is here, I'm going to go with her to see my sister in Sarasota. I just drive locally to Ruskin, shopping, and I drive to church every Saturday afternoon. I pick up my cousin and we go together."

*   *   *   *

"The world has changed drastically. I think we lived our best years in the past. Those were beautiful years, raising the children. It's such a changed world in so many respects. Then there was war, but Roosevelt brought in income for the poor people. I think that was wonderful. I do. He had polio, but from what I can remember, he did wonderful things. We don't know what the future is now. The new millennium is changing.

When I was young, we didn't have electric lights. We had gas lamps, and on Queens Boulevard the people came along and lit them up. There weren't many cars back then at all. My father bought a car in 1925. He drove the car, but I don't think he had a licence. I remember the bathrooms. You had the pull a chain to flush the toilet.

All this happening since September 11th brings back memories. The depression was terrible. It seems like it was only yesterday. People were desperate then. Nobody had money for food. The milkman brought milk to the door. Children ran down the street and when you went outside, your milk was gone.

I think schools have changed a lot. When we went to school, the subjects we studied were good for us. What they teach today, the children don't even know anything about our own country. We had geography, history, arithmetic, and reading. At the time I went to school, there were two teachers in the room. I remember Mrs. Feldman. There was the seventh grade here, and the eighth grade there. She would assign us work to do, while she taught this class. We had fifteen in the class, and we learned.

I finished high school, and then I went to work. I worked for the American Express on 65 Broadway in New York. I worked for them for nine years.

I got married in 1929 during the depression. I lived in this apartment, got married, and paid forty-five dollars a month. It was an expensive apartment. It was only one bedroom and bath, but it was brand new. A lot of the people couldn't pay their rent. Some people with two children were living in the back apartment. They were paying thirty-five dollars a month, but he lost his job so they moved. A lot of people in the whole complex weren't paying rent. When these people moved out I asked the janitor if I could have that apartment for the same amount. So I got in for thirty-five dollars. We were lucky because I had a job. I was getting fifty dollars a month and my husband was getting sixty a month. He was working on a tugboat in New York harbor. So we made out good.

We bought our first car in 1939. We paid eleven hundred for a new car. When they predicted that in years to come things would be so much more expensive, it was hard to believe. We paid ten cents for a loaf of bread then, and milk was so cheap. Everything was reasonable. I guess you get paid in comparison to your expenses at that time.

I had three children. I got pregnant and didn't work after that. I have eight grandchildren and nine great-grandchildren. I can tell you all their names and birthdays. I think the children were more disciplined then. They weren't rowdy. They were brought up nicely and respected adults.

We moved around some, but then lived in Brooklyn for twenty-four years raising the children. We sold that house and moved to Marathon, down by the Keys, and then Cape Coral. We bought two hotels there. My husband was retired and we wanted to come down to warm weather.

We drove over the Everglades to get to the Keys. That has changed so. The old Everglades you could see everything, including the alligators. Men were fishing for the catfish. But today it's being built up.

My mother died when she was seventy-three. It was an unfortunate accident. She fell down the stairs. My father lived to be eighty-seven. He had a heart pacer and was disabled I had two sisters and a brother and I'm the oldest. One sister passed away three years ago from cancer of the colon. My other sister is in a nursing home in Sarasota. It is a very nice home.

I write her letters once or twice a week. I love to write letters. I used to go often, but I can't go up to see her with my macular degeneration. They are closing the nursing home and she needs to move out, so my daughter is staying to help. We may move her to Brooksville. My brother is in that home. He lives in Brooksville near his daughter. His wife died suddenly last year.

I was a volunteer for fifteen years in Cape Coral. I took care of patients. When their food came, I'd help them. I helped the nurses. It's very interesting. I met all these volunteers. They're all so giving, so dedicated to the hospital. They raise so much money with the benefits when they have cake sales and jewelry sales, everything. They make about a hundred thousand dollars a year. They still send me the literature, but I don't know any of the people anymore.

When my husband passed away, he died of cancer of the kidneys, the children said, "Mom, when are you going to sell the house?"

It was on the river, a beautiful spot. It had a large lawn and too much responsibility. I was glad to get rid of it. After I sold my house, I came here and I liked it. I wanted something with a garage. The real estate woman showed me this, and it was all furnished.

I have silk tree and silk flowers, no real plants. I don't take care of animals, and I don't take care of plants. I just go and I don't want to bother anybody. I think stress brings on aging. I don't get angry. It's just not in me, I guess.

I had a face-lift when I was eighty-seven. They did my eyes. I get wrinkles around my mouth, and they can't do anything about them. How do you get rid of them?"

"Do you want to live to be old?" I asked.

"No," Julie said firmly. "Whenever God's ready to take me, I'm ready."

"Mom is funny," Julie's daughter, Blanch, said. "She'll be with an eighty-five year old and she'll say, 'You're so young'."

"Several people didn't have anybody to travel with," Julie continued. "So after my husband passed away, I went with them. I went to Hawaii, Poland, and Italy.

In June I stay with my daughter in New Jersey until September. All the family is up there, and I get to see them. We got up in the morning September 11th, the day I was supposed to leave. Someone called us and said, "Put the TV on." That's when we found out what was happening. We knew people who died. In Stratton Island, thirty firemen died. It was a terrible tragedy. I felt terrible. It was unbelievable that anything like this could happen in this country. It was unbelievable. I was very upset. I had a flight that was the day after, and I had to cancel it for another flight five days later. Coming back on that plane in New York, I was in terrible stress. Blanch dropped me off at the airport and got me a wheelchair. I didn't need one, but they took care of me. The crash was on my mind. The crash. It took me two days after I got home to get it out of my system. The side of my face was flickering. I thought I might be having a small stroke. I was under terrible stress."

Julie paused and then changed the topic. "I have the most wonderful daughter, and the most wonderful family. My family is the most important thing to me, and my faith."

"What you give, you get back. She's wonderful too," Blanch said. "She's the best mother you could have. She's very giving and helps people. Whatever you need, she'll give."

"That's what life is all about," Julie stated, "to give love and give yourself to others. Isn't it true? If we had more of that on this earth, everybody would be happier. It would be a peaceful life."

JOHN & MARIE
DONNELLY, AGE 95 & 70

Newlyweds
Burlington, Iowa

I wasn't sure how to title this chapter, ping-pong pro or newly-weds. I found John through a newspaper article in the Sun City Center paper. It wouldn't have mattered if I had never seen the article, as he was known by many people in Sun City Center, and at least three or four people gave me John's name, saying "this is the guy you MUST interview." When I called, John wanted to meet me at my house. Although I declined, nobody else had made that offer before. John checked his calendar and said he could squeeze me in for an hour the following week.

John lives in a large white stucco house with white trim. It is located in a wealthy area of Sun City Center, where each house on the block has a flag flying in front. When I arrived, a man was mowing the lawn. The landscaping and lawns in this neighborhood are all professionally kept. A sign in the front of the house greeted me with "Welcome to the Donnelly's."

John opened the door and introduced himself and his wife Marie. He was wearing a beige T-shirt displaying the State of Arizona, and shorts. He doesn't wear glasses and his hearing is sharp. John is bald, except for around the edges, which is several inches long. Only a few age spots on his otherwise smooth skin give away his age, which appears closer to eighty than ninety-five. Marie is a slim woman who wears glasses. Her brown hair is starting to fade to a lighter shade, but isn't showing much gray. She was wearing a shirt with embroidered butterflies. Being newlyweds still on their honeymoon, John and Marie held hands and gave each other meaningful, loving looks throughout much of the interview.

The high arched ceiling gives the full-sized living room an extra large appearance. A floor to ceiling mirror filling up one full wall further exaggerates the open space in the room. The furniture is a contemporary flower pattern.

"You're timing is perfect," John began. "I just got back from my massage."

"Did you both get massages?" I asked.

"No," Marie said. "I didn't. I get one every other time. He goes weekly."

"I hear you two are newlyweds."

"Yes, we are," she said. "I just turned seventy."

"I'm ninety-five."

"You're robbing the cradle, so to speak," I replied.

"I need her to keep me going." John squeezed Marie's hand under the table.

"That's what he says." Marie laughed.

"How long have you been married?"

"Since June 10th last year. Almost eight months," Marie replied. "We knew each other for about six months."

"Getting to be old stuff," John laughed.

"What's it like to be on a honeymoon at ninety-five years old?"

"Well, it isn't 150%, but it is 100%. We went to Don Cesar's for a long weekend. It's a big old hotel in St. Petersburg."

"It was a blessing that we didn't go away for our honeymoon," Marie said. "Four days after we were married I had a gall bladder attack. I never had gall bladder problems before. I had back surgery just before we got married."

"I lost my wife in 1989. I was living in a retirement home, and she died three months after we moved in there. I lived there twelve years, then I met this lovely lady and I moved right out."

"I had this house."

"I'm paying rent. A pretty good rent," John said.

"All you're doing is helping. I lost my husband twenty years ago and made it fine on my own."

"Marie was only forty-eight when her husband died," John said. "We met because I'm a Good Samaritan and take people who can't drive to the doctor. I was taking a lady to the eye doctor and was sitting there, and a friend of mine was sitting here, and they got talking. She got up to go and I said, "Are you married?"

She said, "No," so I said, "I'll call you up." I asked her to go to a dance with me that night, but she wanted to check me out with the lady first."

"This was a real estate agent," Marie said, "and fortunately I was lucky this time that I was listening. I called the real estate agent, and didn't get her right away, but I kept calling until I got her.

"Who is this guy, John Donnelly?"

And she said, "I've known him for twenty years and he's very nice. You'll have a lot of fun with him because he loves arts, theatre, and opera."

"Did he tell you how old he was?" I asked.

"No, but I knew he was older. I would have guessed eighty. I didn't really think of age until we got more serious, and then my friends asked, "Do you know what you're getting in for?"

I said, "I don't care. We love each other so much it doesn't matter."

"I got a little write up about myself in the Senior Connections magazine," John said. "I was elected the healthiest citizen in three counties. Did you see it?"

"No, I saw the one on table tennis and called information. I called a John Donnelly and he said, 'No, you have the wrong one, but I had lunch with him last week.' He gave me your number."

"You had to send in a three-hundred word essay about yourself, and here is what I sent in." John popped up and down, looking for the magazine articles about himself. "This is my Christmas letter that I wrote that tells about me.

They have five-year age brackets in the senior games, which are for people over fifty years old. They have a national tournament every other year and I've been to five of them: Syracuse, New York; Baton Rouge, Louisiana; San Antonio, Texas; Tucson, Arizona; and Orlando, Florida. I got a gold metal every time, but there are only two or three people left in my age bracket. There are five hundred table tennis players, but only three in my age bracket of ninety-five to one hundred. With only three people, you get a metal just for going. Gold, silver, or bronze, you get one for sure. I got a first twice and three times I got the silver. The first time I went, I was ninety-one and there were six or seven of us. It's been every other year. Next year it's going to be in Hampton Rhodes, Virginia. I hope I can go. I won't drive that far, but we go down to Sarasota and Tampa a lot."

"He is so busy," Marie said. "One guy interviewing him said, 'Even Forest Gump couldn't keep up with him. I don't know how his wife keeps up with him.' He's going all the time."

Marie brought his calendar to show me John's schedule, which was full everyday for four months ahead.

"I get up about seven on Monday. Wednesday, Friday, and Saturday to play table tennis. I started table tennis in 1980. I came down here and there was a big billboard outside that said '132 scheduled activities in Sun City Center'."

I said, "Where's table tennis?"

"We don't have it."

"So I put an add in the paper 'Anyone who wants to play table tennis call John Donnelly.'

Ten guys answered me. The first year we were in the back room of our church playing on one table. Then they found a place for us and we got five nine hundred dollar tables. We play four times a week.

I was interested in table tennis way back in high school. After that, I didn't play for a number of years. When I was a stockbroker in Cedar Rapids Iowa, a young man came to work who liked to play. We would go to the YMCA and play for about half an hour every night. He was a good player.

Two days a week I pitch horseshoes, and the third morning I sing in a chorus. My singing voice is still good enough for the Lake Towers chorus."

"He sings pretty good," Marie interjected. "He sings in church every Sunday. We try to go swimming in the afternoon. We walk a mile every morning, and he plays chess. We go out all the time to the ballet and theatre."

"We square dance twice a week. I'm poor at it," John said.

"Well, you're just taking lessons," his wife said. "Can you imagine starting to learn square dance at ninety-five? You know, that's pretty good."

"I belong to a poetry club which meets once a month," John said. "I want to get my poetry organized into a little book. I want about twenty copies for my family. I don't know when I'm going to get the time.

I'm in charge of a monthly church newsletter. They want to save postage, so I have about seventy people deliver the paper. We put that paper together the last Tuesday of every month. Then we deliver the papers. I've been in charge of doing that for about ten years. There are people who can't work so I always have to find new people. Calling people gives me a little something to do. I do everything. Three guys, including myself, take nine hundred papers and pile them up in twenty-six piles for people to deliver. I deliver papers to the hospital portion of Lake Towers."

*   *   *   *

"I was born in Burlington Iowa, a small town of about thirty thousand people. I remember as a boy one of the main businesses was the livery stable where you could rent horses and carriages to go places. I remember the ice wagon trucks, and we would hang around and get chips of ice to put in our mouths. There have been big changes. Well, computers are the biggest invention. And cellophane.

I had two sisters but both are gone now. I was the oldest. Marie was an only child. I had a family reunion down here two years ago at Christmas time. My sister came and she died shortly thereafter. I was glad I had the chance to see her.

I got a bachelors degree at the University of Iowa, and had a bit of graduate work, but not enough to get a degree. The year before I graduated, in 1929, out of 150 men graduating in economics school, everyone got a job, and the next year nobody got a job. I was making money working around the campus using a carpet washing machine. I was making a good living at it.

I became a stockbroker. I was one of the first fifty people hired by the social security administration in 1935 out in the field. They picked two from every state—a manager and a servile went out into the state and started writing social security numbers.

The year after I graduated, my first wife was doing graduate work in violin. I'm the only University of Iowa student that went to all the recitals one year, just because he wanted to hear the music. She had to go because she was a graduate student. I sat down beside her and took her home. That was when it all started.

We were married fifty-five years and had three kids. My daughter lived in Spain for twenty years. We traveled to Europe fourteen times and visited her. We went almost every other year. We were members of the Chicago Counsel on Foreign Relations for several of those years, and they would hire a charter plane to take the members to London or Rome, and bring us back from Paris or Berlin. We were on our own for two weeks of that time. We always ended up in Madrid to visit my daughter. She came back in 1980 after her husband died. She's been a great comfort to me.

My son, John, was an economic professor at the Washington State University. He retired a couple of years ago and moved to Tacoma, California. He's very active in an organization called Seeds of Learning. He's a very good craftsman, does beautiful woodwork, and he's been down to Salvador building schoolhouses with Seeds of Learning.

My other son lives in New Jersey, and works in New York City. He was in the first big bomb blast in the World Trade Center. It took him two hours to get out of the building. He moved out of there about a year ago working for an engineering firm uptown, but he had an appointment that very afternoon in the World Trade Center. He has two children.

My mother died at age forty. She had a strangulated bowel and had successful surgery. She was getting better, but they didn't have antibiotics and she died of an infection. It was the only time I saw my father cry. My father had a brain tumor at age sixty. He had an operation on his head at the Mayo clinic in Rochester in February, and seemed to be doing pretty well for several months, but it came back in August and he died in early December.

My wife and I moved into the retirement home and she got sick a month later. She was in the hospital for the last ten days.

My health is pretty darn good. I have minor problems, but I'm still healthy. I've always been in love with somebody. I had a girl friend for years after my wife died, but it didn't work out. We're good friends again because after she left I met this lovely lady. Now we're all together. We play bridge and go to concerts together. With Marie, it was absolutely love at first sight. But I thought, no chance, she's already married."

"I told you I wasn't."

"I know, but I wondered ahead of time, before I even asked you."

"He's so nice. It works together."

"A lot of my friends are dead now, but I'm pretty active in the life of the community. If I die, ten or fifteen people will probably come to my funeral."

"A lot more than that," Marie said. "It was funny, when I first started going with him he would say, 'I know this person, I know that person.' If we got into a discussion with anybody, there was always somebody who knew him. He knows a lot of people at church and people in town."

I added, "I notice you said *if* you die. It sounds as though you're not planning on that."

"Not exactly. Not any particular day. Our immediate plan is to go to Spain in October. My grandson in Denver Colorado is going to get married in Spain, in the church where my daughter was married. I'm looking for a young chick you know."

"Marie, you have no gray in your hair. Is that your natural color?" I changed the topic, ignoring John's comment.

"Yes. I wouldn't do anything to it until I have to. They call it a mousy brown. I've got a little bit of gray just starting in the front.

If you want to know something, older men take good care of you. They don't want you to run off with anybody else."

"Will you stay?" John asked with mock concern.

"You don't have to worry about that. You're married to me so I won't go running off. He'd better take good care of me."

John concluded. "I wish I could give you some big secret of success. I occasionally have a social drink, but not much. I never smoked a lot. I just smoked a cigarette on the way to work, at lunch, but not at home. I quit in 1950, when I was about forty-five years. I eat judiciously. I like chicken and fish, and ham once in a while. I drink a lot of cranberry juice. For eight years I've gotten a massage once a week—that's one of my secrets of success."

Tony Grillo, 94

A conversation over breakfast
New York

John Donnelly referred Tony to me. The two men go to the same massage therapist, but have never met each other. Tony said he had a busy day and invited me to join him for breakfast. We met at his house, and I was the passenger while he drove to his favorite restaurant.

I met Tony at his small white stucco house with sky blue trim. Tony had landscaped the yard with a small rose garden and cactus plants. He is tall, thin, balding man wearing a long-sleeved checkered country shirt with red suspenders and a navy blue sports cap. His most noticeable feature is his smile. After a few minutes introduction, he decided he'd prefer to drive since I didn't know the way to his favorite breakfast place.

Once seated and having looked at the menu, he began talking. "I eat anywhere from fifteen to eighteen eggs a week. I love eggs. I started way back when we had chickens. I would make a hole on each end of the egg and blow it out.

I don't eat at home—too lazy to wash the pots and pans. My house-keeper comes in once every two weeks to clean up. I have a new stove, which I use for storage, and I rarely use the toaster oven. I have a new refrigerator. Many people say, "Nothing like home cooking." It all depends on who's cooking. When a man cooks, he doesn't cook like a lady. She may say a pinch of this, or that much—how much is a pinch?"

The waitress arrived and Tony ordered, "I think I'll have three eggs, grits, toast, and give me a little bacon.

I was having coffee at night, too. My buddy is a nature-pathic doctor who also gives acupuncture. He told me not to take anything with coffee. I try to keep away from the coffee. I didn't give up smoking cigars because the doctor told me to. I gave them up because they were ninety cents. Now they're over six dollars. The only thing I'm taking is Coumadin. The doctor is concerned that I might get a blood clot because I had a heart attack years ago.

I eat what my body says. What does my body say tonight? "Too early," it might say. One night it may want chop suey, the next night Italian food, and the next night a steak, or rack of lamb. All of a sudden I get the bright idea that I might want chicken tonight. I go to Colonel Sanders Kentucky Fried Chicken to get some fried chicken. I eat some fruits and vegetables, about half and half. I'm not too keen on them.

One thing I always believe in is having a good breakfast. I don't believe in having a donut and a cup of coffee. I'd just as soon drink herb tea, chamomile, peppermint, or sleepy-time. My cholesterol is 160. I have three eggs."

"Everyday?"

"No, not everyday, sometimes I have four.

When they talk about bacon, they give bacon to a poor little mouse that weighs two ounces, and they tell a guy like me, a six-footer, not to eat bacon. You'd have to eat a ton of it to hurt you.

To stay healthy, eat three times a day. In the morning you eat like a king, noon a prince, night a pauper. It takes six hours to digest a meal.

I eat very slowly. When you go to sit down in a restaurant, what are you rushing? I may have problems from a big heavy meal at night. If I eat meat once a week, that's a lot. Growing up, if there wasn't meat on the table we didn't eat.

Doctors' info you can throw out the window. Eat what your body says—ask your body. Best not to overeat. You can eliminate that if you eat a regular meal and appetizer or a meal and a desert.

Eat a little of everything. Fruit, vegetables are good for you. Some fish. You couldn't be healthy on a doctor's limited meal. Taking vitamins is a good idea too. My naturopathic doctor said eat all the eggs you want, so I eat three or four steady.

When we're going out, people say, "Let's find out first what Tony's body is asking for." They know me by heart.

I might say, "Tonight I can go for anything—fish, meat, rack of lamb, pink salmon."

Sometimes my doctor says, "You don't listen to me at all."

So I said, "How many other patients do you have my age?"

"Don't think I have any."

I listen to my body. The doctor says, "You must be doing something right."

Staying healthy is very easy.

When I was young, I was working with my brain. Then I could do anything, whether I was playing basketball or anything. But when I got to be about eighty years old, I started listening to my body. My brain would say, "You can do that—you've been doing it for years," but the body says, "No, you can't play the way you did. You have to play nice and easy." I very seldom use the word "old."

Exercise, yes. I find something to do. Too many men I see sit in front of the idiot box TV and do that. They don't do anything, then they can't get up." Tony stood up and touched his toes. "When I see a man with his belly sticking out, I know he takes good care of his automobile, but he doesn't care for his body. He just forgets about it. I exercise every morning. I don't do anything strenuous, because you really start feeling your aches and pains about eighty years old. You don't want to strain yourself. I'm not out to build muscles anymore. I want to keep the ones that I have nice and flexible. I do old fashioned exercises that I started in grade school, move arms up and down, and kick your legs up and down, try to bring your knees to your chin, but they don't go that far any more. Stretching exercise is very important. I do that before I get out of bed, stretch one leg and then the other one. I have a friend who is seventy-five and can't get up, but he looks at the idiot box most of the day.

I walk to the golf course. I quit playing two years ago because the doctor told me to keep away from the sun. I had skin cancer removed from my nose. That's why I wear long sleeves. How can you play golf and not be out in the sun? I also go to the recreation building,

No matter how well you take care of yourself, you still go down. You loose your hair, and the eyes go, you lose your teeth. I have my own teeth on the bottom but a plate up here.

The funny thing, I have a whole day to do something, and sometimes I'm too busy to get a haircut (I had quite a bit at one time, and it was black). I was busy yesterday doing paperwork, getting my figures together for my income tax. This morning I took the sheets off the bed and took the laundry down to have it done. Today I'm going to the bank and then I'll pick the laundry up this afternoon. I wouldn't be surprised if when I get home, somebody will have called to ask to go for a ride, go out to lunch, or dinner.

Usually by twelve or twelve thirty, a friend calls up and says, "What about lunch?" I say, "Of course." I never like to miss a meal. I have to have three meals a day and snacks at night. I'll go out for lunch at one. I usually say one because restaurants are busy between twelve and one, and this guy is a fusspot.

I've been getting massages for years. Once I had something they call a Russian. It's on three different levels. One man is hitting you with a big bunch of leaves. Then there's another man who throws cold water on your head because you're in the steam room. The other is a Swedish massage. A regular massage.

I didn't know a thing about the computer, but I bought one anyway. I'm having a lot of fun with it. There was one night I ended up in Australia and the scenery was beautiful. I don't know how I got there, though. The first thing I learned was e-mail."

*   *   *   *

"I come from an Italian family. My father couldn't speak English. My mother passed away when I was four and I was the only child. I have a stepmother and she had four children. I saw them being born because I was already five years old when father got married again. I saw them all being born, and I saw them all pass-away. My father lived to eighty-one.

I never even finished grade school. I only made it to seventh grade. At that time I may have only been fifteen years old, but even at that age I could do plenty of work. Schooling in those days wasn't too important. A girl in an Italian family wouldn't even be considered to go to college, and a boy would have to show an awful lot of smartness before he could go to college.

I can remember when the boys were going to war in World War I. I was ten years old. I remember the war because of the soldiers. A boy from the neighborhood was leaving, and we gave him a party. I can always remember all the men getting together. There was no such thing as a woman being in a barroom at that time—it was all men. Us kids would sneak in, and they were singing and what not. World war I lasted four years, but we were only in one. The war started 1914, but we didn't go in until 1917. It was over in 1918.

World War II, they took me when I was thirty-six. I went to basic training. Good thing I was in good shape at that time. We had to go on an obstacle course, climb ropes, and jump over things. One morning they shipped me to another camp closer. Louisville was thirty miles away, so you could get a bus, but the buses were full. The next time I took a jalopy and went whenever I wanted.

One time a lieutenant had broken down, his car wouldn't start. I worked on it awhile. I was older than the young kids and I told him. "My rear end is dragging. Basic training is getting to be too much."

It's a good thing that I was a Good Samaritan and fixed that car. He gave me a card to go to classification, and told me to ask for Sergeant Mendel.

Sergeant Mendel said, "I think I can use you. It's very easy. You'll decode TWS, which is nothing but a telegram. I want somebody who can keep quiet and not tell anybody."

I said, "You're now talking to the three little monkeys, can't see, can't speak, can't hear."

I got a job in classification. Although it was only six months of my career in the Army, I enjoyed it.

In an Italian family, whatever the father is, a carpenter, an electrician, a plumber, the oldest son becomes the same. My father was a house builder, so I became a carpenter, a builder. I had to learn carpentry on the outside, how to balance beams. I worked for one fellow for two years. I didn't care to go to work very much. I was kind of stupid.

I knew about the building game now, but thought there's an easier way to make a living. I thought I'd try to sell. I had a friend in a real estate and insurance office. He lived quite a way from me. I said, "I'd like to establish an office in this area"

He said, "Sure." So he gave me a tip how to get into the insurance business. I didn't have to pay anything, but I had to represent his company.

Then I took a test to get my real estate license and it was easy because of my experience in building. The insurance test I failed the first time, but they give you another one in thirty days, in New York. For thirty days I sat and didn't leave the house, went over all the copies of policies, and read the fine print. I could have taken the insurance in small pieces, liability, and then take compensation, but no, I had to take the whole insurance test at one. The second time I passed it. I had my own insurance agency. That's what I stayed in the rest of my life.

We were starting out from scratch. I didn't have an office, so I'd have people call me at my house. The first year was a hard one, and the second was fair. The Mrs. was working and that helped. We could eat anyway. The third year I started seeing black ink instead of red ink. The first girl I hired was eighteen dollars a week.

What do you do when you get old age? You either have a lot of money or you get into stocks. That's what I did. One customer of mine came into my office, I said, "Dave, I want some kind of an income when I get older."

He said, "One way is to buy mutual funds or you can buy municipal bonds—they go for a long time, fifteen or twenty years. They pay a dividend every year."

I started about 1957 in Long Island. I had a few thousand dollars and I don't think there was anything less than 6 percent. Now, I just want the income coming in. That was the best thing I did in my life. It comes in steady, and I don't have to worry.

That's where I started. There's no better experience in the world than being in business and being with people. You can't find that in college. I have a lot of young friends who took out insurance with me. They went to college, but I'll be frank with you, they do very well with what they study, but the outside world, they don't know anything.

I married a girl who had five sisters. Not one of them had children. I was married thirty-eight years and my wife died in '85. You want to know something…seventeen years ago today, at this hour, I buried my wife. The eighth of February."

"Has it been difficult being alone?" I asked.

"No. At first it was. I walked in the house and the dinner is made, and my bed was made. Now I have to do it. I look at it this way, maybe the guys who get married again weren't really happy with the first wife, or they wouldn't want another one. Sometimes a couple brings someone along to make it a foursome, but I don't date. It wouldn't be the same. I don't want to live with anybody. I'm never lonesome.

I don't have a worry in the world. That's something else that's very, very important—don't get into anything where there's any stress. Some say money's everything. Naw, I know some very nice people who are living a nice life, but they don't need a bundle of income.

Being in the insurance business there's a lot of stress. I could take it, but right now if you gave me an agency that made a million dollars a year, and you gave it to me for nothing, I wouldn't want to take it. I don't want the stresses. I have enough money for one person. You read about a guy who makes seventeen million dollars in one year? He's not a happy man. Money doesn't make him any happier. Some of the richest people are the lousiest people to deal with.

I've been in England, Italy, Ireland, Switzerland, and across the country three times. You'll see the very best right here in your own country. Even though I've gone three times, I haven't seen anything of what you could see. Travel around the United States first, then Canada.

Brice Canyon is beautiful. It's fifty miles north of the Grand Canyon. You've never seen anything in your life like Brice Canyon. You're looking down toward the valley, and there's the mountain, and it's all different colors, orange, white, dark brown. In one place it looks like a steeple of a church, and it's all different colors, oh, what a sight! At Yellowstone I saw Old Faithful just on time.

Alaska, I went there too, and I'd like to go there again. And I might just do that. Thinking of Alaska, one morning I was talking to a couple of friends of mine and his wife brought up something about traveling, asking her husband to go somewhere.

By the time we got through, I said, "You got me to the point where I feel I should be going somewhere tomorrow morning. I don't even know where to go."

Somehow or other Alaska came up and I said, "That is a place I've never seen. I think I'd like to see it. Tomorrow morning I'm going to Alaska."

The lady said, "I'll come with you."

I said, "be ready about eight thirty; we'll go down to Kennedy airport."

I know she was kidding so I went alone. The funny part was I went down to Kennedy and went to the counter and said, "I'd like to go to Alaska. Do you have a ticket?"

"There is a flight in about twenty-five minutes. I can get you on that one if there's a cancellation."

"Ok, I'll be right around here."

I go over and have another breakfast.

She said, "Give me your name and I'll call you over the loud speaker."

I didn't get a call. When I went up there it was after twelve.

She said, "There's a flight going at five." So I did that.

But I forgot to tell you, when I had no ticket and couldn't go on that plane at noon. I said, "I'll tell you what—it doesn't matter if it's not Alaska. If you have a trip to Hawaii, I'll take that, too. There were a couple people behind me by that time. She leaned over and said, "Are you running away from somebody?"

I just felt like taking a trip. I always did take trips, at least one short trip a month. I'd go to Cape Cod, the Catskill Mountains, or Massachusetts. There are so many places in the Catskill Mountains to go. I go with a couple that likes to go to Biloxi. I'll gamble if I'm there, but for me to go out of my way to gamble, no. If I got a call right now when I get back home asking, "You want to go to Boston?" Sure.

I was like that all my life. Sometimes my wife would come home— we lived on the outskirts of New York City, so she'd come home Friday night and look pretty tired. I'd say, "No cooking, pack your suitcase and we're going down to the city."

We'd go Friday night and come home Sunday night. We'd stay in a motel, see a play, a good show, a good meal, taking the tours around New York City. We went there at least once a month, a couple of weekends. Things were cheap then. I was married in '38, and I went to a honeymoon in Havana. It was a very nice place.

My wife was such a Catholic. It was embedded in her. She went to Catholic grade school, high school, and college. If I went to church on a Sunday, that was enough. I don't have to go now because I'm old. When you reach a certain age, you don't have to go. You can be in your own bathroom and say a prayer from your heart, and it means more than somebody going to church seven days a week and saying a routine prayer with no meaning.

When I said I would like a youngster, her answer always was, "If God wanted us to have children, we would have children." She felt it would be talking against God. I think it was just the opposite. I think we would be happy to see two youngsters have a home. I could only go so far, or she'd get angry. I said, "We aren't going to live forever. Wouldn't be nice if we had a girl and a boy?" My problem is that my family is all gone, she's all gone, and her family is gone—every one of them.

That's my only mistake, I think. I don't know if I should blame my wife or myself. There were children in the orphanage, a cute little girl, and little boy. The nearest I could bring her to having youngsters in the house was on Christmas time and Thanksgiving. Back in the thirties, we would bring a boy and a girl from the orphanage. They'd be so excited, and we'd get a kick out of it, especially if we gave them four or five single dollar bills.

I'm the godfather of two youngsters. They're like my own. One girl takes care of my house just outside of New York City. I spend six months here and six months back home, although I never in my life made plans for anything, except for getting married and going on our honeymoon. I'll be doing something this summer, but I never plan. What I usually do is go to Cape Cod in the summer time for two or three days. I go on a Friday for a visit, and come home Monday. I have a lot of cousins in upstate New York. Jewish, Irish, German, Italian, you mention it, we have it. One place I enjoy has ballroom dancing.

You know that I've got a mind of my own. I'm not a follower. I put my watch on my right hand. Someone says to me, "Everybody wears their watch on the left arm."

I'm not everybody, I'm an individual. Everybody doesn't eat four eggs in the morning either. In the morning you're supposed to have eggs, or cereal, or oatmeal. I can have steak or spaghetti in the morning if I feel like eating that. I'm a little different from the average person.

I have a birthday coming up soon. I'll be ninety-five."

LAURA, AGE 97

Old Enough to Vote
Wayzata, Minnesota

Dorothy Apgar from the Newly Near Shop gave me her friend Laura's name, phone number, and age. Laura asked me not to use her last name, as she doesn't want to give her age away. Her last name is of French derivation.

Laura lives in an upstairs apartment. The stairs are narrow, with large gaps between each stair. There is no elevator. Numerous lighted model-homes were in her apartment window, giving it a festive appearance.

Laura was on the phone when I arrived. It was a long distance call to Wisconsin, and she talked for some time while I waited and had time to look around. Her living room looked like a 1900 museum display. She had Oriental and braided rugs on the floor. Numerous decorative plates and old photographs decorated the walls, and antique cranberry glass was in a display cabinet. Furniture, bought in antique stores, was an interesting mixture of gold, some red, and some blue with patterns. There was an old phonograph in the corner.

Laura appears to be a healthy woman in her late seventies, although Dorothy had told me she is ninety-eight. Laura was wearing a blue flowered overshirt, blue cotton slacks, and decorative slipper shoes. She is petite, her smooth skin is nearly wrinkle free, and her hands have only a hint of arthritis. She has some rounding in her back.

When Laura got off the phone, she explained, "They're friends of mine who are coming down from Wisconsin. They were here last year, and we had such a good time that they're coming down again the end of the month.

I keep my house and do my own work. It looks as though I don't do very well. I have my piano. I do my ironing. I do everything.

I did volunteer work at the woman's hospital here for a while. I worked in the gift shop, but I didn't like it. I went to Oregon and Washington for the summer, and when I came home I didn't go back. I'd like to volunteer at the library, but without transportation I stay home a lot. I'd have to walk a mile to get the bus. It's not safe to walk in this town. My friends and my niece take me.

I drove until I got scared a few years ago. It was on Dale Mabry [a major street with heavy traffic]. It was an old car. An old man was in the car and he turned right in front of me. I missed him by a coat of paint. I got so frightened I never wanted to drive after that.

My friends are all in their sixties or seventies. My friend Margaret loves to fish. I told her I'd go crabbing with her someday.

I like to go out to the strawberry fields. I went last year and picked strawberries and I picked tomatoes twice this year. I give most of them away. I make strawberry jam and freeze it for my nieces. I do regular cooking. I made muffins this morning.

I do needlepoint and make my own patterns. I think I'm going to design a different color for the piano bench. They are so expensive. I used to have a friend who was an artist and she designed all my things for me, but she died a few years ago, so I design them myself. I used to make all my clothes, but I don't do that anymore. I don't need that many clothes.

My niece comes every week, and we go shopping, and I have a friend who calls me and says, "Let go out to lunch." She eats out every day.

I can't do that. You get the same thing—there are no vegetables, you get a salad and meat or whatever, and that's your meal. I like some vegetables.

I'm just sick of being old. It's a bug. If people don't know how old you are, you're okay. But you're a dead duck if they know how old you are because they start talking down to you, and you're not equal anymore. You can be with a crowd, and they'll ignore you, and everybody else is in the conversation."

"How old are you?" I asked.

"I'm old enough to vote."

"I need to tell people in my book."

"What difference does it make how old you are? Oh, look at her." Laura changed the topic to her cat, who had just entered the room, "She's so adorable. I'm so delighted she's come out. She's so antisocial. I have a niece who comes, and she runs and hides. She's giving your purse the once over. She is named Sweetheart and has blue eyes. She's a pretty good kitty. I have to share the bathroom with her. I would love to have two bathrooms, but I won't move.

How did you meet Dorothy?"

"I saw an article about her in the newspaper," I replied.

"She knows everybody's age."

"I want to be accurate, that she gave me the right age. I think she was wrong and you're younger than she told me."

"What'd she say?"

"She told me you're ninety-eight."

"No, I'm ninety-seven." Laura couldn't let this mistake stand.

"This house is fabulous—it's like a museum." I said.

"It's Victorian furniture, a mish-mash of all kinds of stuff. This phonograph was in our attic at home. I need to get a coupling for the horn, it's hanging by a thread. We had all the records stolen but my niece was able to find some at an antique store. I left the old photographs at my sisters. I have a picture of my aunt and sister when she was three. I don't have any of my mother.

The china is English. It's an open pattern, Singapore Bird. I've got five sets of dishes. No wonder I don't have any room. I love dishes. I have one set of twelve, and the rest are eight.

These are famous houses in the window, and they're all done to scale. I leave them in the window all the time. Sometimes I remember to light them, and sometimes I don't. The one up there on the shelf is the old church in Boston. The light went out and I need to put a new bulb in it.

Would you like a cup of coffee? I just made some cupcakes. It's a good thing I have a walkie-talkie phone, (referring to her cordless phone). I was doing all these things. We've been on that phone for an hour."

The kitchen chair was covered with newspapers, books, and needle-point projects. There was a step stool in the middle of the floor. Laura moved everything to clear a space for me.

Going into the kitchen, I noticed the advanced musical composition on the piano stand and asked Laura, "Do you play that? It looks hard."

"I'll tell you, I've never taken lessons. I do it on my own. This is one of my hobbies. I do anything I want to do. I sometimes try things I don't know how to do, but I'm learning. I like to read history, travel, something factual, I don't like junk. I never read novels. That's some-body's imagination and I have enough of my own. We're not supposed to have a piano here, and I gave my piano away when I moved here. I was in a music store one day, and I saw this one. You can control the sound on it. You can have it as loud as you want so I bought it right away. I said, "This is for me." I can play it at two in the morning if I want to, and nobody can hear it. I can turn the sound down.

I was a guest in Germany, and I didn't know what to get my host, so I made a needlepoint pillow with a detailed checker design. That's what I'm doing for my piano bench. I made the pattern and I don't have a lot left to do. It's not hard to do, you have to keep going the right direction, one going up and another coming back. I love doing it.

The telephone rang, and I didn't get the chance to dip them in butter and sugar." She referred to the freshly baked muffins. "My kitchen is upside down. I started to paint the inside of my cupboards because the paint is white and they just absorb every single mark. See how dirty they are? I went to Home Depot last week, and I got white enamel.

I would have finished already, but I'm fighting a cold. I'm lying low, and not doing very much, just painting the inside, but not the outside. I love this kitchen because there's room in it, but I hate those cupboards. I put lemon oil on them and I have sanded them. I have done everything, and they're still sticky. Now I got some kind of gold and put that on. That lasted about four days and dried up and fell off. I give up. I just give up.

Isn't the weather turned nice now? It's just right. I have my plants covered up. I have to go outside and bring those things (paint clothes covering the plants to protect them from a freeze) inside. We'll probably have some more cold weather. I don't like cold weather.

Cream?" She poured the coffee and served with steady hands.

"I drank it with sugar when I was a kid. I never drank tea with sugar. My father drank it that way. Mother always used milk and sugar in hers. I cannot stand sweet tea or coffee. It tastes like medicine to me."

*   *   *   *

"The farm is the best place in the world to live. I grew up on the farm. I had a brother and sister, and I was the oldest. It was wonderful. We had a big house with four bedrooms. We had dogs and cats that I enjoyed. I never did anything with the animals in the barn. We had a wonderful flower garden, tulips, jonquils, and other flowers. We didn't have a butterfly garden. I'm not a butterfly person; every butterfly is a glorified worm. They eat everything. We had a pea garden at home and we couldn't keep up with them.

I remember when I was a kid. I was a country kid, and went to high school in town. I sang in the chorus. We took the trials for a play and I took the lead. There were two girls who were popular, and they didn't like it that I took the lead, but I didn't let that get me. I know what kids can be. I was a peaceful kid, very sensitive and very perspective. My father always said I could get along with the devil. I don't argue with anybody. Their judgment is just as important to them as mine is to me, so I let them have it.

We used to hang our clothes on the clotheslines, but now we don't want to have lines. That's obscene, we are defeating the purpose of conservation.

Mother used to wash clothes. We had our own washing machine and our own electricity. You could have a power line running right past your house, but you couldn't get electricity for any amount of money. When Franklin Roosevelt came, everybody could get electricity. They branched it out into the country. So everything is electrified now, but it doesn't have to be. We had our own generator. People used to say, "Isn't that wonderful. You don't have to pay the light bill." They didn't know how much it cost to run a generator. We had a big bank of batteries, and they were very expensive. So I often think of it, and they say, "Oh, you can't live without air conditioning." Florida hasn't always had air conditioning, but air conditioning made Florida. I wouldn't live here without it. Everything is damp and mildews. I'd go back to Minnesota, as much as I hate snow and winter, I'd go back. But that's what made Florida, air conditioning.

I was going to tell you about the ice story. There was this pond and it had rubber ice. Do you know what rubber ice is? It will almost hold you up, and if you run over it fast, you won't go down. Well, we weren't supposed to be there, but we were. We were all running across this ice, taking our turns and some kid jumped on it and the thing caved in. We all got wet. So, it's March, and we had to go home wet, and we had a lot of explaining to do. It was a shallow pond, we couldn't drown in it, but it was just the idea that we weren't supposed to be on the ice. I didn't get in trouble, just got a talking to. My folks were very liberal in lots of ways.

My mother lived to be eighty-nine but my father died at fifty-four. He had cancer. They probably could have saved him today. My sister is twenty years younger than I am. My brother was killed. He managed a trucking firm. There was a tree on a hill, and for no reason, the tree broke and rolled down the hill and killed him.

We lived on a big farm, and I was going out to Oregon to visit my aunt. I stopped and visited friends, and they invited me to stay for Thanksgiving, Then after Thanksgiving they suggested that I get a part time job before Christmas, and said this shop needed somebody. There was a beautiful, fancy shop. I said I'd never get to work there. About one o'clock, Mrs. S., who became my boss, said, "We're in a jam. Do you think you could come down this afternoon?"

So I came down, and she said to me, "Do you know how to iron?" I had ironed all my life so she put me to ironing handkerchiefs. I had to put them in a box, and tie them with ribbon. I had never seen such extravagance. Handkerchief orders were three to four hundred dollars. They were all special monogrammed; some were imports and some were domestic. I ironed all afternoon, and she said to me, "Can you come tomorrow?" and I said, "Yes."

So this went on, Christmas came, and she gave me a lovely gift and a check. She said, "Can you come after Christmas? We're going to need help."

She had an annex. On day I came and she said, "I'm going to do a dirty trick. I'm going to put you in the annex. I don't have anybody there." So they put me in the annex, and there was something in the window and I sold it. Because the window was almost bare, I filled and decorated the window. She was so pleased that became my job. I decorated her shop, the window, and the annex.

When the heat went out in this little annex she closed it and asked me to work in the shop. I worked there twenty-two years. We had a lot of special orders, a lot of dining, and a lot of colors. And I'd just go in there and do the very thing I like.

I never married. My mother and I used to come to Florida every winter. I took two weeks with pay, and two weeks on my own. When my mother got older, I quit working and went to live with her on the farm.

Dorothy Apgar is a busy person. I came down to manage a linen shop, and Dorothy had a rug shop, not too far. She came into my store and we talked, and she said, "Someday I'll have you over for lunch." I never thought any more. We talked, but people say things like that and you never hear from them again.

But one day she came over and said, "When is your lunch hour?"

I said, "I can take it anytime."

"Come on over. We'll have lunch together."

She lived right back of where I worked. That's how I knew Dorothy. I stayed here all that summer, and in the spring I went back home. I didn't stay at my job too long. My boss was very, very difficult. His wife said, "You want people to manage, but you won't let them."

I have wonderful friends. I have friends who have a beautiful motor home, and I'm always invited to go with them. I've been from coast to coast with them. Last summer I went to Germany, Poland, and Czechoslovakia with Dorothy. Sometimes she picks me up and then I stay with her a few days.

I'd like to go to Mexico for a month or so if I could find someone to go with me. I wouldn't go to Mexico in the summer time though. This summer I'm planning to go to Wisconsin where my friends live, and visit my sister in Minneapolis. I go anytime anybody says to go.

I like flowers. We had a nice flower garden at home. We had flowers in every room in the house. It's been so dry that I'm glad for every drop of rain we get. I have some petunias that I need to plant. I went to Home Depot last week and bought some. I'm growing a pineapple from a cutting. I have an airplane plant but it won't bloom until its pot bound. I didn't have much luck with geraniums. I used to pick gladioli in front of my apartment, but they cut them all down. I'd like to get some black eyed susan's. I'd put them on the porch and they'd cascade over.

Everything is changing. If a building is good, they tear it down and build higher and uglier ones. Some people have drastic changes in their lives, and they keep going. My niece wants me to get a computer. With all the other stuff I have, I don't have the room for it.

There was a wonderful program on last night. Did you watch it? *Mark Twain* directed by Ken Burns, who is absolutely a genius. He did a jazz program. Jazz is the only art we have that's truly American. He did a wonderful program on that. Channel 3 and 16 (educational channels) are my favorites, I don't have cable. I don't care for the movies. I like something that's factual. I never watch the soaps. I don't know how people watch those things—they're nothing but immoral stories. TV could be the most wonderful learning medium that's ever been, and they use it for all the wrong things. There are so many good things that could be on that thing, but all afternoon soap operas are all they have on. Sometime the educational channels have stuff that is just junk.

I like to read biographies and history. I'm wondering how they teach history, and if they project it the right way. When I went to school, I was taught that there was no place as honorable as the United States that we *never* were the first ones to shoot in a war. Somebody else always started it. That's just not true. Look what we did with Mexico. We stole all of Texas and California from them. That was during Grant's time. He was told to go in there and pick a fight with them so there would be a way of taking the land away from the Mexicans. I don't think that's right. This country has got plenty of things that are disgraceful. We had slavery and look what that has brought us. It isn't over yet. These young black hoodlums read all this stuff and they think it's their chance to get even.

There are new things coming up all the time in the medical field, even cloning, which I do not believe in. It hasn't been too successful with animals because they breed in some of the weaker points. I don't know what I think about stem cells.

I probably won't live to see it, but I think that someday there will be nudity on the streets. It will be everywhere. They are just as close to it as they can get. I went to Publix one day, and there was a girl who was wearing three patches. They used to sell hotdogs here on the Gandy Bridge just wearing a T-back. It's against the law now. You see these girls with short-shorts and just a bra in the grocery store. You know in Germany they go to the beaches nude, and most of Europe is very lax. I've never been to a foreign beach. I'm not a beach person. I don't like the sand, and I won't go into the water. They have all kinds of crawly things that are repulsive. I'm not too fond of swimming pools, either. I like water in the bathtub and drinking water in a tumbler.

I'm not religious or churchgoing, but I could go to any church if a friend invited me, even the Jewish Synagogue. There's only one God. Why make such a big issue of the way you're going to heaven? This quarreling, the way they're doing in Ireland, and in the Holy Land, now that's not religion at all. I don't care what church I go to, or any. I respect everybody's religion. I don't care if they are a Moslem, or Catholic, or Jew, or what. Some of my very best friends are Jewish, and I love the Jewish people. Just because their religion and their beliefs are different doesn't make them any different.

"Hi, Sweetie," she addressed the cat. "It's so strange that she'll come out while you're here. When the neighbors picked her up she was half starved. I didn't want a cat, a bird, nothing to keep me home. She came and claimed me, and won't have anything to do with anyone else. She's a dear little thing, but she is so timid. I'd give her away except I love her. I have a friend who stays with her, but if she can't, then I have to stay home to care for her."

"What is your secret for staying healthy and living long?" I asked.

"Who knows? If you can find out, you'll make a fortune.

My health is excellent and my vision is very good. I had cataract surgery and can read without glasses."

Laura stood up and reached down to pick up a tiny crumb she spotted on the floor.

"I always have vegetables and meat, and if I have ice cream, it doesn't last very long. I love ice cream and fruit pies.

I don't have any arthritis. I sometimes get a muscle spasm in my back. I've had that since I was thirty years old. It's a mystery. Who knows where my good health comes from?

I avoid taking medicine, we doesn't know the long-term effects of it. You take medication, and then you find out you shouldn't have been taking it, or you find out it conflicts with something else you are taking. I take an aspirin once in a while if I feel I'm getting a cold. I couldn't sleep last night, my nose was bothering me, so at three I got up and took an aspirin. I don't know if it does any good, but it makes me feel good that I'm doing something for myself.

I know I should walk, but I don't. At home I had a big flower garden that I took care of. Just to walk for no reason, I never did much of that. I wrap the garbage up and put it in the dumpster. It's across the street. I just walk down the stairs and take the garbage out at night. Walking the stairs, they say, is good for you. I walk the stairs anytime I want to. I don't make a rule that I have to have exercise. I just do what I have to do.

I have a friend who does my hair. I color my hair. I'm gray here, in front, but I'm not gray anywhere else. It's a kind of reddish blond. To prevent wrinkles, I wash my face with soap and water, and that's it. I think that the people have been hoodwinked into all the expensive stuff that doesn't do any good at all. You might as well put Crisco on your face, and the cost of it! Some of it is forty dollars. I like money too well for that. I just don't think it does any good.

I'm going to Seattle sometime in the spring, and I'm going to Wisconsin and Minneapolis in the summer."

ALICE SAND, AGE 99

Book Club Member
New York

One day, when I was putting flyers up at the Sun City Center Community Center, I accidentally stumbled into an art class. The teacher was gracious enough to let me tell the class what I was doing. Nobody in the class admitted to being over eighty, but one woman took my flyer and promised to give it to her friend, Alice, from her monthly book club. A few weeks later Alice called and we set up an appointment the following day. Although her car was in the driveway, Alice wasn't home. This hadn't happened before, and I later found out that Alice was in the hospital. Eight weeks later we rescheduled the meeting. Alice's calendar was full for three days, but she was free the following week.

A lice had moved out of her house and was living in a two bedroom, one bath, senior apartment complex. There were pull cords and people available in case of emergency.

The apartment was furnished with wicker tables and comfortable revolving chairs. A blue flower boarder decorated the walls along with several multicolored stencils that Alice had painted. She told me this kind of work is called a theorem.

Alice is a petite, independent woman. She is short with upright posture, and thin. She has very few wrinkles although the skin under her neck is loose. Like the majority of people in this book, she has all her own teeth. She was wearing khaki slacks, a sky-blue shirt, and a brace on her right wrist.

"I've been busy," she began. "I'm closing on my house this coming Monday. After the heart attack, my daughter came down for a couple of weeks and said I have to sell my house and move. I've only been here three weeks, so I'm not settled yet. I can't reach things to put them where they belong. My daughter wanted me where I was protected. This is really very good. You get three meals a day if you want them. I only get dinner. I always cook breakfast.

This apartment isn't the way it's going to be, but it's what I brought from the other place.

I've had all sorts of bad luck. I fell out of bed and broke a wrist. I don't know why I did that. I had a heart attack about two months ago.

I play a lot of bridge. That's good for everybody. I think it keeps your mind going. I'm a quilter and I make wall hangings. I've been crocheting, knitting, quilting, and playing cards. I won yesterday. It's the first day I was back. We play for quarters.

I go to church, but I haven't since I broke my wrist. It's been an important part of my life although I'm not very active here. I'm a Presbyterian.

When I have time, I will take an exercise class. I have to walk up for my meals. They have the freshest vegetable salad. I get that fresh every day. I think their meals here are remarkable. I don't eat very much meat, but when I do, I like lamb best.

I go to a reader's book review in Ruskin. We meet and exchange our opinions of the book. They are all very intelligent women. I just listen. I haven't been able to go the last two times, but it's very interesting. It started out with about four and the last time I was there, there were about fifteen or sixteen people. We meet once a month and read the same book. Now I'm reading *A Heart of Stone*. I'm not too crazy about it. I called the other day and said it's way over due. The librarian said not to worry about it. I like that Ruskin library. There are so many computers, and so many children around. They give you marvelous service.

Except for this heart attack, my health has been good. I've got a bit of arthritis. It comes and goes. The day I had my heart attack, I went to see the movie *A Beautiful Mind*. Then my friends said, "Let's go eat," but I said, "Take me to the emergency room." It must have been very mild. I had to have blood transfusions. I was in the hospital five days.

My daughter said I can't live alone any more. They have an emergency thing to press. The other morning the phone rang and they asked me if I was all right. The machine went off. I don't know why.

I can't figure out why I fell out of bed, but I caught myself on my arm and broke my wrist. The doctor put in a metal thing. I support it. It's still too young.

I have a fit when I have to make someone wait for me. I went to this doctor Tuesday. He made me wait an hour in a cold room. I was all set, the x-ray was right in front of him. All he did after that was tell me I could drive. I was kind of perplexed. I'm going to see the doctor this afternoon. I hope he changes…after you have a heart attack they give you a million pills. I take seven a day, and I'm going to see if he can change that.

I belong to church organizations. University Women is a big organization that works for women's rights. They keep an eye on the government. They have a good bridge group, Theta. I'm a Kappa Alpha Theta. It's with education. They're interested in everything that goes on. In college they have fraternity houses and I lived in the house for three years. Mostly now, I just give them money. I'm not much in politics. I play bridge and vote, but I don't go out and wave a flag. I never did.

I have a lot of friends. I have one who's two months older, but she's not in good health. My grandson says we're the old biddies."

*   *   *   *

"There were four girls growing up, and I was number three. I was the only small one and was always at the end of the line. I've always been the smallest at five feet. I loved school and I had the best teachers that were possible in high school. Then I went to the University of Michigan and got a BA in language. I learned Latin in College. I taught French and Latin. I loved to teach and I loved the kids. I had the cream of the crop. I enjoyed it and the kids enjoyed me. They took Latin away so I ended up just teaching French. I taught until 1968, and then stopped teaching.

I'm worried. We didn't have all this fighting and terrorism. I used to walk through the school building; never thinking anybody would ever touch me. I wouldn't do it now. I don't think schools are as safe. I had reported children using drugs and nobody did a thing about it. I don't know what's going to happen.

I met my husband in school. We both graduated. I was married for fifty-three years. He went with the insurance company the week after he graduated, and he stayed there the whole forty years. He became the vice-president of an insurance company. I didn't have to work, but after my kids went to college I was bored.

It was an ideal life. We had a two hundred acre farm outside of Glen Falls New York. We always had a garden wherever we went. He wasn't a very good weeder, but he had a tractor and a cart. He'd take people around to show them. Most of it was wild. We had a pond that attracted deer and beaver. They cut down the best trees to build their dam.

We traveled overseas with his job. I've been to Europe nine times and I've been to Las Vegas. I took my grandson to China. That was a great trip. When my husband was alive we went to Africa and Egypt and Morocco. I went to France one summer. My husband died seventeen years ago. After he left, I went to Australia. I want to go to Panama but...

My son lives in New York. I have two kids and they're both college graduates. I have a grandson. He and I are very, very close. He just took a walking tour in Peru. I would have liked to go with him. I don't know if I'll be going on any more trips. It depends on what happens.

I'm not interested in dating. I had the best there was, and that's it. He was ideal. Only we thought I'd go first because I was a couple of years older than he was.

I want to be of value somewhere or other. I ate dinner with a couple who takes food into the jail. She teaches teenaged kids. I'd really like to do something like that, but I don't know if I could do that. I haven't volunteered lately, but I taught English as a tutor.

I think it's been a marvelous century. If you have to live a century, this is one to do. Everything happened. Everything has developed up to the computer. I have a computer, but I push the wrong button a lot of times. I use e-mail everyday to talk to my daughter in Cape Cod. That's where I will probably end up, but I didn't want to do it right away."

CELEBRATION OF GASPARILLA DAY

The final person in this book spoke of Gasparilla Day. Unless you come from the Tampa Bay area of Florida, you probably don't know that Gasparilla is a weeklong Tampa celebration in honor of Jose Gaspar, a local, and most likely imaginary, pirate. Many of the wealthiest and notable local citizens dress up as pirates and "invade" the city from pirate ships that land in Tampa Bay. A large parade follows the invasion, with pirates shooting cap guns and throwing plastic beads from their floats to the children waiting below. Parties and drunken celebrations continue throughout the day and night.

Herbert Carrington, 103

Greeter
Thomasville, Georgia.

I called several local African-American Churches, attempting to find minority men over eighty and was given Herbert's name. There were two Herberts in the phone book, the man I interviewed, and his son, who joined his father and supplied moral support.

The old wood framed, one story house, going back to the early 1900's, has white peeling paint and a red porch with columns. It is one of the nicer homes in the rundown neighborhood. The high ceiling is a design that allowed circulation and cooling before air conditioning was available. Burglar bars are on the door of this home and all the homes on the block. The yard is kept up and needs only minor work.

I was interviewing the oldest person in this book, a hundred and three years. A white-haired man with glasses and smooth skin greeted me at the door. He was wearing a red plaid shirt and pants, and was five to ten pounds overweight. He appeared to be between eighty and eighty-five, certainly under ninety.

"Hello," I introduced myself to the gentleman who opened the door. "I'm here to talk to your father."

"I'm the old man, yes, uh-huh!"

"It's not your father I'll be talking to?"

"Yes, it's me, honey!"

"I guess I'll have to take your word for it."

"Hi," a younger man, who had just arrived, entered the house.

"That's my son, Herbert, Jr.," the old man said.

"He can't be a hundred and three!" I addressed the son with amazement.

"Sure he is."

"He's got to be lying by a good twenty years." I laughed.

"How are you?" The son put out his hand to shake.

"I'm Linda."

"I'm Herbert, Jr."

I noticed the father was looking through his wallet. "He's going to show me his ID."

"He delights in doing that."

"I'll bet nobody believes him."

"Here's my driver's license. It says I was born in 1898. That makes me a hundred and three."

"I believe you."

Herbert, Sr. laughed with delight.

"They have me wrote up so much, the newspaper had me a week ago, on and on and on.

I've been in three Gasparilla articles, St. Petersburg Times had me a week ago, and another. I don't want to be in the paper no more—it looks kind of silly."

"No, I'm writing a book."

"That's okay."

"Nice house," I commented.

"Thank you, it's comfortable. This antique furniture is from turn of the century. It's old, old, old. This chair foot is like a goose's foot, and the handle [arm rest] comes around looking like a goose face. You never see anything like that today.

I live alone here, but I've got two sons nearby, about five minutes away. My wife has been dead twenty-five years.

I own quite a bit of property, so I keep busy doing something all the time. I cut the grass around the apartments myself. People say I keep doing too much. I don't do the maintenance, but I hire people to come in and do the work, and I pay the bills. All morning I had a man fertilize my orange trees out there."

"All told he has thirteen apartments. He has a triplex, and four duplex, and three single structures," Herbert, Jr. said. "He does the groundwork, and has a riding mower. He's in perpetual motion."

"I'm selling four houses, too. They're paying me," Herbert, Sr. boasted.

"I work. I go to the Tampa Yacht and Country Club, to the parties and special occasions. I was there about sixty years as a maitre-d. I retired. Now my title is "host." I be at the door to greet people. I get them to come in, and then I leave. I don't work everyday now.

We have Gasparilla at the Yacht club. We serve around two thousand people for breakfast. I go tomorrow night. I'll be there to pass out the sandwiches.

For my one-hundredth birthday there were around sixteen hundred people there. It was the biggest birthday party at the Yacht Club.

I go out with friends for lunch quite a bit. I'm known too well through the city, you know. On my hundredth birthday, Jim Davis, the congressman, flew a flag over the capital. He came down and personally presented it to me."

Herbert got up to show me the flag that he had put away in a wooden cabinet. He also showed me a scrapbook with pictures and birthday congratulations from the local mayor, past mayor, several senators, and other well-known people.

"I get up in morning, check the obituaries, eat breakfast, and take a walk. I have a lot to do. People are moving in and out of the apartments. Monday somebody is coming to paint the apartments. I keep busy doing something. Last night I was at Home Depot buying mini-blinds.

I always used to grow snapdragons and give them to people. I gave some to the mayor, Sandy Freedman. They come from a local nursery, but this year I can't get any plants.

I'm Catholic. I go to church. I got baptized when I was eighty. My friends made me do it so I could go to church with them. I go to quite a few funerals of friends I've known more than fifty years."

*   *   *   *

"I was born in Thomasville, Georgia. We had one sister and five brothers. I didn't get much education, about fifth or sixth grade. I was the oldest one, and they're all dead but me. My parents died young. My sister just died in March. She was ninety-six. My mother went to Julliard and played the piano. She died early and my grandfather did farm work in Georgia. He took the kids.

Cotton was the main thing when I came along. Cotton and peanuts. On the farm I would do anything my grandfather wanted me to do.

Plow the mule or pick the cotton. I just didn't like that farm life. I left and I've been working for myself since I was fourteen or fifteen."

"The farm life really wasn't that bad at the turn of the century," his son said. "There were prosperous farmers up there until that blasted boll weevil came through and just devastated the cotton industry."

"That's right. I got out before the boll weevil. I'll tell you the way it was. I was doing different jobs supporting myself. I was a chauffer and drove cars in one family for almost twenty-five years. I'm a pretty good mechanic, too. I worked all my life. When I came to Tampa, my first job was helping build the Gandy Bridge in 1921 and '22.

I've had four wives. I divorced them. They're all dead I suppose. I've got two sons and a daughter. She lives in Miami. I have nine grand-kids, and one great grandkid. Here's my pride and joy." Herbert showed me the picture of a toddler sitting next to a Great Dane. "Here's my little great-grand. They have a nice white carpet, and the mother has the dog trained to stand by the door until she wipes his feet. She tells him night-night, and he goes right upstairs. There are no great-greats. I started late. I had a lot of wild oats to sow.

I've got a companion, but it's not like it used to be. She's sixty-five or seventy. I've been with her about ten years. We go to movies together, things like that. Not that much romance any more."

Herbert got up and brought a yellowing newspaper clipping to show me. "I bought my first car from Jim Ferman, Sr.. It was a used, green, 1921 Chevrolet. He says I'm his oldest living customer.

Those days we had a wood stove. My grandfather had a nice home, five bedrooms. I didn't do washing. My grandmother and my aunts had washboards, no washing machines or dryers. I had a bicycle until I grew up. I repaired my own cars and fixed my automobile tires, just take them off and patch the tubes. Things were cheap those days. You could buy a loaf of bread for a nickel.

I've traveled a little bit. I was in Washington, D.C, New York, Pennsylvania. I worked in a shipyard out of Philadelphia during the war. I worked at a proving ground. That's a testing ground where they send the ammunition to see if it works. That was World War I. The cannons were tested there. I wasn't but sixteen or seventeen years old. I drove a horse. They didn't have tractors in those days. I drove a horse, pulling a scoop. Aberdeen was just a proving ground and I was just a common laborer.

When the children were born, George Steinbrenner gave me tickets to all the World Series with my grandchildren. George Steinbrenner is a nice fellow. I used to travel to the World Series. Now the kids are grown and I'd rather sit home and watch television. I don't read much."

Herbert, Jr. was squirming in his seat with his father's modesty. "He's traveled a lot in recent years. He's been to the Bahamas, Puerto Rico, California, and Las Vegas. He's an avid reader. He reads the paper everyday from cover to cover, both the St. Pete Times and the Tampa Tribune. He keeps abreast because of his social schedule. He goes through the obituary first to see which of his friends have passed. Most are younger than him. There are a lot of his friends at the club that he's known since they were toddlers."

"I was in the Yacht Club fifty years. I never had any problem and they always treated me as a gentleman. We had separate bathrooms and water fountains. We knew that was the way it was in those days, and we accepted it. White for one and colored for the other. That's the way it was until Martin Luther came along. He's the one who straightened that up. We couldn't go into a white restaurant until Martin Luther King. He's the man who did all that for us. If my wife and I went to California, we could go into any motel or hotel to sleep. Before Martin Luther King we couldn't do that. We had to go on the side of the road to eat. We couldn't go in no hotels, or restaurants. Some restaurants had little windows, and they would push the food through the hole."

Herbert, Jr. said. "He's the bionic man. He had corneal transplants at ninety years of age and he's the oldest person to ever have a triple bypass at ninety-five. He has had cancers, but they are in remission. He goes to the best doctors. He will call the doctors at home. He's known them since they were kids. He has a very close relationship with the physicians. Up until the arthritis just recently, he was very spry. Only in recent months he began to use a cane. He's real modest about that, when he goes to the club he doesn't take it with. When he walks in the neighborhood nobody bothers him. They put up a protective shield."

"I worked all my life. I think that attributes to my health. I've always been busy doing something. I take Centrum vitamins, one a day. My knees have arthritis right now. Yah." Herbert laughed. "The trouble is they tell me there is no cure for it. Both knees have arthritis. I see and hear well, and I've got a pretty good head of hair. Medication for prostate cancer costs me thirty dollars a pill, but I'm getting along fine. I plan to leave something for my children and grandchildren. That's all I care about.

I walk everyday, about ten blocks. I used to walk outside, but now I walk in the mall. I like to eat most anything, but with diabetes you can't eat everything, you know. Ya live to be a hundred years old and then get diabetes. I love sweets and I can't have them. I cheat a little sometimes," he laughed. "I like bacon and eggs and grits for breakfast, and for lunch I might fix a hamburger. Steak or broiled fish, lamb chops, something like that. I have vegetables all the time, and I like all fruits. I like strawberries with whip cream and short cake. Put a lot of whip cream on it."

"Are you always this cheerful?" I asked.

"Ya, better to smile. People say, 'Shoot the sherbet to me, Herbert'."

0-595-27079-4